BY THE EDITORS OF CON
WITH JEFFREY W. ELLIS, M.D.

Medical Symptoms
& Treatments

BEEKMAN HOUSE
New York

CONTENTS

Copyright © 1982 by Publications International, Ltd. All rights reserved. This book may not be reproduced or quoted in whole or in part by mimeograph or any other printed means or for presentation on radio or television without written permission from:

Louis Weber, President
Publications International, Ltd.
3841 West Oakton Street
Skokie, Illinois 60076

Permission is never granted for commercial purposes.

Manufactured in the United States of America.   10 9 8 7 6 5 4 3 2 1

Library of Congress Catalog Card Number: 81-82227
ISBN: 0-517-346923

This edition published by:
Beekman House
Distributed by Crown Publishers, Inc.
One Park Avenue
New York, New York 10016

Illustrations: Teri J. McDermott, M.A., Medical Illustrator

Cover Photo: Brooks & VanKirk Photography
Cover Design: Frank E. Peiler

Note: Neither The Editors of CONSUMER GUIDE® and PUBLICATIONS INTERNATIONAL, LTD., nor the author or publisher take responsibility for any possible consequences from any treatment, action, or application of medication or preparation by any person reading or following the information in this book. The publication of this book does not constitute the practice of medicine, and this book does not attempt to replace your physician or pharmacist. The author and publisher advise the reader to check with a physician before administering or consuming any medication or undertaking any course of treatment.

INTRODUCTION

Most of us want to — and are expected to — assume responsibility for our own and our family's health. But where do we start? How can we intelligently take an active role in our own health care? Where do we learn what we need to know about our bodies and how they function in health and in illness?

This book answers those questions. *Medical Symptoms & Treatments* is a guide to the most common health problems that many of us encounter. Each condition or disease is described along with its possible complications, its causes, and its risk factors — the factors that increase an individual's risk of contracting or developing the disorder. But probably of the most importance to you are the sections on symptoms and treatment of each disease. Many people know little about disease, but everyone has a personal knowledge of symptoms. And everyone wants to know what the symptoms indicate and how they can be treated.

Medical Symptoms & Treatments is not a comprehensive medical encyclopedia, and it is not intended to be. Rather, it is a guide to those diseases and conditions that you will most commonly face or hear about. Furthermore, this book should by no means take the place of your doctor. If anything, this book should make your communication with your doctor more profitable and more informative. By being informed both about your body and

about the illnesses that may afflict it, you will be able to help your doctor help you. You will know when to see your doctor, how to describe your symptoms, and what to ask about treatment. In short, you will be able to participate actively along with your doctor in your own health care.

To get the most out of this book, you should know how to use it effectively. You will want to start at the beginning of the book with the section on symptoms. This section is devoted to a discussion of the most common symptoms of disease — such as pain, fever, cough, indigestion, and others — and you will learn how to recognize a symptom and how it may be treated. Armed with the information in this first section, you will better understand the discussions of symptoms and treatment within each individual disease topic.

Because you may be familiar only with the symptoms of the area of the body which is affected, the book is divided into sections based on systems of the body. Within each section the most common disorders of that system are dealt with. For example, disorders originating in or affecting the stomach and intestine are discussed in the section entitled "Problems of the Digestive System." Preceding the discussions of the individual diseases is an introduction to the digestive system — descriptions of its organs and of how the system as a whole normally functions. To under-

stand disease as a departure from the normal healthy state of an organ or system, you should understand what is normal and healthy. These introductions, not only to the digestive system but to every body system, give you a reference point for becoming familiar with the way your body should work. You are strongly urged to read the introductory descriptions of each body system before you read about any diseases within that system.

In order to make *Medical Symptoms & Treatments* as useful as possible, the editors of CONSUMER GUIDE® have included numerous detailed illustrations. Each introduction to a body system has an illustration of that system so that you can see the normal structure of the system as well as how its parts relate to each other and to the rest of the body. In addition, there are illustrations throughout the rest of the book that are designed to clarify the information in each section and to expand your knowledge about the disease.

Use *Medical Symptoms & Treatments* as your home adviser about health and medical problems. Use this book to increase your understanding of your body, to learn to recognize what is normal and abnormal, and to establish a more profitable relationship with your doctor. With this book as your guide, you can now become an active participant in your own and your family's health care.

COMMON SYMPTOMS

Maintaining good health is a vital concern of everyone. Most of us are aware of what to do to promote health — proper diet, appropriate exercise, and adequate rest are only a few of the good health habits that guarantee fitness and vigor. However, many of us forget that understanding illness is also important to insure health and vitality. By recognizing symptoms of illness, we can better prevent, diagnose, and treat problems that threaten our good health.

A symptom is evidence of a disease or disorder — it indicates departure from normal well-being. Sometimes a symptom in and of itself constitutes the disorder. For example, indigestion may be your punishment for eating that last wedge of whipped cream pie before bed. On the other hand, indigestion can be a sign of cancer in the intestinal tract or even of a heart attack. In these cases, indigestion is more than a temporary disorder in and of itself, and you need to be able to tell the difference.

At other times, a symptom is a defensive reaction of the body — an attempt to restore the body to normal health. Falling into a faint in an overheated room, for instance, is the body's method of restoring adequate blood supply to the brain by lowering the head to the same level of the heart. However, fainting may be a sign of a serious illness, and again you need to know when fainting should be reported to your doctor.

Your ability to recognize and understand symptoms of illness is important to your doctor. When you go to the doctor with a medical problem, you should be prepared to describe your symptoms exactly. You should note their time of onset and the nature of your activity when they occur (eating supper, shoveling snow, lying down). Be prepared to describe the rapidity with which your symptoms appear. Sometimes the symptoms themselves provide fewer clues than does the manner in which they occur.

To do all of this well, you must learn to be observant about your body. The following descriptions of some of the more common symptoms will help you become alert to changes in your body. This section will also offer some guidance on when to seek medical attention. As an additional aid, you may want to read the introductions to each body system in the book. These sections discuss the normal functioning of the body systems and may help you recognize when your body is not working the way it should.

Pain

Pain is the most common symptom for which people seek help. Pain is an unpleasant sensation of discomfort ranging from mild to agonizing. Pain results from the stimulation of specialized nerve endings in the body. The pain signal then travels along these nerves to the brain, at which point you become aware of the pain. This all happens in a fraction of a second.

Pain serves a useful function. It is a protective mechanism because it often forces the sufferer either to remove the cause or to withdraw from the source. Pain can also be a warning of potential damage to the body.

There are many causes of pain, including disease, injury, abnormal changes in the body, and others. In addition, it may result from psychological factors such as the headache pain arising from tension in the muscles of the head and neck during times of emotional stress.

Pain is not always felt at the spot from which it arises. For example, the pain of the heart condition, angina pectoris, may be felt in the arm rather than only in the chest. This is called "referred pain."

There are different ways of experiencing pain. It can seem crushing, as in angina and other disorders associated with the heart; burning, as in heartburn or ulcer; or aching, as in arthritis.

Your doctor will probably ask several questions in order to diagnose the possible cause of your pain. Often the two questions that are the most revealing are: "What brings it on?" and "What provides relief?" For example, the pain of indigestion and certain intestinal disorders may be brought on by eating, but the pain of an ulcer, which may be similar, is often relieved by eating.

In some cases, the cause of pain is difficult to diagnose and, in fact, may never be discovered. In addition, most normal healthy persons occasionally have brief twinges of pain — in a joint or muscle, for instance — that have no cause and disappear on their own.

The ideal treatment for pain is prompt removal or treatment of its cause. Often, however, this is either not possible or very time-consuming. In these cases, the pain itself may have to be relieved. The most common remedy is the use of analgesic drugs or painkilling medication. Aspirin is probably the best-known example of a mild nonprescription pain-killer. In addition, your physician may prescribe more potent pain-killers which should be used according to instructions. Other types of drugs, either prescription or over-the-counter, may relieve the pain of a specific disorder. For example, antacids are considered to be helpful in easing indigestion.

Surface treatment of pain — applying heat or cold and massaging skin or muscles—may also be helpful. These treatments are especially beneficial if they simultaneously promote healing of the affected part, thus eliminating the cause of pain. Naturally, too, adequate rest of the affected part may relieve pain.

It is essential to remember that pain is an important defense mechanism of the body. Unexplainable pain that persists for more than a few days or keeps recurring should be investigated.

Fever

Fever is a rise in body temperature above the normal range. Normal body temperature is considered to be 98.6°F. to 99.6°F. A fever is a body temperature over 101.5°F. when measured with a rectal thermometer, 100.5°F. with an oral (mouth) thermometer, or 99.5°F. when measured under the arm.

Fever is one of the body's de-fense mechanisms. A regulatory center in the brain controls the temperature of the body. This built-in thermostat helps the body maintain normal body temperature despite changes in the external environment such as unusually hot or cold weather. However, during an illness, such as an infection, the body's thermostat may respond by setting itself at a higher than normal level. It is thought that the microorganisms causing the illness cannot survive the higher body temperature.

There are other reasons for a fever besides infections. Disorders in that portion of the brain that regulates temperature may trigger fever. These disorders may include stroke, brain tumor, or brain injury. A heart attack or some forms of cancer also may cause fever. However, infections—such as colds, influenza, measles, and many others—are the most common causes of fever.

The early signs of fever may include chills or sensations of heat, flushed skin, increased pulse and breathing rates, and general muscular aches and pains. Sometimes, though, a fever is so slight that these symptoms are not noticeable.

The primary aim in treating fever should be to diagnose and treat its cause. Fever itself is not a disease, and treating the fever by attempting to lower the body temperature to normal should not be confused with treating the illness that is causing the fever. Furthermore, attempting to reduce the fever is not always recommended. To do so diminishes any help the fever may offer the body's defenses in overcoming the illness. Also, artificial lowering of the temperature may mask the course of the underlying cause of the fever.

Nevertheless, prolonged fever may cause weakness and dehydration (depletion of body fluids). Thus, attempting to lower the fever somewhat will usually make a patient more comfortable. Aspirin or an aspirin substitute like acetaminophen will effectively lower a fever; using these drugs and increasing fluid intake are often recommended. However, any drug treatment — especially for children — should be discussed with your doctor. Aspirin, for example, has been linked to Reye's syndrome, a serious complication that may follow a virus infection like influenza or chicken pox in children.

If you do not or cannot use a fever-reducing drug, sponging or bathing with tepid water may be effective in reducing the fever or in providing comfort. Additionally, clothing and blankets should be sufficient for comfort, but the patient should not be kept too warm.

Medical attention should be sought if the fever is high (103° to 104°F.) for 12 to 24 hours, if a moderate fever (101° to 102°F.) lasts for several days, or if there are wide fluctuations in the temperature. If the fever disappears but returns several days later, a doctor should be consulted. This usually signals a new or additional infection. And, of course, anyone with a fever that causes convulsions or that is higher than 105°F. should obtain medical help immediately.

Fatigue

Fatigue is a feeling of weariness and of a lack of well-being. There is also a lack of energy, vitality, and enthusiasm, even for many normally pleasant projects. Some people confuse fatigue with weakness. Weakness, however, is an actual loss of strength, sometimes to the point of dizziness and fainting.

Fatigue is often a normal companion of disease. Sometimes fatigue is the first, or at least an early, symptom of illness. Everyone has experienced the sudden fatigue that often occurs just before a severe cold or influenza. Fatigue may also precede the other symptoms of hepatitis, infectious mononucleosis, and other infectious diseases.

Fatigue that occurs easily but is relieved by rest is often a common sign of heart disease. Lung disorders, such as emphysema, which prevent adequate amounts of oxygen from reaching the blood, may lead to a feeling of being run-down and tired. Other disorders that may be accompanied by fatigue include certain gland diseases, anemia (a deficiency of red blood cells which carry oxygen to body cells), various nutritional deficiencies, and some diseases of the nervous system.

Fatigue may also come from working too hard. The work can be either physical or mental. Fatigue that cannot be explained by overwork or illness is usually caused by some psychological factor such as anxiety or depression. In fact, many cases of fatigue that are blamed on overwork may actually be emotional in origin. Some physicians and mental health specialists believe that almost all fatigue not caused by physical illness is a result of psychological problems.

Symptoms that accompany fatigue include nervousness, anxiety, depression, irritability, headaches, difficulty in concentrating, and sexual disorders. Other symptoms, particularly in those persons whose fatigue is caused by psychological factors, are an inability to sleep even with an overwhelming need for sleep, early morning waking, and fatigue upon awakening.

As is the case with many other symptoms, the most successful treatment for fatigue is often treatment of the underlying cause. Fatigue that is caused by medical disorders should disappear with successful treatment of these disorders. Fatigue resulting from psychological factors may be eliminated when these factors are pinpointed and properly managed.

Edema

Edema is swelling caused by the accumulation of excess fluid within the body's tissues. It is a general symptom of many diseases and disorders that range all the way from minor to life-threatening. Some edema is very common and perfectly normal. This includes the slight puffiness, particularly of hands and feet, that many people experience during hot weather. Edema is also common just before a menstrual period and during pregnancy. Excess weight and tight clothing may also lead to edema.

The fluid that accumulates in edema comes from the blood since excess body fluid is normally removed by the blood and excreted through the kidneys. There is a normal, constant exchange of fluid between the blood vessels and the remainder of the body's tissues. Edema occurs when that exchange does not function properly, allowing too much liquid to leave the blood vessels and/or too little fluid to enter the blood vessels from the body tissues. A change in pressure within the blood vessels because of heart disease, high blood pressure, or a blocked vessel may trigger the imbalance in fluid exchange. Damage to blood vessels—caused by injury, infections, or other factors — is another cause of edema. And, of course, kidney failure causes the excess fluid to remain in the body rather than to be excreted through the kidneys and urinary system.

Edema is sometimes confined to a small area of the body. For example, the swelling that appears around a tiny splinter in your finger is edema. But edema also may occur over large areas of the body, causing widespread swelling and puffiness. Widespread edema may not be noticeable at first, because the accumulated fluid is distributed over such a large area. Thus, a person may gain several pounds from the weight of the excess liquid before noticing any puffiness.

One of the earliest signs of edema is difficulty putting on or removing a ring that formerly slid on and off easily. Another sign may be an inability to wear a pair of shoes that previously fit. If widespread edema is not diagnosed and treated, it may progress to the point that the swelling becomes obvious in such areas as the ankles, legs, and face.

The most serious forms of edema occur within the body. For example, heart disease may result in internal edema, particularly of the heart and lungs. This may place an extra strain on these organs even to the point of becoming dangerous.

Simple or temporary edema may often be relieved by decreasing dietary salt, since salt causes the body to retain fluid. Severe edema — or that which threatens the function of internal organs — may be treated with a diuretic, a type of drug that stimulates the kidneys to produce more urine and thus rid the body of excess fluid. If edema is discovered to be a symptom of an underlying disorder (for example, heart disease), treating that disorder will often eliminate the edema. Prolonged or widespread edema — particularly when it has no discernible cause such as hot weather or an approaching menstrual period — should be investigated by a doctor.

Indigestion

Indigestion is discomfort that is related to eating. The term indigestion means "inability to digest foods." For many it is an uncomfortable feeling of fullness, pressure, or slight pain. Gassiness also commonly occurs. Some people call constipation, diarrhea, heartburn, or nausea "indigestion." Although they are related to the problem of indigestion, these symptoms will be discussed separately in this book.

Indigestion can usually be traced to some eating problem. It could be as simple as not chewing thoroughly, eating too fast, eating too much, or eating in an emotionally upsetting environment. Some people get indigestion when they eat particular foods. For many, spicy, fatty, or oily foods are the culprits. This type of indigestion may be caused by an allergic reaction to the specific food. Smoking, too, often leads to indigestion. This is especially true if you smoke immediately before or after a meal.

Other causes of indigestion are linked to disorders of organs associated with digestion. These organs include the esophagus (the passageway from mouth to stomach), stomach, intestines, gallbladder, liver, and pancreas (a gland located behind the stomach). These disorders may be as serious as an ulcer or even cancer. Therefore, you should see your doctor about any indigestion that persists or that you cannot control yourself.

In some cases, a feeling of indigestion is caused by problems not related to food or the digestive system. Many people suffering heart attacks may have a sensation similar to indigestion as an early symptom. Tumors that are unrelated to the digestive system and emotional problems may also cause feelings similar to indigestion.

You can help your doctor solve your indigestion problem by describing it as fully as possible. For example, the doctor will probably want to know exactly what and where your feelings of indigestion are. When and for how long you suffer indigestion is also important, especially in relation to when you eat. You may also have to describe what you normally eat and drink and under what conditions you have your meals and snacks.

Sometimes the doctor is unable to determine the cause of indigestion by questioning you or by a simple examination. In such a case, your doctor may turn to other diagnostic procedures. These may include X rays or a stool analysis.

Prevention is often the best treatment for indigestion. Eating balanced meals in a relaxed setting, eliminating foods that are suspected of causing problems, and avoiding smoking at mealtime can be beneficial. If indigestion does occur, an antacid will often provide relief. However, antacids should not be used if you

have kidney disease, since one of the ingredients (magnesium) of antacids may interfere with kidney function.

Heartburn

Heartburn is an uncomfortable burning pain felt behind the lower part of the breastbone. The pain may extend up into the upper chest or lower neck, or both. Heartburn gets its name from the fact that it is felt in the area of the heart; however, it is not caused by a pain in the heart or by a heart attack.

Heartburn is usually caused by the backup of digestive juices from your stomach into the esophagus — the passageway between your mouth and stomach. These juices are a type of acid and thus can irritate the tissue in the lower esophagus. Partly digested food that may accompany the juices can add further to your discomfort by also irritating surrounding tissue.

You are most likely to get heartburn ten minutes to one hour after eating. Overeating, highly seasoned foods, alcoholic drinks, coffee, acidic fruit juices, smoking, and aspirin seem to trigger heartburn. Lying down after eating or bending over may allow the backup of stomach acids into the esophagus, thus aggravating heartburn.

Heartburn is a common complaint of pregnancy as the growing baby presses on the stomach and esophagus. It usually disappears shortly after delivery.

Heartburn is somewhat relieved by standing or sitting upright. In addition, drinking something soothing like milk and eating small meals frequently can ease heartburn. Antacids that are available without a doctor's prescription may relieve severe heartburn.

If you tend to get heartburn often, try to determine what usually triggers it and then avoid those factors whenever possible. Also, you may want to try several antacids to find the one that works

best for you. (Antacids, however, should not be used if you have kidney disease, since one of the ingredients of antacids may interfere with kidney function.)

If your heartburn is not relieved after trying the appropriate remedies and if it is severe, call your doctor. There is a possibility that persistent heartburn may be a symptom of peptic ulcer or some other more serious disorder.

Loss of Appetite

Loss of appetite—or anorexia—is the lack of the desire to eat. It is a common symptom of many mild illnesses. In extreme cases it can cause weakness and decreased resistance to infections.

Appetite, or hunger, is usually regulated by two centers in your brain. They are a "feeding center" and a "fullness center." Working together, these centers regulate your hunger depending on your body's need for food. Damage or disease in these areas of the brain can affect appetite, but this is extremely rare.

More often people lose their appetite from as simple a cause as fatigue or a bad cold. In such instances, appetite returns in a short time. More severe problems, such as various cancers and glandular and intestinal diseases, may cause longer periods of appetite loss. In these cases, medical attention is necessary.

Psychological problems such as anxiety and depression can also cause loss of appetite. If anorexia stemming from emotional reasons lasts a long time or frequently occurs, the doctor may recommend psychological counseling.

It is essential to remember that whenever appetite does not return quickly and there is no obvious cause, such as a cold, you should consult your doctor.

Nausea and Vomiting

Nausea is an intensely uncomfortable feeling in the stomach

area that is accompanied by an urge to vomit. Vomiting is the forceful ejection of the contents of the stomach through the mouth.

Vomiting is triggered by a site in the brain called the vomiting center. This center receives, through impulses along nerves, information from the digestive system and from the mechanisms in the inner ear which control your sense of balance. When this information indicates the need to vomit, the vomiting center sends out nerve signals that cause you to vomit.

Most episodes of nausea and vomiting are temporary and sometimes even advantageous in that harmful substances are expelled from the body. However, prolonged or repeated vomiting can lead to serious loss of essential fluids and salts in the body as well as to nutritional deficiencies. Severe persistent vomiting may also cause damage to the tissue in the esophagus (the passageway from the mouth to the stomach) or upper stomach.

Nausea and vomiting can result from such common and harmless conditions as motion sickness and pregnancy. Eating spoiled food, overeating, eating foods that disagree with you, drinking too much alcohol, emotional upset, and certain drug side effects are other common causes. More serious causes of nausea and vomiting include severe injury and pain, serious disorders of the digestive system (such as peptic ulcers or gastritis), heart disease, gland disorders, and others. Vomiting not preceded by nausea may be associated with brain injury.

A person who is nauseated may experience chills, sweating, drowsiness, headache, and rapid heartbeat and respiration. In addition, there may be salivation— excessive flow of saliva in the mouth.

Both nausea and vomiting usually subside once the cause has been removed or corrected. Vomiting after eating disagreeable foods or during morning sickness of pregnancy may require little or no treatment. However, there are measures which may help relieve the discomfort. Tea and non-cola beverages, especially ginger ale, are usually tolerated quite well (it is important to remember that a person who is vomiting needs to drink plenty of fluids to replace those being lost). Solid food should not be eaten, although soup or broth is usually recommended. When vomiting has stopped, light foods such as crackers or toast should be tried before returning to a normal diet.

There are also medications that help control the urge to vomit. In cases of severe or prolonged vomiting, your doctor may suggest one of these drugs. However, if you are pregnant or think you may be pregnant, inform your doctor so that the medication recommended will be safe for use during pregnancy.

Anyone who vomits regularly or frequently without being able to pinpoint a cause, and/or anyone who sees blood or red or dark brown spots in the vomitus should seek medical assistance immediately. In some of these cases, the doctor may want to examine a sample of the vomitus.

Diarrhea

Diarrhea is abnormally frequent and liquid bowel movements. Diarrhea is most often a defensive attempt by the body to rid itself of irritating or toxic substances.

There are two general types of diarrhea. One is short-term, or *acute*, diarrhea. This is the more common form. It begins quickly and lasts no more than two or three days. The other is long-term, or *chronic*, diarrhea. This form may also come on quickly, but it becomes persistent, coming and going repeatedly or remaining constantly present for weeks or months.

Although a common symptom of many ailments, diarrhea—particularly chronic diarrhea — can become dangerous. It can lead to loss of body fluids and essential salts and eventually to nutritional deficiencies. Long-term diarrhea may also be a warning of serious problems, for example, colitis (inflammation of the colon) or cancer somewhere in the digestive tract. For this reason, you should contact your doctor if you have diarrhea for more than three days.

Since diarrhea is the passage of bowel movements containing excess water, the basic cause of diarrhea is a malfunctioning in that part of the intestine that absorbs water from waste material as it moves through the intestine. This malfunctioning may have many causes. Acute diarrhea is usually caused by an infection. The organisms that are responsible may be viruses, bacteria, or tiny, one-celled life forms called protozoa. The organisms may enter the intestine when you eat contaminated food or they may accompany a general infection. These organisms either attack the intestine directly or produce substances that irritate it.

Other common causes of diarrhea include changes in the diet, drugs taken for other disorders (particularly antibacterials which disturb the normal bacteria balance of the intestine), stress, strenuous physical exercise, and food allergies.

Diarrhea may be accompanied by symptoms other than frequency of bowel movements. These symptoms include nausea, cramps or other pain in the abdomen, gassiness, fatigue, and fever. Your doctor will need to know about these symptoms as well as your diet, your emotional state, and any changes in habits. The doctor may also examine you thoroughly and request a sample of a bowel movement. This sample will be analyzed for color, consistency, odor, and presence of blood, and chemical content. All of this is necessary to determine the cause of diarrhea.

Treatment often depends upon the cause of the diarrhea, since eliminating the cause—for example, an infection — will probably eliminate the diarrhea. In addition, there are measures to relieve the distress of diarrhea. Rest is essential as is an adequate fluid intake to replace fluid loss. Diet is also important. The meals should be light — perhaps at first restricted to soups and broths—and frequent. As more solid food is included in the diet, the food should be cooked rather than raw. Irritating foods, such as fried foods, bran, fruits and vegetables, spices, coffee, and alcoholic beverages, should be avoided.

If diarrhea persists, your doctor may suggest an anti-diarrhea medication. These medications, however, should be used with caution and only according to instructions.

Constipation

Constipation is the occurrence of difficult or infrequent bowel movements. However, it is important to understand that it is not necessary to have a bowel movement every day. Normal frequency may vary from three bowel movements per day to three per week.

As a rule, constipation is more uncomfortable than harmful, but any change in the usual bowel habits can be a sign of something serious such as cancer.

The most common causes of constipation are physical inactivity, lack of fiber or roughage in the diet, inadequate fluid intake, and emotional distress — particularly depression. Another fairly frequent cause is postponing the bowel movement until the urge is no longer felt. Constipation can also be a side effect of some drugs taken for other disorders.

The possibility of other less frequent but more serious causes means that you should contact your doctor if your constipation lasts a long time or becomes extremely uncomfortable. Just a few of these factors, besides cancer, are intestinal obstruction, disease or injury of the nervous system, and endocrine gland disorders.

Constipation is usually accompanied by other distressing problems. The most common of these is difficulty and strain in producing a bowel movement. Others include a feeling of fullness or being bloated, abdominal cramps, headache, and gassiness. Hemorrhoids (swollen veins near the anus — the opening from the intestine to the outside of the body) may also be a result of constipation.

Treatment often depends on the cause of the constipation. In most cases of simple constipation, unrelated to an underlying disorder, changing your diet by adding more fiber foods and drinking more water — up to eight to ten glasses a day—will often solve the problem. Increasing exercise and developing good bathroom habits are also effective. In healthy individuals the intestine should be conditioned to function in response to normal stimulation. Attempting to have a bowel movement at the same time every day is quite beneficial in establishing regularity without drugs. The best time is in the early morning, about 30 to 60 minutes after breakfast. Food that enters an empty stomach activates and increases normal intestinal contractions. During the night, too, residue from the previous day's meals has moved to the rectal area (the last section of the intestine) and is ready to be eliminated.

The use of laxatives and enemas is generally not recommended. Laxatives should be used only when absolutely necessary. The reason for this is that the intestine tends to become dependent on the laxative and may lose the ability to function without the laxative. Furthermore, prolonged laxative use may irritate the lining of the rectum.

Changes in Urine and Urinary Habits

Changes in urine and in urinary habits may be an indication of disease. Unless you can trace these changes to simple and obvious causes, such as drinking more liquids than usual, you should see your doctor if they last more than a day or two. If there is extreme pain when you urinate or if there is blood in your urine, you should see your doctor immediately. There are several other changes that may require attention.

Frequency. If you are urinating more or less often than usual, there may be a problem. Increased frequency, often accompanied by a sense of urgency, is the more common of the two.

Increased frequency of urination commonly results from inflammation of the kidneys, bladder, or urethra — the passageway from the bladder to the outside of the body. Frequency may also be an early sign of diabetes or of an enlarged prostate gland (the male gland that rests at the bottom of the bladder and surrounds the urethra).

A decrease in urinary frequency should also be investigated. This may be a symptom of kidney failure and may become a medical emergency.

Timing. The most common timing difficulty is waking up repeatedly at night by a need to urinate. The term for this is "nocturia." It is normal upon awakening during the night to have a desire to urinate. However, frequent waking with the desire to urinate may be a symptom of inflammatory or infectious disease within the urinary tract or of tumors or other disorders which cause pressure on the bladder. Such illnesses usually cause other symptoms as well, including painful urination, a poor stream, or difficulty in starting. Anyone with these symptoms should see a doctor as soon as possible.

Control. You may have trouble getting the urine flow started or maintaining the flow once it has begun. This may be a symptom of an inflammation of the prostate gland. Or you may not be able to hold back urine — a problem particularly common in the elderly and in women in late pregnancy when the uterus is pressing on the bladder.

Quantity. Producing an excessive amount of urine is called "polyuria." This condition requires a doctor's attention since it may be a symptom of kidney disease, certain types of diabetes, or endocrine gland disorders.

Pain. The most common type of pain during urination is a burning sensation. Often this is felt along the urethra that leads from your bladder (in which urine is stored) to the outside of your body. It may be a sign of a lower urinary tract infection. Excruciating pain across the abdomen or the back may accompany kidney stones.

Color change in urine. If the color and clarity of your urine change slightly from one day to another, there is no need for concern. If you see strong color changes (particularly blood) or extreme cloudiness, especially along with other distressing symptoms such as pain or fever, contact your doctor immediately.

Treating a change in urine or urinary habits means treating the underlying cause. These causes may range from a mild infection to more serious and complex diseases. Accurate medical diagnosis is the first step in treatment.

Cough

A cough is a normal reflex of the body to eliminate dust, dirt, or other irritants (including bacteria and viruses) and secretions from the respiratory system. The very act of coughing may cause more coughing — air moving rapidly across the sensitive throat lining can irritate the throat and provoke more coughing.

A cough often results from minor aggravations such as inhaling irritating fumes, drinking very hot or very cold beverages, breathing icy air, or mistakenly drawing food into the airways. However, it is also a symptom of more serious respiratory disorders such as influenza, pneumonia, or tuberculosis. Persistent coughs (those that last more than two or three weeks) or those without other respiratory symptoms may suggest diseases of other organs such as the brain or heart. Certain brain injuries may activate the cough center in the brain. A cough may also be an early sign of congestive heart failure.

The type of cough—productive or nonproductive—partially determines its treatment. Productive coughing is often caused by a bacterial lung infection. When bacteria attack the lungs, the lung tissue produces large amounts of secretions in defense. The accumulated secretions irritate the lungs, resulting in coughing that brings up fluid. That is why the cough is called productive — it produces fluid. A yellowish or reddish fluid in particular indicates infection and requires a doctor's attention.

Nonproductive coughing does not bring up fluid. It occurs when nasal passages drain into the throat or when smoke, dust, pollen, or other irritants enter the respiratory system. It may be touched off, too, by drinking liquids that are too hot or by eating highly spiced foods.

Because coughing has the vital function of expelling foreign substances, it should never be totally suppressed. However, it may be necessary to control a cough that is disrupting sleep or aggravating another condition. People who are over the age of 65, those with heart disease or excessively high blood pressure, and those in otherwise poor health may need to control coughing. This may be accomplished by using a cough suppressant or a cough expectorant. A suppressant helps to inhibit the cough while an expectorant encourages the discharge of mucus from the respiratory tract, thus perhaps shortening the course of the illness.

Often nonproductive coughing results from insufficient moisture in the air. The respiratory passages become dry and irritated, and coughing develops. This is particularly common in winter months when the humidity is lowest. The use of a humidifier or vaporizer to add moisture to the air may provide greater relief than any drug.

For other than the mildest, short-lived cough with obvious causes, a doctor should probably be consulted to determine the cause of the cough and to suggest appropriate treatment.

Nasal Congestion

The nose becomes congested when blood vessels in the nose enlarge and begin to leak fluid into surrounding tissue. The enlarged blood vessels reduce the size of the nasal cavities, allowing less air to enter with each breath. The fluid leaking out of the blood vessels also helps fill the nasal cavities and makes breathing more difficult.

A stuffy nose is a symptom of the common cold, influenza, allergy, bronchitis, and a number of other disorders. Constant nasal congestion may occur when structural abnormalities within the nose interfere with flow of air into the nose and when certain drugs are used on a daily basis. Drugs for high blood pressure, for example, work by dilating or enlarging blood vessels including those in the nose. Any persistent nasal congestion requires a doctor's attention.

Nasal congestion is not a serious problem in itself. However, it can be annoying enough to keep you from some of your usual activities and to interfere with normal sleep.

Nonprescription decongestants (in the form of nasal sprays, nose drops, and inhalers) shrink the swollen blood vessels and stop them from secreting fluid. However, they also shrink the blood vessels in other parts of the body, and they may raise blood pressure and increase heart rate. They may also cause nervousness and sleeplessness. Decongestants should not be used by people with high blood pressure, heart disease, diabetes, or thyroid disorders.

In addition, decongestants should be used for only a brief period—three days is usually advised — to avoid "rebound congestion." These products work by constricting the blood vessels. Their repeated use tires the constricting vessels; the fatigued vessels relax completely, making the nose more congested than it was before the product was used. Thus, the term "rebound congestion."

Occasionally, the doctor will prescribe specific medication to be placed in the nose. In addition, a vaporizer or humidifier will help breathing by adding moisture to the air.

Sore Throat

Sore throat is a painful irritation of the throat. It may be as mild as a "scratchy" throat or so severe that swallowing even liquids causes great pain.

The most common cause of a simple sore throat is a cold. During a cold, the nose may be blocked, forcing you to breathe through the mouth. This dries and irritates the throat. In addition, the throat may be sore from coughing or from the secretions draining into the throat through ducts in the back of the nose.

Inhaling irritants or allergy-causing substances such as smoke, pollen, polluted air, or dust can also cause a sore throat. Additionally, these irritations may stimulate drainage from the nose into the throat which in turn becomes even more inflamed. Swallowing hot or stinging liquids or foods may be responsible for a sore throat as well.

A more severe sore throat may be caused by a specific infectious agent present in the throat, middle ear, nose, or sinuses (the sinuses are air-filled cavities in the facial bones that connect with the nasal passages). If a sore throat is accompanied by fever, achiness, and fatigue, or if the throat and mouth are extremely red or have yellow or white spots, it is probably caused by a bacterial (usually strep) infection and should be seen by a doctor. Left untreated, a strep throat could lead to a serious disorder like

rheumatic fever, a heart disease that affects the heart valves and may cause lifelong health problems. Cough and stuffy nose are not characteristic of a strep throat, but the patient may have a strep throat along with another illness. If strep throat is present, antibiotics will be given to combat the infection and to prevent rheumatic fever, and aspirin or an aspirin substitute may be recommended to reduce pain and fever.

If the sore throat lasts more than a week, if it occurs without a cold or a congested nose, and if no obvious irritant can be found, it needs to be evaluated by a doctor. Such a sore throat may be the symptom of a more serious illness, a blood disorder, or a severe infection.

The simple sore throat of a cold is treated by relieving the other cold symptoms. If the inflamed throat results from breathing through the nose, a nasal decongestant may be suggested to assist breathing. Sucking on a piece of hard, sour candy often stimulates soothing saliva flow to the throat. While the throat is sore, the patient should refrain from smoking and talking.

If coughing irritates the throat, a cough suppressant may be beneficial (although a cough suppressant is not always recommended if it allows mucus to accumulate and cause further difficulties). A sore throat may also be somewhat relieved by gargling every hour with a solution of one-half teaspoonful of table salt in a cup of warm water.

Nosebleeds

A nosebleed is bleeding from inside the nose, caused by a break in the blood vessels in the inner lining of the nose. Nosebleeds may occur after an injury to the nose, from breathing dry air for an extended period of time (which dries and irritates the inner lining of the nose), or even from repeated blowing of the nose. Constant nose picking may also cause irritation that eventually leads to

bleeding. More serious causes include tumors in the nose, high blood pressure, and other blood diseases. However, bleeding from the nose is usually not a symptom of serious illness, and most cases can be easily managed.

Recommendations for treatment vary widely. One effective procedure is the following: have the patient sit up and lean forward to prevent swallowing of the blood. Pinch the soft portion of the nose together for about five minutes, or until the bleeding stops, and then gently release. If the bleeding has not stopped, have the patient apply cold packs to the bridge of the nose and sit still for 15 to 20 minutes. If bleeding still persists, see a doctor. The nosebleed may be occurring far back in the nose and may need to be cauterized to stop the flow. Cauterization is the use of heat to seal off the blood vessels.

A person who suffers from frequent nosebleeds as a result of dry air may benefit from a humidifier in the home to add moisture to the air. Anyone with frequent nosebleeds should also take care not to blow the nose too harshly and to blow through both nostrils simultaneously, that is, without closing one while blowing through the other.

A nasal decongestant — which shrinks the blood vessels — may be helpful if the nosebleed seems to occur during a cold or other respiratory infection when the nose is tender. However, decongestants should not be used by people with high blood pressure, heart disease, diabetes, or thyroid disorders.

Very frequent nosebleeds require medical attention. Once the possibility of serious disease has been ruled out, the doctor may decide to cauterize small blood vessels in the nose to keep them from bleeding.

Itching

Itching is an uncomfortable sensation in the skin that produces the desire to scratch. It has been described as a stinging, burning, or crawling feeling. The biological reactions responsible for itching are not clearly understood. It is known that the sensation arises in nerve endings in the skin when they are stimulated.

Some causes of itching are easy to determine. Examples are insect bites, small cuts or scrapes, hives and other allergic reactions, fungus infections, and other clearly visible causes including the rash that accompanies chicken pox and other infectious diseases. The itching clears up when the cause is eliminated.

Many cases of itching with no visible cause are triggered by psychological stress. This type of itching often affects the scalp, but it also occurs frequently in other areas such as the forearms. Removing the stress or learning to handle it is the most effective way of dealing with this kind of itching.

Other relatively common causes of itching are dry skin and reactions to drugs. If the dry skin is only a small area, it can be treated with skin lotions or creams. If large areas of the body itch because of dry skin, bath oils may be helpful. In some cases, a doctor may recommend that baths be limited to two a week, since excessive exposure to water can dry out the skin. You may also want to switch brands of soap to see if soap is aggravating the problem. If a drug reaction is causing the itching, you should consult your doctor. *Never stop taking a drug without consulting your doctor.* If you must continue taking the drug, you may be able to change the dosage to eliminate the itching. On the other hand, the doctor may be able to offer suggestions on how to relieve the itching while you are taking the medication.

If your efforts to relieve the itching fail or if the symptom persists for more than a week, a medical examination is recommended. Under these circumstances, your itching may be a symptom of a more serious problem, including diabetes, thyroid disease, kidney failure, liver disease, or cancer.

Rash

A rash is a skin eruption which most typically appears as red patches, blisters, or spots and is often accompanied by itching. A rash may be confined to one part of the body or it may be more widespread involving extensive areas.

A rash may develop from something as ordinary as exposure to sun, heat, cold, chemicals in household products, or fabrics —for example, wool. Some people may break out in a rash after eating certain foods. These rashes are often allergic rashes. For example, the patient has developed an allergy or sensitivity to a certain food—such as strawberries—and a rash is a symptom of the allergy.

A rash is also a common symptom of some diseases. Measles, rubella or German measles, chicken pox, and shingles are infectious diseases which are characterized by distinctive rashes. Certain sexually transmitted diseases, such as herpes and syphilis, also display distinctive rashes.

If a rash appears and then disappears after a day or two without returning, there is little need for concern. If, on the other hand, a rash reappears regularly, it may mean an allergy, and you should see your doctor. There may be nothing you can do other than relieving minor itching and irritation, but you will want to try to identify and avoid future contact with the irritant. If a rash is a symptom of an infectious disease, there will be other symptoms that will probably confirm the diagnosis. A rash that lasts for more than a few days and that cannot be identified should be seen by a doctor.

A rash often disappears when its underlying cause disappears or is successfully treated. In the meantime, your doctor may have suggestions about relieving the annoying symptoms of a rash. Often a soothing lotion, such as calamine lotion, or a warm bath may offer relief. However, you should consult your doctor before treating any rash.

Hives

Hives (also called urticaria) is an inflammatory condition of the skin characterized by rapidly changing welts or raised lumps. Hives are most often caused by an allergic reaction—an adverse response to a substance to which the body is sensitive. This offending substance is called an allergen. The body's response to the allergen causes body cells to release histamine, a powerful chemical that, when released from the cells, causes hives.

Most cases of hives are caused by allergies to food, including shellfish, pork, strawberries, eggs, milk, tomatoes, and chocolate. Certain drugs, food dyes, molds, and bacteria can also cause hives, as can contact with animals. Sometimes stress or emotional disturbances triggers a case of hives.

Red or white welts may appear all over the body or only in certain areas. The welts vary widely in size and may come and go rapidly, sometimes lasting only a few minutes, sometimes a day or two. Usually, however, the outbreak lasts for a week or so. It causes intense itching and occasionally fatigue, fever, and nausea. There may be difficulty breathing if the allergic reaction leads to swelling of the throat and a constriction of the airways into the lungs.

Hives can be prevented by avoiding the allergen once it is known. Antihistamines taken immediately after exposure help to control swelling by preventing the released histamine from causing symptoms. To be effective antihistamines may have to be taken several times a day and the type and dosage may need to be adjusted periodically to avoid sleepiness, the most common side effect of antihistamines. Depending on the allergy and its severity,

13

other drug therapies may include corticosteroids to reduce swelling and the use of inhalers to ease breathing.

Dizziness and Vertigo

Dizziness and vertigo are similar sensations and are often confused with each other. However, they are different. Dizziness is an uncomfortably distorted sense of one's physical relationship to the surrounding space and objects within it. There is a feeling of unsteadiness and sometimes of swaying, weakness, lightheadedness, or faintness. Vertigo is a false sense of movement — a perception that one is spinning or that one's surroundings are spinning. This, too, is accompanied by feelings of swaying and by the other sensations that are associated with dizziness.

Dizziness and vertigo are often the result of a malfunction in those parts of the body which are responsible for maintaining balanced posture and for providing us with information about the body's position and movements. These parts include the eyes, a balance-sensing mechanism deep inside the ear, and certain areas of the brain. In addition, disorders in the nerves that lead from these parts to the brain can cause dizziness and vertigo. Similarly, any problem within the specific areas of the brain that connect with these nerves can lead to dizziness or vertigo. This is because balance is dependent upon the brain's proper processing of the information it receives from the rest of the body through the nervous system.

Therefore, any injury, disease, or deterioration of the eye, ear, nerves, or brain can cause dizziness or vertigo. This explains why these symptoms accompany such a wide variety of problems, ranging from bumps on the head and ear infections to migraine headaches and epilepsy.

However, an occasional feeling of dizziness or vertigo is not cause for alarm. Becoming too warm, overtired, tense, or nervous can cause dizziness. So can standing up quickly after spending some time lying or sitting down. Frequent, repeated, or severe attacks of dizziness or vertigo, however, require medical attention.

The symptoms of dizziness and vertigo may be somewhat similar. Both dizziness and vertigo are often accompanied by nausea, vomiting, and a sense of weakness. However, vertigo displays other signs as well. A person with mild vertigo can walk, but only unsteadily and often veering to one side. A more severe attack of vertigo can cause falling down, paleness, and sweating as well as nausea and vomiting. In addition, the eyes may move continually and rapidly, causing the person to think that surrounding objects are moving.

There is no specific treatment for occasional dizziness other than identifying and treating its cause. Recurrent dizziness or vertigo, on the other hand, should be investigated by a physician since it may result from a disorder in the eye, ear, or nervous system.

Fainting

Fainting is a temporary loss of consciousness. It is usually a result of reduced blood supply to the brain.

There are several internal mechanisms that protect your brain by preventing blood from collecting in the lower part of the body because of simple gravity. One such mechanism is the body's ability to constrict, or reduce the size of, blood vessels in these areas. Another is the ability to increase the rate of the heart, thereby increasing the heart's output. Still another is the natural effect of muscle, limb, and breathing activities which aids the blood's circulation. Interference with any of these mechanisms can cause you to faint. Because fainting usually results in your falling down, it brings your head to the same level as your heart. This makes it easier for the heart to supply the brain with the blood it needs.

Most fainting is harmless — a defensive reaction by the body to restore the temporary reduction in the blood supply to the brain. It is usually triggered by a hot and crowded place, emotional stress, unusual fatigue, or hunger. However, occasionally more serious factors may cause a person to faint. These include various drugs (such as some high blood pressure medications) and certain diseases (such as anemia, hypoglycemia, diabetes, heart disease, atherosclerosis, bleeding peptic ulcers, and epilepsy).

Before fainting, most people feel quite sick. There is confusion, lightheadedness, and spots before the eyes. The face turns white or ashen gray, and often the skin is cold and moist. Nausea, and sometimes vomiting, also may occur.

Fainting can be avoided if you lie down upon noticing these signs. Hanging your head between your knees and breathing deeply may also help to prevent fainting. Both these actions serve to get the brain at or below the level of the heart, which helps increase blood flow to the brain. Spirits of ammonia and smelling salts are not reliable aids and may cause vomiting.

To help someone recover from a faint, certain steps need to be followed. The individual should be lying down, preferably with the feet higher than the head. Loosen clothing, splash cool water on the face, and make certain there is plenty of fresh air. Recovery should occur within seconds of falling, although a sense of disorientation may prevent the person from returning to activity for a few minutes.

Recurrent fainting should be discussed with a doctor.

Hemorrhage

Hemorrhage is the technical term for bleeding. Often the term is used to refer to heavy or un-

14

controlled bleeding, either externally or internally.

Hemorrhage occurs because blood vessels are torn or broken. Blood normally clots within seconds or minutes of an injury to a blood vessel, thus halting the loss of blood and preventing death. In severe injuries, however, the blood's clotting mechanism is inadequate. Furthermore, in certain blood diseases such as hemophilia, the blood-clotting mechanism is disturbed; in these cases internal bleeding may occur in any part of the body often with serious consequences.

The effects of hemorrhage depend upon what part of the body is affected and how much blood is lost. However, severe hemorrhage produces symptoms that are easily noticeable and that demand immediate medical attention. These symptoms include rapid pulse, dizziness, faintness, and often collapse and shock. The patient may become pale, cold, and sweaty with a drop in blood pressure and a rise in pulse rate. If the blood loss is not halted, death may occur.

An internal hemorrhage may also show symptoms, even if the bleeding is slight. Bleeding in the intestinal tract from a peptic ulcer or cancer of the colon may cause black, tarry stools. Bleeding in the stomach, may lead to blood in the vomit. A hemorrhage in the kidney or urinary tract may be revealed by blood in the urine.

Frequent hemorrhaging always requires a doctor's attention. Likewise, hemorrhaging that doesn't stop within a reasonable period of time (minutes to hours depending upon the severity of the wound) should be seen by a doctor. Blood in the stool, urine, or vomit should always be reported to a doctor at once.

Treatment of an internal hemorrhage involves correcting the cause of the hemorrhage. This may necessitate surgery. An external hemorrhage is treated by applying pressure with a sterile gauze bandage on the bleeding site. In an emergency situation, simply pressing on the wound may check the blood flow.

In situations where the bleeding cannot be controlled, the patient will probably be hospitalized where the lost blood can be replaced by blood transfusions. If the bleeding continues, it may be treated surgically by tying off or sealing the bleeding vessels.

Shock

The term shock describes a sudden drop in blood pressure or a collapse of the circulatory system. This results in a serious reduction in the blood supply to all parts of the body. Shock is an extremely dangerous condition; if it is not treated quickly, death usually occurs.

Generally, shock occurs when a great deal of blood or body fluid has been lost. It can also occur when blood vessels dilate (expand), causing blood to pool or collect in one part of the body and not circulate effectively. Shock may develop with severe infection, burns, wounds and broken bones, hemorrhage, excessive vomiting or diarrhea, insect stings (in individuals who are allergic to the insect's venom), heart attacks, and certain drugs. Shock is a possibility in virtually every serious accident, burn, poisoning, or injury.

Symptoms of shock include weakness, rapid but weak pulse, paleness, cold and clammy skin, sweating, chills, thirst, nausea, shallow breathing, and very low blood pressure. If untreated, shock may progress to unconsciousness.

Shock should be considered in any emergency situation after immediate life-saving first aid is given — for example, after bleeding has been stopped or after making certain that the victim's air passages are open. The patient should lie flat, or with the head lower than the body (unless the head has been injured), and should be kept warm. Do not give food or water.

Contact a doctor. A person in shock should be hospitalized as soon as possible where emergency treatment can be given to restore lost fluids and to raise blood pressure. Shock is considered a medical emergency requiring immediate attention by trained medical professionals.

INFECTIOUS DISEASES

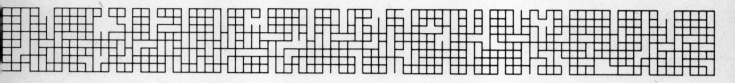

The human body is both surrounded and inhabited by many living organisms. Most are so small that they are invisible to the naked eye. For this reason, they are called *microorganisms*. Many microorganisms are harmless or even beneficial — for example, certain bacteria that normally live in the digestive system help digest food. Occasionally, however, a microorganism capable of causing a disease invades the body. Diseases of this type are called infectious diseases.

Infectious diseases are contagious; that is, they can be passed from one person to another. They can be transmitted by skin contact, by contaminated food or drink, or by airborne particles containing the microorganisms. In addition, animal or insect bites are another means of transmission. (If an insect, for example, bites an infected person, the insect can carry and pass the disease by biting another person.)

The two most common types of infectious diseases are bacterial infections and viral infections. Bacteria are one-celled microscopic organisms. They normally exist in the body by the billions. Most are harmless; some, like those in the digestive tract, perform useful functions.

On the other hand, others are disease-causing, or pathogenic, bacteria which either (1) attack the body's tissues directly or (2) cause damage by secreting poisonous substances called toxins.

Fortunately, bacterial infections are frequently curable; certain bacteria can be killed by drugs called antibiotics. Other bacterial diseases can be prevented by vaccination (this will be discussed in greater detail later in this section).

A virus is the smallest known microorganism. Viruses are responsible for diseases as prevalent and relatively harmless as the common cold and as serious as meningitis. Viruses live and reproduce only within living cells, and only certain cells are susceptible to a specific virus. You may be host to many viruses without suffering any adverse effects, but if enough cells are attacked, you may become sick.

There is no effective medical treatment for viral infections. Because a virus lives inside a cell, any treatment designed to kill the virus is also likely to harm the cell. In addition, there are thousands of different viruses — each with different properties — and an agent effective against one virus probably will not affect the others. Although there are vaccinations for some viral diseases, therapy for most viral diseases is limited to treating the symptoms.

Despite the prevalence of disease-causing microorganisms, your body is not defenseless against these invaders. The body fights infections in three ways: by preventing these organisms from entering the body; by attacking those that do manage to enter; and by inactivating those organisms it

cannot kill. Sometimes, too, the body fights disease by developing defensive symptoms. Fever is an example. During an illness, the body's temperature regulator may respond to the illness by raising the body's temperature. It is thought that the microorganism causing the disease may not be able to survive the higher body temperature.

The skin is the first barrier that guards the underlying tissues of the body. Additional protection is offered by sweat which contains antiseptic (germ-killing) substances. Where there is a natural opening in the skin, there are also defenses. For example, tear glands in the eyes secrete fluid with bacteria-fighting properties to bathe the eyes. The saliva glands in the mouth and the tonsils in the throat help prevent microorganisms from attacking the mouth and throat. Many openings in the body as well as internal passages are lined with mucous membranes. These delicate layers produce mucus, a slippery secretion which moistens and protects by repelling or trapping microorganisms.

Internally, certain body organs fight infection. The liver and spleen — a large gland-like organ located in the abdomen — for instance, filter out harmful substances from the blood flowing through them. The lining of the stomach produces acids that attack germs in food that has been eaten. And the body's lymph sys-

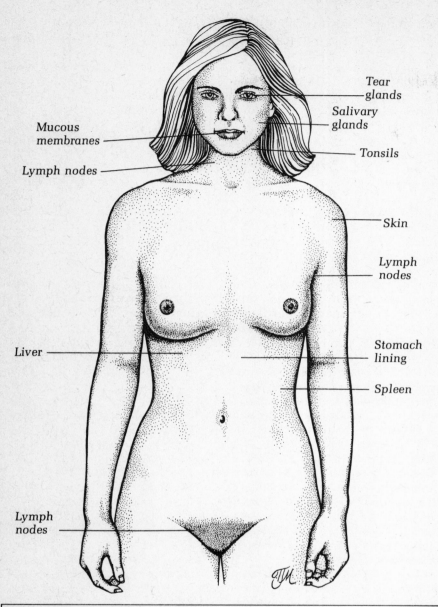

Mucous membranes

Lymph nodes

Liver

Lymph nodes

Tear glands

Salivary glands

Tonsils

Skin

Lymph nodes

Stomach lining

Spleen

The body has many natural defense mechanisms to fight infection.

tem manufactures white blood cells whose job it is to attack and kill invading organisms. The lymph system is a system of vessels which carries lymph, a watery fluid containing white blood cells, throughout the body. Lymph drains from the blood vessels and body tissues, carrying away waste products. The waste products, including germs, are filtered out of the lymph by small glands called lymph nodes. Within the lymph nodes, unwanted microorganisms are trapped, attacked, and destroyed by white blood cells. This is one of the body's primary and most

efficient lines of defense.

The lymph system also manufactures antibodies. Antibodies are protective substances that the body produces in response to an invasion of a hostile organism. Antibodies counteract invading bacteria or viruses by inactivating them so that they are powerless. Antibodies that neutralize toxins (poisons) produced by bacteria are called antitoxins.

The body's production of white blood cells and antibodies in response to an invading disease organism is called the immune reaction. Immunity is the body's ability to resist an invasion of

disease-causing bacteria and viruses. Once antibodies have been made to fight a certain microorganism, that germ no longer poses a threat to the body. That is why one attack of a disease often prevents that same disease from infecting the body again—the first attack causes antibodies to be produced and these antibodies protect the system against subsequent attacks.

Immunity can also be provided artificially. This is the underlying basis of immunization or vaccination. A vaccine is a preparation containing the offending organism — usually in a weakened form that will not cause the actual disease — that is introduced into the body. The vaccine stimulates the body to produce antibodies against the disease. These antibodies remain in the system for a long time (often for life), and the body is thus prepared to resist the actual disease.

Besides vaccination, there are other measures that can be used to help the body's natural defenses fight off an infectious disease. Bacterial infections can often be conquered by medications called antibiotics. Antibiotics, too, are a product of nature. They are substances produced by living microorganisms that kill other microorganisms. Penicillin, for example, comes from a living mold called *Penicillium*. Penicillin is one of the most commonly used antibiotics, along with streptomycin, tetracycline, and erythromycin. Each of these is effective against specific diseases and work by either destroying bacteria or by preventing their reproduction.

Sulfonamides (or sulfa drugs) are synthetic drugs that are also effective against infections. This type of drug is often prescribed for general infections of the body or localized infections in the urinary and intestinal tracts.

Unfortunately, these medications do not attack viruses. Viruses, therefore, account for most of the infectious illnesses today, since no effective cures have been developed. However, some viral diseases can be prevented by immunization. There are vaccines for measles, rubella (German measles), mumps, and some strains of influenza—all of which are viral diseases. There is no effective vaccine available yet for chicken pox or shingles.

Researchers are continually searching for new ways to help the body combat infectious diseases. Medical advances against these diseases have already been dramatic—not too many years ago infectious diseases were uncontrollable and thus a constant danger. The understanding and control of infections has been one of medicine's greatest accomplishments.

CHICKEN POX

Chicken pox is a usually mild but extremely contagious disease that is characterized by an itchy, blistery rash. Most people have chicken pox as children and do not get it again. During the course of the disease, the body manufactures antibodies, or protective substances that circulate in the blood to combat the virus. These antibodies prevent the virus from causing the disease a second time.

Although chicken pox does not recur, the same virus that causes it also causes shingles, a nerve disorder. Since a previous infection with chicken pox is necessary to get shingles, it is believed that the virus remains inactive in the body after recovery from chicken pox. However, why shingles occurs in some people many years after they have had chicken pox and how the virus survives in the body are not well understood.

Chicken pox seldom leads to serious complications in otherwise healthy children. However, infection of the blisters is common. This sometimes happens because the person scratches the blisters, and bacteria enter where the skin is broken. Also, if the rash spreads to the eyes, it can cause pain and may damage the eyes.

On the other hand, chicken pox may be a considerably more

dangerous disease for anyone who already has a chronic disease, especially a disease such as leukemia or other forms of cancer. Both the chronic disease itself and the treatment for it may reduce the body's ability to fight infection. The same difficulties apply to anyone who is taking steroid drugs. In such cases, pneumonia or encephalitis (inflammation of the brain) may occur and can cause death.

Other rare complications of chicken pox include kidney infections, heart problems, arthritis, inflammation of the testes in men or boys, and Reye's syndrome, a form of encephalitis. Chicken pox causes about 100 deaths per year in the United States, mostly in persons either under five years old or over 20 years old.

Chicken pox is caused by the varicella zoster virus. It is so contagious that anyone in a household where the disease occurs will almost certainly get it, unless he or she has had it already. In schools, once one child contracts chicken pox, about half of the classmates will also get it. The other half will have had it before. Chicken pox is usually contagious for about six days after the rash first appears. After that time, the blisters have generally all crusted or scabbed over.

Chicken pox travels from person to person through contact with the blisters or anything contaminated by them. It is also possible that it travels through the air, since chicken pox may be caught from an infected person before the rash has developed. However, some researchers believe this is because one or two spots may appear before the rash is generally recognizable on the body. It is also possible to get chicken pox through exposure to shingles.

Almost everyone will get chicken pox at some time. In urban areas in moderate climates, most children have chicken pox between the ages of five and eight. Those who live in tropical countries are less likely to have it as children, apparently because the

virus is less common in the tropics. In the United States, less than 20 percent of cases occur in persons over 15 years old. Babies under six months old whose mothers have had chicken pox are usually immune, because antibodies from the mother are passed to the baby before birth and can remain in the child for that long.

Chicken pox can appear at any time of the year, but outbreaks occur most often in winter and spring.

SYMPTOMS

In children, the first symptom of chicken pox is usually the rash which is very itchy. It begins as

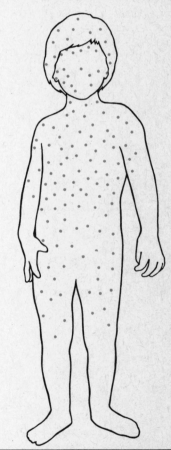

The rash of chicken pox begins as small, itchy red spots on the scalp, face, and trunk and later may spread to the arms and legs. The spots become larger, fluid-filled blisters which then burst and scab over. Unless scratched, the scabs eventually fall off and leave no scars.

small, red spots usually on the scalp, face, and trunk. The spots become larger, fluid-filled blisters in a few hours. Over the next few days, the blisters fill with pus, burst, and crust or scab over. During this process, new spots appear in the same location or elsewhere, and go through the same changes. New spots appear two to four times in a two- to six-day period. They may spread to the arms and legs and occasionally to the soles and palms. The most troublesome areas for the rash are in the eyes, in the mouth, and in the throat.

The other main symptom is a mild fever (101° to 103°F.) that rises as the rash spreads and then disappears as the rash goes away. Some children have a slight fever and a dragged-out feeling a few days before the rash begins, but this is more common in adults. Adults usually have higher fevers, a more severe rash, headaches, and muscle aches and take longer to recover than children. Unless a bacterial infection develops on the skin, the chicken pox rash usually heals completely without leaving scars. Recovery from all symptoms usually takes ten days to two weeks.

A physician diagnoses chicken pox by the characteristic rash and by confirming that the patient has been exposed to the disease. The incubation period — the time between being exposed to the virus and actually having symptoms — is ten to 21 days, so the doctor will look for evidence that exposure occurred about two weeks before the symptoms began.

TREATMENT

There is no cure for chicken pox. In most cases, the only necessary treatment is the application of soothing lotion (for example, calamine lotion) to the rash to reduce itching, and baths in tepid (not hot) water to keep the skin clean and reduce the risk of infection in the rash. Bathing will not spread the rash, because the viruses are destroyed in the water. If the itching is severe, the doctor

may recommend trimming the fingernails and wearing gloves at night to minimize scratching. If the rash becomes infected, the physician may prescribe an antibiotic ointment.

Aspirin is usually not recommended for the fever in chicken pox because it can increase the risk of complications. For example, the use of aspirin during the course of a viral disease has been linked to Reye's syndrome, a type of brain inflammation. Your doctor may suggest an aspirin substitute if needed.

Consult the doctor if breathing problems, high fever, extreme drowsiness, severe headache, vomiting, or staggering occur during the course of the disease or within several weeks of recovery. These symptoms may indicate serious complications, including Reye's syndrome.

Researchers are working to develop a vaccine to prevent chicken pox, but no vaccine is generally available yet.

INFECTIOUS MONONUCLEOSIS

In infectious mononucleosis, or "mono," a virus attacks the lymph glands around the throat, causing sore throat, swollen glands, and fever. The disease usually lasts about six to eight weeks.

Mono is contagious and spreads by contact with moisture from the mouth and throat of an infected person. Infectious mononucleosis is sometimes called the "kissing disease" because it may be passed through kissing. It can also be transferred by sharing drinking glasses, toothbrushes, or anything else that comes in contact with the mouth.

Mono almost always ends in complete recovery, but sometimes the swollen glands in the throat, combined with a throat infection, can make breathing difficult. Occasionally, too, the infection spreads to other parts of the body besides the throat and lymph glands. For example, the disease

can lead to hepatitis, an infection of the liver. Yellowing of the skin and the whites of the eyes, called jaundice, is a symptom of this complication. The spleen, which is a part of the lymph system, may become swollen and may even rupture, or burst. Pain or tenderness in the abdomen is a sign of spleen problems. All of these complications are serious and should be treated immediately.

A person who has mono may contract a second bacterial infection, because of reduced resistance to attack by these infectious agents. Other complications can occur, but are much less common. These are kidney damage, damage to the nervous system, bleeding in the tonsils and adenoids, and bleeding in other organs that have been infected by the virus. However, only about one case of infectious mononucleosis in 3,000 ends in death because of complications.

Mono is caused by a virus, which scientists have identified almost certainly as the Epstein-Barr virus, discovered and named in the mid-1960s. Medical researchers believe that the Epstein-Barr virus infects some persons in early childhood. These early infections are very mild and produce few symptoms or even none at all. Those who have such infections as children are not likely to get infectious mononucleosis as young adults, even if they are exposed to the disease, since they have developed an early immunity to the virus.

In a young adult who has not had the Epstein-Barr infection before, the virus enters the lymph glands and attacks the lymphocytes. Lymphocytes are a type of white blood cell that is made in the lymph glands. When these cells come in contact with the virus, they change shape and begin to multiply excessively. It takes several weeks for enough of these changed cells to accumulate in the body to cause a reaction, so at first there are no symptoms. Symptoms begin gradually, with a mild sore throat, a feeling of tiredness, and a fever. As the body begins to fight the infection, the symptoms worsen. Then they gradually diminish again and finally disappear.

Teenagers and young adults are most susceptible to infectious mononucleosis. It sometimes occurs in children, but seldom affects anyone over 35. There is some evidence that the disease occurs most often in wealthier communities of industrialized countries, possibly because fewer persons raised in affluent communities have Epstein-Barr infections in early childhood. These childhood infections may be due to poor sanitation, but this has not been definitely established.

Partly because many people are immune to the disease, it does not spread as quickly or as widely as other infectious diseases such as flu. There have been few confirmed reports of epidemics of mono, where large numbers of persons in the same area have the disease at the same time.

SYMPTOMS

Because mono develops slowly, it may take several weeks to realize that a person with the disease does not have a cold or a case of the flu. A sore throat that lasts two weeks or more, swollen glands around the neck, armpits, and groin (the juncture of the lower part of the abdomen and the inner thigh), a persistent fever (usually at about 102°F.), and a feeling of tiredness (known medically as malaise) are hallmarks of the disease. In a cold or flu, such symptoms would last only a few days or a week at the most.

The symptoms of mono are often mild, but they can be quite severe, with a throat so sore that swallowing becomes difficult and fevers as high as 105°F. Some people also experience a rash, pain in the eyes, or extreme discomfort in bright light (photophobia). Jaundice, or yellowing of the skin and the whites of the eyes, may occur. This indicates that the liver is affected.

To determine if a person with these symptoms does in fact have infectious mononucleosis, the physician will take two blood samples two weeks apart. The first sample will be tested for an excessive number of white blood cells, the presence of abnormally-shaped white blood cells caused by the virus, and for antibodies (protective substances) made by the body to fight the Epstein-Barr virus. The second blood test is done only if the first one shows signs of the disease to measure the number of white blood cells again. If the count is still high, the diagnosis is confirmed.

TREATMENT

Once infectious mononucleosis has been identified, there is little that can be done about it. The disease is caused by a virus, and viruses usually cannot be treated with drugs. The treatment for mono, as long as no complications develop, is to stay in bed, to drink lots of liquids until the temperature returns to normal, and then to gradually resume normal activities as strength returns. Some people take as long as six months to recover completely, but six to eight weeks is more common. The last symptom to disappear is usually the tired feeling, which may also include depression. Mono may flare up again in a milder form within a few months of the first infection, but it almost never appears again after a year has passed.

The doctor may prescribe antibiotics if a bacterial infection develops along with mono. In severe causes, corticosteroid drugs may be prescribed to reduce swelling. The doctor may also check to see if the spleen is swollen and may recommend avoiding strenuous activities, such as heavy lifting or pushing, that may cause a sudden rupture of the enlarged spleen.

If severe complications occur, hospitalization may be necessary.

INFLUENZA

Influenza is commonly known as "the flu." It is an infectious disease, caused by a virus, with fever and respiratory symptoms. Influenza is an uncomfortable illness, but it is usually not dangerous in otherwise healthy adults. It often occurs in epidemics, in which large numbers of persons in a community, or even an entire country, get the disease within a short period of time. About every ten years, influenza causes a pandemic, or worldwide epidemic. When epidemics or pandemics of influenza occur, many people die from complications of the disease. The worst flu pandemic in this century was in 1918. That year, there were 21 million deaths attributed to influenza. Since then, treatment and prevention procedures have improved, and deaths usually occur only in the very old, in the very young, and in persons who have chronic diseases.

The most common complication of influenza is pneumonia, or infection of the lungs. This can take one of several forms. The most dangerous is viral pneumonia caused by the influenza virus itself. This type of penumonia becomes severe very quickly, and, because it is caused by a virus, antibiotics are not effective against it. Viral pneumonia complicates influenza most often in those who have heart disease or some other chronic disease that has weakened the individual's resistance to infection. It is often fatal.

Bacterial pneumonia can also follow influenza. It is not as serious, because it can be treated with antibiotics. However, in someone whose resistance to infection is low, and especially in the elderly, this type of pneumonia can also be fatal.

Other less serious respiratory complications can result from influenza, including croup in children and bronchitis.

Another life-threatening complication of influenza is Reye's syndrome. This disorder affects children between the ages of two and 16. It is a type of encephalitis, or inflammation of the brain, that is accompanied by deteriorating changes in the liver.

There are at least two types of viruses that cause influenza: influenza A and influenza B. Within each type is a number of different "strains" of the virus that are named after the place where they were identified. That is why there might be an epidemic of "Hong Kong" flu one year and "Russian" flu another.

After an outbreak of flu, the virus strain that caused it changes its structure. The antibodies, or protective substances made by the body to combat the virus, no longer work against that virus. Scientists have been studying this characteristic of influenza for many years, and they can now predict with some accuracy (but not infallibly) what type of virus to expect each year. However, about every ten years an entirely new strain appears, and almost no one is immune to it, either from vaccination or from previous exposure. It is at those times that pandemics occur. It is not known exactly how the viruses change or where they go between epidemics.

Once an outbreak of flu begins, everyone who is not immune to the particular virus causing the disease is susceptible. However, influenza affects children most often. Favorable conditions for spread of the disease are low humidity and temperature in the environment; for this reason, influenza almost always occurs in the fall and winter months. Crowding, for example, in schools and other institutions and on military bases, also encourages the spread of influenza. It is thought that influenza is transmitted by airborne particles that come from an infected person's respiratory system. The viruses probably enter the body through the respiratory system as well.

SYMPTOMS

The incubation period for influenza — the time it takes for symptoms to develop once the body has been exposed to the virus — is one to three days. Sometimes it is as short as 18

A vaporizer to add moisture to the air will help relieve the respiratory symptoms of influenza.

hours. The symptoms begin suddenly with fever, chills, headache, muscle aches, and sometimes total exhaustion. The fever usually lasts about three days and may go as high as 106°F. Temperatures of 100° to 104°F, however, are more common.

While these symptoms are developing, the person may also have a dry cough and a runny or congested nose. These symptoms become more noticeable as the fever, aches, and chills subside. The respiratory symptoms worsen and last for three to four days. The cough, along with weariness and sometimes depression, can last for two weeks or more after the other symptoms disappear.

During an outbreak of influenza, physicians can often diagnose the disease from the pattern of symptoms. In an epidemic, about 85 percent of those who have flu-like symptoms have the disease. Flu rarely occurs in isolated cases.

TREATMENT

Influenza cannot be cured, but there is an anti-viral drug that can reduce the severity of the symptoms. The drug can also prevent influenza in certain circumstances. Since it can have some unpleasant side effects, the drug is usually used only when the patient is especially susceptible to complications. Furthermore, it is only effective against influenza A viruses.

In most cases, the treatment for flu is like treatment for a bad cold or a fever. Bed rest is usually necessary. The physician may recommend extra fluids and an aspirin substitute to reduce the fever and muscle aches. Nasal sprays or drops, cough medicines, and a vaporizer in the patient's room to add moisture to the air will help relieve cold-like symptoms.

When pneumonia occurs with influenza, the symptoms often include difficulty in breathing, blood in the material produced by the cough, and a bluish color to the skin. Consult a physician at once if these symptoms occur.

An influenza vaccine, or "flu shot," is put together each year by researchers in an attempt to prevent the spread of the current virus or viruses to those persons who are most susceptible to complications. It is made up of several different strains, and is given in the fall for the flu season ahead. This vaccine can protect against the strains comprising it for several years, but it is not necessarily effective against new or different strains.

Some people have reactions to the vaccine itself, ranging from inflammation at the vaccination site to mild flu symptoms. Very rarely, more serious problems occur such as nervous system disorders. To reduce the likelihood of such reactions in children, the vaccine is given to them in two small doses four to eight weeks apart. In adults who have had flu shots before, only one dose is necessary. The vaccine is between 67 and 92 percent effective.

MEASLES

Measles is a contagious disease caused by a virus. Another name for the disease is rubeola. Measles affects mainly the respiratory system, the eyes, and the skin. It is uncommon today because a vaccine has been developed to prevent it, but it used to be one of the more dangerous of the childhood diseases.

Measles is considered dangerous mainly because of complications. The most serious ones are pneumonia, or infection of the lungs, and encephalitis, or inflammation of the brain. Pneumonia causes 90 percent of the

deaths from measles, although today deaths from measles rarely occur.

Measles can also lead to severe ear infections, particularly in young children. Other possible complications are bronchitis, laryngitis, and severe swollen glands in the neck. Such disorders can make the disease last longer than usual or cause a relapse — a return of the symptoms after apparent recovery.

There may also be a connection between measles and a very serious and often fatal disease of the brain called subacute sclerosing panencephalitis, or SSPE. However, this disease is very rare, and the link between it and measles has not been definitely established.

Measles spreads from person to person through droplets of moisture in the air from an infected person's respiratory system. It is possible to catch the disease from an infected person up to four days before that person's symptoms begin and up to six days after the rash develops. Some researchers believe that the virus actually enters the body through the eyes.

Today most children are vaccinated against measles by an injection given around the age of 15 months. Persons born between 1957 and 1968 are now the most likely to get measles. Those born before 1957 probably had measles as children, and by 1968 most children routinely received an effective vaccination. Another susceptible group is babies over six months old who have not yet been vaccinated. Most babies are immune to measles from birth to six months old because they acquire temporary immunity from their mothers before birth. The vaccination is still not given at six months, however, because it has a relatively low effectiveness rate before 15 months of age. The vaccination is delayed until it is most likely to work, since the risks of exposure to measles are small. If a baby is exposed to measles, however, consult a physician: measles is a dangerous disease in anyone under three years old. Measles is

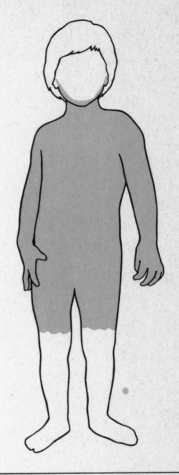

The measles rash usually begins on the face, the neck, and behind the ears. The rash appears as dark red spots that merge together as they spread over the body as far down as the knees.

also likely to be serious in individuals who have chronic, or long-term, diseases.

SYMPTOMS

Measles usually begins with symptoms like those of a bad cold: runny nose, nasal congestion, sneezing, a dry cough, and a fever between 102° and 104°F. By the third or fourth day, the eyes become red and swollen and may be sensitive to bright light. Then the fever drops. Inside the mouth, red spots with tiny white centers appear. These are called Koplik's spots, after the man who discovered them.

On the fourth or fifth day, the rash appears and the fever goes up again. The rash usually begins on the face, the neck, and behind the ears, then spreads to the rest of the body. The spots are light pink, flat, and about the size of a pinhead at first. As they spread the spots grow larger, become raised, and sometimes run together. They turn a dark red and then a brownish color. About a week after the rash first appears, the skin begins to come off in small flakes. Discoloration of the skin may last for as long as two weeks after the rash begins. The other symptoms usually disappear within seven to ten days of the start of the disease.

Measles can be diagnosed by a physician from the characteristic symptoms. If there is an outbreak of the disease, the physician will probably know about it, since measles is relatively uncommon. The incubation period, or the time between exposure to the disease and the first symptoms, is eight to 12 days. A test on nasal discharge, blood, or urine can be conducted if necessary to confirm the diagnosis.

TREATMENT

There is no cure for measles. Treatment is aimed at making the person as comfortable as possible. A vaporizer will add moisture to the air in the patient's room and may ease the cold-like symptoms. Dim lights will be more comfortable than bright ones if the eyes are painful. Most physicians recommend using an aspirin substitute to reduce high fevers, especially in children, because aspirin may increase the risk of complications. The skin should be washed without soap, because soap may irritate the rash. The doctor may suggest adding baking soda to the bath water or applying a soothing lotion to the rash to relieve itching. Warm, moist compresses may make the eyes more comfortable.

If the person has chest pain, problems with breathing, increased coughing, earache, or extreme drowsiness, consult the physician. Such symptoms may indicate complications.

If a susceptible person has been exposed to measles, a physician can sometimes give an injection of gamma globulin. This substance works by supplementing natural resistance to infection, and it can prevent the measles virus from causing symptoms or make the symptoms less severe in some cases. It is usually used only when the exposed person is under three years old or already has some other serious illness.

The United States Public Health Service is trying to eliminate measles altogether, so all confirmed cases are reported to health authorities. Children and others who have not been vaccinated against measles should be vaccinated if possible. The vaccine is 95 percent effective.

MUMPS

Most people have mumps as children. It is a contagious disease caused by a virus. It is also called "epidemic parotitis," because it spreads rapidly from person to person and because it causes swelling of the parotid glands — the saliva glands beneath the ear.

Although mumps can be painful and uncomfortable, it seldom has long-term complications. The most dangerous complication of mumps is encephalitis, or in-

flammation of the brain. This is the only complication of mumps that carries a risk of death. One possible result of mumps encephalitis is hearing loss, or even deafness, usually on one side only. The hearing may return to normal after several months.

Pancreatitis, or inflammation of the pancreas, can also be a complication of mumps. The pancreas is a gland near the stomach that produces digestive juices and the hormone insulin. Symptoms of pancreatitis include stomach pain, vomiting, chills, fever, and weakness; however, these signs disappear, leaving no damage. It is possible, but rare, to develop diabetes after having pancreatitis.

Other rare complications of mumps include arthritis, blood disorders, heart problems, and nervous system disorders, all of which are temporary.

Mumps has a reputation for causing sterility (the inability to conceive a child) in males who have reached sexual maturity. Although mumps often cause swelling and pain in one testicle — the male sex gland — and the affected testicle may atrophy, or shrink, it will almost always return to normal with time. Sterility hardly ever occurs.

Mumps is caused by a virus that spreads from person to person through contact or through air-

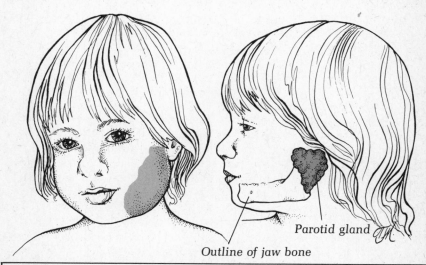

Parotid gland

Outline of jaw bone

Mumps is a viral disease that infects the salivary glands, particularly the parotid gland beneath the ear. The infection results in a painful swelling of the face in front of the ear.

borne moisture from an infected peron's nose or throat. It is also possible to catch mumps from someone who either has the disease without having symptoms or who has not yet developed the symptoms.

Most adults have had mumps even though they may not remember it. The symptoms are sometimes mild, or nonexistent. Once you have had mumps, even without symptoms or only on one side, you will not get it a second time. There have been reports of persons who have had mumps twice, but many researchers believe that one of the cases must have been diagnosed incorrectly in virtually every instance.

Mumps usually occurs between the ages of six and ten, and 85 percent of cases occur before age 15. The disease is most often seen in the spring, but it can develop at any time of the year.

SYMPTOMS

Mumps usually begins with fever, headache, and loss of appetite. Complaints of earache follow. The most common and characteristic symptom, swelling of the parotid glands—the saliva glands just below the ear along the jawline — usually appears next. The swelling starts on one side and often spreads to the other side a few days later. However, sometimes only one side is affected. The inflammation may be minor or extremely painful. It may be difficult to eat or even to swallow.

There may also be a fever between 101° and 103°F. In boys, one or both testicles may become swollen, which may be extremely painful. This is known medically as orchitis. In girls, the ovaries — female sex glands — may be affected, but the problem usually causes little discomfort. Other glands and organs may also become swollen including the other saliva glands, the breasts, the liver, and the brain.

If the brain is affected, there may be a mild form of a condition called meningocephalitis, or inflammation of the meninges (the coverings of the brain) and the brain itself. The patient may have a stiff neck, headache, high fever, drowsiness, dislike of bright light, and possibly delirium. In spite of these severe symptoms, recovery is usually complete without damage to the brain. If the symptoms appear after the other symptoms of mumps have disappeared, or if they are extremely severe, the person may have encephalitis, which is more dangerous.

A physician diagnoses mumps by examining the swollen glands and tracing exposure to the disease. The parotid glands often have a particular form and texture in mumps. In boys, swelling and pain in the testicles are also signs of the disease. The incubation period, or the time between being exposed to the virus and beginning to show symptoms, is 14 to 21 days.

In some cases, these characteristic symptoms do not appear. If mumps is suspected, the mumps virus can then be found in the blood, urine, or saliva — the secretions from the saliva glands.

TREATMENT

There is no cure for mumps, so treatment is aimed at reducing the person's discomfort as much as possible. Bed rest is usually not necessary. A person with mumps may prefer soft foods and liquids. Fruit juices, however, may sting because of their acid content. The physician may prescribe painkilling drugs if the glands are severely swollen, and either warm or cold compresses on the glands may help. For boys or men, steroid drugs may be prescribed if the testicles are extremely swollen, but the drugs may be ineffective. Also, ice packs may ease the pain. Most cases of mumps clear up completely in about ten days.

A vaccine is available to prevent mumps. It is usually given in combination with measles and rubella (German measles) vaccines during a child's second year. The mumps vaccine is 95 percent effective in preventing the disease.

RUBELLA

Rubella, or German measles, is a contagious viral disease with mild, cold-like symptoms and a short-lived rash. The disease usually is not dangerous, except when it occurs in pregnant women. Especially in the first three to four months of pregnancy, rubella can affect the fetus, or unborn child, causing serious, lifelong problems. A vaccine is available to prevent the disease, and rubella is now relatively uncommon. The last major outbreak was in 1964-1965.

Although rubella is generally a mild infection, it can lead to encephalitis, or inflammation of the brain. This occurs in only about 1 in 5000 cases. It can also lead to a blood disease called thrombocytopenic purpura. Both of these disorders can be fatal, and they cause most of the deaths associated with ordinary rubella. In older patients, especially women, rubella sometimes causes joint pain, but this usually lasts only about two weeks.

The most serious complication of rubella, however, is congenital rubella syndrome, or rubella infection that is present at birth. A woman who gets the disease during pregnancy, runs the risk of spreading the virus to the fetus itself. Congenital rubella syndrome can cause a wide range of problems. The most common of these are congenital heart defects. Others may include hearing and vision problems, blood disorders, brain disorders that can cause retardation, and growth disorders. Up to 20 percent of infants born with rubella die, most of them by the age of six months. Most of the others are permanently impaired in some way.

A blood test can be taken to determine immunity (resistance) to the disease. Because of the serious consequences of this infection for pregnant women, it is recommended that women of childbearing age who have not been vaccinated against the disease find out if they are immune and have a vaccination if necessary. It is not harmful to be vaccinated if you are already immune. However, because of a slight risk of infection for the fetus, vaccination is not recommended for pregnant women. Also, a woman receiving the vaccination should wait at least three months before becoming pregnant.

Rubella is caused by a virus. The infection is spread from person to person by airborne particles from an infected individual. It is possible for an infected person to spread the virus as early as one week before the rash appears and as late as five days after the rash fades. It is also possible to get the infection from a baby with congenital rubella syndrome until the child is about a year to 18 months old. Rubella seldom occurs twice in the same person, but cases of second infections have been reported.

SYMPTOMS

The symptoms of rubella usually begin with a runny nose, swollen glands in the neck, and a slight fever (up to 101°F.). After about two days, a rash develops on the face and neck. The spots of the rash are about a tenth of an inch in diameter and light red or pink. They are flat at first, then become slightly raised, and fade within a day or two. As the first spots fade, more spots develop on the trunk and arms. The rash lasts only two to three days. The swollen glands may persist for as long as a week, and all other symptoms have usually disappeared by then. If joint pain develops, it may last another week.

Rubella is difficult to diagnose because the symptoms are so mild and are also quite variable. For example, the disease can occur with no rash and resemble an ordinary cold. An especially serious case may be confused with a mild case of measles. Nevertheless, if rubella is suspected, a physician can identify it definitely with a blood test. Also, if there is an outbreak of the disease, exposure contacts can be traced. The incubation period, or the time between

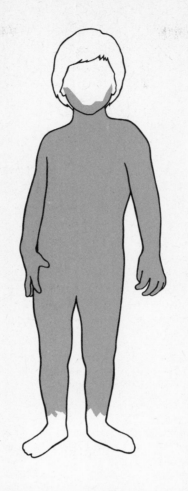

Rubella, or German measles, produces a light pink rash that first appears on the face and neck and gradually spreads over most of the body.

contact with the virus and the beginning of the symptoms, is 14 to 21 days.

TREATMENT

Usually no treatment is necessary for rubella. If joint pain develops, aspirin or an aspirin substitute may provide some relief. Otherwise, drugs usually are not needed. Bed rest may be suggested, but usually the person feels well enough to be up and somewhat active.

The rubella vaccine is given routinely in combination with measles or measles and mumps vaccines to children at about 15 months of age. It is 95 percent effective.

The United States Public Health Service is attempting to eliminate rubella to prevent the problems caused by congenital rubella syndrome. Because of various programs aimed at vaccinating as many persons as possible, the number of cases of the disease has dropped significantly in recent years.

SHINGLES

Shingles, also known as herpes zoster, is a nerve infection caused by a virus. The virus attacks one or more nerves which become inflamed and swollen. The infection is painful and is accompanied by a blistering, itchy rash on the skin above the affected nerve. This rash is almost identical to the rash of chicken pox, and, in fact, the two diseases are caused by the same virus, varicella zoster.

The most common complication of shingles is a bacterial skin infection at the site of the rash. Such an infection can delay healing of the rash and cause scarring of the skin.

There are also other less common complications. When shingles occurs in the nerves of the face, it may cause eye disorders such as corneal ulcers — eroded spots on the transparent covering across the front of the eyeball. It may also lead to Bell's palsy, a disease in which one side of the face is temporarily paralyzed. Similarly, shingles in other parts of the body can cause temporary paralysis of the area over the affected nerve.

Occasionally, shingles becomes generalized, and the rash spreads over the entire body. This occurs most often in persons who have an underlying disease such as Hodgkin's disease, leukemia, or some other form of cancer. In those who already have such a serious disorder, shingles can cause death, but this is rare.

Shingles occurs almost entirely in those over the age of 15, and more than half of those who get shingles are over 45 years of age.

The disease occurs with increasing frequency in older age groups. Previous infection with chicken pox is necessary to get shingles. (If you are exposed to the virus as an adult and have not had chicken pox, you will get chicken pox, not shingles.) It is believed that the varicella zoster virus remains inactive in the body after recovery from chicken pox, probably in one or more spinal nerves.

Why shingles occurs at any given time and why it only occurs in some individuals is not known. Some research has shown that the virus may be reactivated in some cases by a blow to the affected part or by some other emotional or physical upset. Such a connection was found in 65 percent of the cases studied, but no cause was found for the disease in the rest of the cases.

Another theory that may explain why shingles occurs relates to the antibodies, or protective substances, that are manufactured by the body to fight a chicken pox attack. According to some researchers, the number and strength of those antibodies diminish in time in some individuals, making them susceptible to another attack by the virus. Because some antibodies remain, the person gets shingles rather than chicken pox.

Shingles rarely occurs more than once. If shingles does recur, a physician should be consulted. In many cases, recurrent shingles is a sign of another more serious disease that should be treated promptly. These diseases include leukemia, Hodgkin's disease, and disorders of the immune system—the system that protects the body from infections.

SYMPTOMS

The first symptoms in shingles are an abnormal sensation such as prickling or tenderness in the skin over the affected nerve and burning or shooting pain in the same area. Two to four days later, the rash appears, also in the same part of the body. The rash begins as small, red spots. The spots enlarge

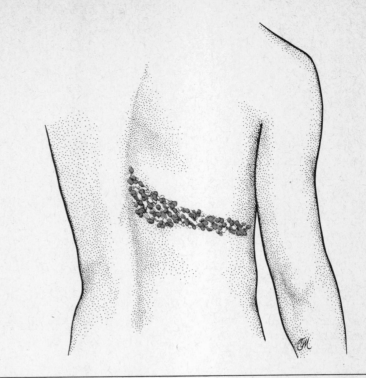

Shingles is a viral nerve infection which is characterized by a blistering, itchy skin rash following the path of the affected underlying nerve. The rash is almost identical to the rash of chicken pox, because both chicken pox and shingles are caused by the same virus —varicella zoster.

and blister and sometimes run together. They then fill with pus, burst, and crust over. This development of the rash is the same as in chicken pox, but it takes longer and is confined to the area above the infected nerve. New spots appear and complete the same process. The rash is very itchy, and the skin beneath it is red and swollen. In most cases in which the person with shingles is under 60 years old, the rash clears up after two to three weeks. The pain usually continues for three or four weeks (although it may continue to appear for a month or more). In those over 60, however, the pain may persist for several months, even though the rash disappears.

Shingles usually affects a nerve on the chest, the back, the neck, an arm, or a leg. The rash appears in a band or strip, often along a rib, and usually only on one side of the body. Facial nerves are also involved fairly often.

The disease is difficult to diagnose at first, because the initial pain can resemble a heart attack, appendicitis, pleurisy, a slipped disc, or one of many conditions, depending on what part of the body is affected. The rash and its characteristic pattern, however, are unique, and the problem can be identified as soon as the rash appears.

TREATMENT

There is no cure for shingles, so the main goal of treatment is to reduce the pain. Some sort of analgesic—or painkilling drug—is usually prescribed. It is also important to prevent the rash from becoming infected by keeping it clean and by avoiding scratching.

For older patients, some physicians prescribe steroid drugs to reduce inflammation in the nerves. This treatment must be started soon after the disease begins or it is not effective. Steroid treatment is not advised when the person has an underlying disease, because steroids can block natural resistance to infection.

ALLERGIES

Ragweed pollen

Cat dander

Foods—milk, eggs, wheat

Insect venom

Medications

House dust

Poison ivy

Feathers

An allergy is an increased sensitivity to an environmental substance. These offending substances are called allergens, and some of the more common ones are shown here.

An allergy is the body's unusual reaction or increased sensitivity to an environmental substance that does not normally affect other individuals. No one knows exactly why some people are sensitive to certain substances while others are not. What is known, however, is the fundamental mechanism which causes an allergic response.

Basically, an allergy is a response of the body's immune system. In simple terms, the immune system functions as follows: when foreign substances invade the body, the blood forms certain substances called antibodies to protect the body against future invasions of the foreign material. In the case of measles, for example, the antibodies formed by having the disease or by being vaccinated (injected) with the measles virus fight off the second attack of the disease, thus providing immunity against a recurrence of the illness. An allergic reaction, on the other hand, although caused by the same immune response, does not protect the body against the invading substance but rather makes the body unusually sensitive to the foreign material. The result is an adverse reaction to the offending substance, called an allergen. The antibodies produced as a reaction to the invading allergen cause the body cells to release histamine, a powerful chemical that, when released from the cells, dilates small blood vessels, constricts smooth muscles—

such as those in the air passages or digestive tract — and causes hives.

Because the antibodies to a particular allergen tend to accumulate over time, a person rarely experiences an allergic reaction on the first encounter with the allergen. But after the first or even several exposures, allergy symptoms may appear. It is essential to remember that any allergy can appear, or disappear, at any age.

In general, there are four categories of allergens:

1. Inhalant—a substance that is breathed in, such as dust, pollen, feathers, animal dander (tiny scales from the skin of an animal). Example of allergy: hay fever.
2. Contactant — something that is in contact with or touches the body, such as poison ivy, cosmetics, dyes, fabrics, detergents. Example of allergy: contact dermatitis.
3. Ingestant—a substance that is swallowed or eaten, including certain foods and oral medications. Example of allergy: food allergy.
4. Injectant—a substance that penetrates the skin, such as insect stings or drugs given by injection. Example of allergy: insect venom.

An allergic reaction can be mild enough to be almost unnoticeable or may be severe enough to threaten life. The watery eyes and runny nose of a mild case of hay fever may be merely annoying to some people. Others, however — for example, those who are allergic to insect venom or certain drugs—may go into anaphylactic shock if stung by a bee or if they are treated with the offending drug. Anaphylactic shock is a serious acute reaction, characterized by breathing problems, hives, collapse of blood vessels, and occasionally by vomiting, diarrhea, and abdominal cramps. If not treated promptly, such a reaction can be fatal.

Most people, however, suffer less severe complications. The swollen nasal tissue and blocked sinuses (air-filled cavities within the facial bones) accompanying hay fever may cause sinus infections, headaches, and diminished senses of taste and smell. Itching and inflammation of the skin may be an annoying effect of a contactant allergen. And hives, often the reaction to a food allergy, may also be associated with swelling of the mouth, throat, and airways, causing intense discomfort and perhaps breathing difficulties.

There is no typical allergy case; allergic reactions and symptoms can occur in any person at any age. However, scientists believe that a family history of allergies may predispose a person to develop a sensitivity to certain allergens. Additionally, a person living in a locale known for its high pollen count is obviously at higher risk of developing an allergy such as hay fever.

Diagnosing an allergy may be simple, but identifying the allergen may be extremely difficult and time-consuming. Sometimes a thorough medical history, including notations of other family members with allergies, combined with a careful review of daily life, especially any recent changes in the environment, may pinpoint the guilty agent. If this kind of analysis does not provide any clues, the physician may decide to test for specific allergies. Skin tests, either scratch or intracutaneous, are common diagnostic procedures. In the scratch test, small quantities of the suspected allergens are applied to tiny scratches in the skin, usually several at a time and in a certain order. After about 20 minutes the doctor observes which substances have caused a reaction. The intracutaneous skin test involves injecting a small amount of the allergens in or under the skin. In both tests, a positive reaction is characterized by a swollen red bump at the application site. However, it is important to remember that many times an allergen which shows a positive reaction may not be the one that causes the most serious allergic illness nor the only substance involved in the allergy.

Skin tests are the cheapest, easiest, and most reliable methods of identifying allergens. However, if it is necessary to avoid the stress and discomfort of skin testing, for example, in young children, in those persons with extremely sensitive skin, or in individuals who are suspected to be extremely allergic to an injected allergen, there is a blood test to diagnose allergies. The test, called RAST (radioallergosorbent technique), uses a blood sample to measure specific antibodies in the blood (you will recall that antibodies, the substances formed by the blood in response to foreign invaders, cause the body to be more sensitive to invading substances). Unfortunately, the RAST is not as accurate as skin testing and is considerably more expensive.

The most obvious treatment for any allergy is to avoid the offending allergen. Many times such a step is easy: if you are allergic to strawberries, you simply avoid eating strawberries. Occasionally, eliminating the cause is more difficult; giving away a family pet is a distressing decision. And sometimes it is virtually impossible to avoid an allergen; a hay fever sufferer cannot leave town whenever the pollen count is high.

Fortunately, there are treatments for those who must coexist with an allergen. The two mainstays of allergy treatment are medications and immunotherapy.

The primary medications are antihistamines to combat the effects of the histamine released in response to the allergen. The antihistamine drugs work by preventing the histamine from causing symptoms. To be effective, antihistamines may have to be taken several times a day, and the type and dosage may need to be adjusted periodically by the physician to avoid sleepiness, the most common side effect of these drugs. Depending on the allergy and its severity, other drug therapies may include corticosteroids to reduce swelling and the use of bronchodilators to ease breathing.

Immunotherapy, or "desensitization shots," takes advantage of the process by which the body develops its own immunity or resistance to invading foreign substances. Beginning with very small amounts, the doctor injects an allergen into the skin in gradually increasing doses. The injections are given at periodic intervals, usually weekly, over a period of several years. If this program of shots is effective, the body slowly develops its own immunity to the allergen. In some cases immunotherapy either cures the allergy or substantially reduces the severity of the reactions. However, immunotherapy is not a practical treatment method for everyone. So far it has been proven to be helpful only for pollen allergies (especially hay fever), insect venom allergies, and possibly allergies to house dust. Allergies to food or to animal dander do not seem to be relieved by immunotherapy. Furthermore, the expense, inconvenience, and discomfort of desensitization shots may limit this treatment to those persons who are incapacitated by their symptoms or who cannot take antihistamines because of side effects.

Common sense precautionary measures can also ease an allergy sufferer's life. Hay fever victims can try to stay indoors during the pollen season or perhaps install air conditioning or air filtration systems. You can replace household and clothing items made of natural fibers, such as wool or feathers, with synthetic products which are less likely to provoke an allergic reaction. If you are allergic to insect venom, you can minimize the chance of stings by wearing protective clothing and avoiding bright clothing colors and perfumes, both of which attract insects. And a final recommendation for new parents with a family history of allergies who would like to reduce a child's chances of developing an allergy: breastfeeding as long as possible plus a delay in introducing cow's milk, eggs, and citrus fruits may eliminate the risks of some allergies early in life.

The following section offers brief descriptions of a common allergy in each of the four allergen categories — inhalant, contactant, ingestant, and injectant.

HAY FEVER

Hay fever is an allergic reaction of the nasal membranes to inhaled substances. Acute seasonal attacks of hay fever are generally reactions to pollen. Typically, spring attacks are reactions to tree pollen; summer attacks are due to grass pollen; and autumn attacks are responses to weed pollen. Year-round hay fever may be a reaction to pet dander, certain fibers, feathers, house dust, or molds.

SYMPTOMS

Hay fever symptoms are usually the same, regardless of the type of allergen involved. The nose, roof of the mouth, and eyes itch severely. A constant thin, watery discharge from the nose is characteristic, and the eyes may water as well. Sneezing and headache are common. Someone with hay fever is often irritable, feels exhausted, and sometimes suffers from inability to sleep and loss of appetite. As the season progresses, the hay fever sufferer may begin to cough and wheeze.

TREATMENT

A severe allergy may best be treated by a change in environment. Someone living in a rural area and who is allergic to weed pollen may find relief by moving to an urban area. An air conditioning system with filters keeps pollen levels low. Relief of year-round hay fever may require giving away the family pet; eliminating carpets, draperies, and feather pillows; or performing daily dusting and damp moppings.

Oral antihistamines will often bring satisfactory relief in a majority of patients. Severe cases may respond to corticosteroids taken orally or sprayed into the nose or lungs. Certain eyedrops that may be prescribed by the physician will relieve itching and redness in the eyes.

In severe cases, desensitization shots may be advisable, especially for those who cannot take corticosteroids or for whom corticosteroids are not effective.

CONTACT DERMATITIS

Contact dermatitis is a skin inflammation resulting from contact with some irritant — the allergen. The resulting inflammation appears on areas exposed to the allergen. Often, contact dermatitis is caused by soaps, detergents, or solvents in household cleaners. Other cases are brought on by certain drugs (such as antibiotics or antihistamines) and by chemicals in foods and cosmetics. A reaction to poison ivy or poison oak is another example of contact dermatitis.

SYMPTOMS

The primary symptoms of contact dermatitis include burning, itching, and stinging sensations on the skin. The itching may be severe. The affected area may become swollen and may develop blisters that ooze a clear fluid. Fluid which becomes cloudy, yellow, or straw-colored may indicate bacterial infection.

TREATMENT

The first order of treatment is to identify and remove the irritant or allergen. The location of the rash is often the first clue to the identity of the allergen. Inflammation on the face may be caused by makeup, soaps, or shaving materials. Certain drugs, for example, some antibiotics and tranquilizers, may cause a rash on those skin surfaces exposed to the sun.

This is called photodermatitis (skin inflammation caused by light). A rash on the neck can be due to cosmetics or even soap or detergent residue left on the collars of shirts or sweaters. If the dermatitis is on the scalp, then hair tints, sprays, or shampoos may be responsible. A doctor can test suspected culprits.

Once the allergen has been identified, every attempt should be made to eliminate it from the patient's environment to prevent recurrence of the dermatitis. If a person must continue taking a drug in spite of photodermatitis, he or she should take precautions to avoid sunlight or cover the skin with clothing or a sunscreen. If the irritant is a soap or detergent, the patient should try switching brands, wearing rubber gloves while washing dishes, and, if possible, avoiding tasks which require the use of soaps or detergents. If cosmetics are at fault, a switch to unscented or hypoallergenic brands may be helpful.

The itching of contact dermatitis may be relieved by orally administered steroid drugs. Topical (rubbed directly on the skin) steroids may also be used, but they do not provide the same relief. Antihistamines are sometimes prescribed but they are not usually as effective as the steroids.

FOOD ALLERGY

A food allergy is an allergic reaction to a specific food. It most often occurs in children, and, fortunately, its incidence decreases with age — most children outgrow it.

It is important to distinguish between true food allergy and food intolerance. A food allergy occurs — as does any allergy — when the body manufactures antibodies against a food allergen. Food intolerance results when there are contaminants, such as bacteria or additives, in the food or when the digestive system lacks certain natural chemicals to digest the food. Either of the factors may cause the body to be unable to tolerate the offending food.

Although any food can become an allergy, the foods most commonly linked with an allergic reaction are milk, eggs, shellfish, fish, peanuts, chocolate, strawberries, and citrus fruits.

SYMPTOMS

The symptoms of a food allergy most commonly occur in the digestive tract and include cramps, nausea, vomiting, and diarrhea. However, the symptoms are not necessarily confined to the digestive system. The patient may also experience hives, rash, headache, nasal congestion, or even anaphylactic shock.

The best way to diagnose a food allergy is to maintain a careful diary of the patient's diet with notations of when symptoms occur. Most doctors also recommend elimination trials. The patient eliminates specific foods — one at a time—from the diet to see if the symptoms disappear. Occasionally, too, skin tests may be used to confirm the identity of the allergen.

TREATMENT

Once the offending food has been determined, the only successful treatment is to avoid it. This may be difficult, but not impossible. It often helps to remember that many food allergies disappear with time.

INSECT BITE AND STING

In most cases, a bite or sting from an insect is only an inconvenience, with brief pain, itch, or slight rash. However, hypersensitive people can have a severe allergic reaction to the insect's venom.

SYMPTOMS

The pattern of the reaction varies with the individual. One person may not experience any discomfort until several hours after the sting; another may react immediately. Possible reactions may include: shortness of breath, palpitations (strong, rapid heartbeat), coughing, wheezing, and light-headedness. The bite area swells and becomes tender or numb. The most serious reaction is anaphylactic shock.

TREATMENT

After a sting, an allergic person should rush to a doctor. Immediate medical treatment includes an epinephrine injection to weaken the reaction.

If an ice pack is available, it should be used over the stung area as soon as possible. A tourniquet is useful for a bite on an extremity, but it should not be tight enough to completely stop blood flow. Both measures will slow the spread of venom through the body.

Many allergic people keep insect bite kits with them that are prescribed by a doctor. These kits contain epinephrine for injecting and other useful equipment.

Once it is established that a person is sensitive to insect bites and stings, desensitization shots may be recommended. At present, whole body extract is used in this therapy. That means that an extract of crushed whole bodies of insects is injected into the patient. The first shots contain very diluted or weak doses of extract, and the dosage is gradually increased. As a rule, this is a lifetime treatment.

Currently, there are those who feel that the desensitization shots should contain insect venom rather than whole body extract. They argue that the allergen is usually venom and that the whole body extract does not contain enough venom to be an effective desensitizing agent. However, at present there is no way of obtaining large quantities of insect venom, so whole body extract continues to be used.

SKIN CONDITIONS

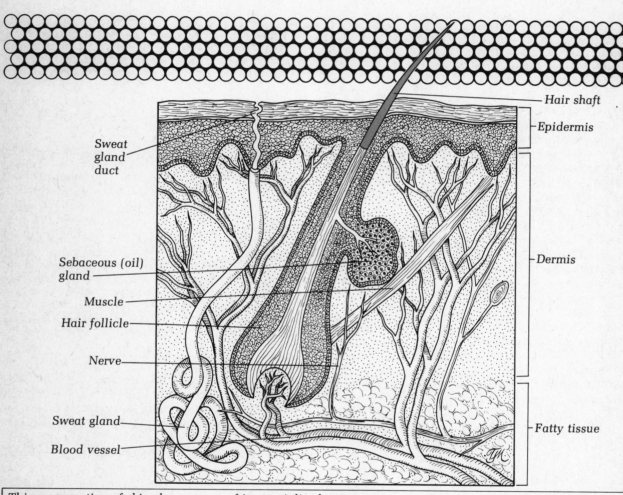

Hair shaft

Epidermis

Sweat gland duct

Sebaceous (oil) gland

Muscle

Hair follicle

Nerve

Dermis

Sweat gland

Blood vessel

Fatty tissue

This cross section of skin shows many of its specialized structures.

The skin is the body's largest organ, weighing about seven pounds and covering about 18 square feet in an adult. The skin is a waterproof barrier that protects the body from invasion of bacteria, dirt, and other elements that may be injurious to health. It helps to regulate the body's temperature, and because it is richly supplied with nerve endings, it also acts as a sensory organ.

Structurally, the skin is divided into three layers. The deepest layer, called the subcutaneous layer, stores fat and supports the blood vessels and nerves which supply the outer layers. It is also the layer in which the sweat glands originate.

The middle layer, the dermis, is sometimes called the true skin because it contains blood vessels, nerve endings, hair follicles, sweat glands, and sebaceous (oil) glands. The blood vessels and sweat glands within this layer play an important role in the body's heat regulation. A rise in the blood's temperature causes the brain to trigger a reflex which promotes sweating. The sweat glands produce a secretion that flows to the skin's surface and cools it by evaporation.

The sebaceous glands, also in the dermis, secrete an oily substance called sebum which coats and protects the skin. This coating also helps to prevent excessive evaporation of sweat from the surface of the skin.

The outermost layer of the skin is called the epidermis. Its main function is to act as a barrier to protect the dermis from injury and disease. The epidermis is composed of layers of cells which manufacture keratin, a tough substance which is found in hair and nails. This layer also contains the pigment cells which determine the color of the skin. In addition, these pigment cells protect the skin from many of the damaging effects of the sun's rays.

The epidermis is continually shedding old cells and being rebuilt. This shedding process is usually invisible unless the surface of the skin is excessively dry or irritated by a skin disorder (for example, psoriasis). Because the epidermis repairs itself quickly, burns and injury to this layer usually result in little injury to the body. However, damage to the dermis can mean severe damage to the body. Breaks in the dermal layer may allow the entry of bacteria and other infectious organisms to the blood vessels. Through these vessels, the organisms can reach all parts of the body.

We often take our skin for granted, but it should be viewed for what it is: a highly complex organ that serves two important functions — to protect us from external environment and to help us maintain a normal internal environment.

ACNE

Acne is the most common disease of the skin, affecting in some way more than 80 percent of the population, usually during the teenage years. Acne appears as small, raised lumps on the skin known as pimples, blackheads, or whiteheads. Acne generally first appears shortly after puberty — that period of time in the early teenage years when a child matures into an adult. However, the condition can persist past the age of 25, particularly in women. Problem acne affects about one of every four persons between the

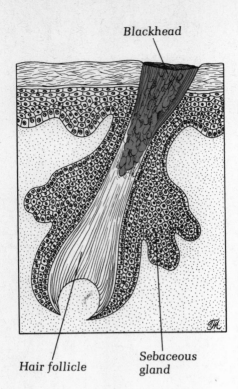

Blackhead

Hair follicle

Sebaceous gland

A blackhead results when excess oil produced by the sebaceous gland clogs the hair follicle. Another word for this is comedone. Although a blackhead is open on the surface of the skin, it nevertheless blocks the normal release of oil from the sebaceous gland onto the skin's surface.

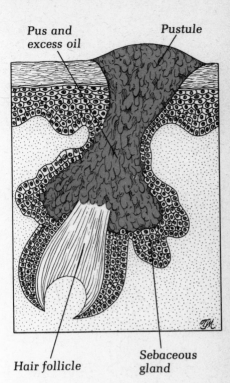

Pus and excess oil

Pustule

Hair follicle

Sebaceous gland

A pustule or pimple occurs when a comedone (blocked hair follicle) is not open on the surface of the skin and thus may become inflamed. Bacteria may invade the inflamed area and even play a role in rupturing the follicle walls. This allows excess oil and pus to escape into the surrounding skin.

ages of 12 and 25 and tends to be more severe among boys than girls.

Acne is not life-threatening, but it can be severe, particularly if untreated. In such cases, the acne eruptions can leave serious and permanent scars. In addition, since acne often occurs during adolescence, when the child may be self-conscious, the condition often results in embarrassment and emotional stress.

It is generally believed that acne is a by-product of the hormonal changes that occur in the body during puberty. Increased production of hormones, particularly the male hormone testosterone, stimulates the enlargement of the sebaceous (oil) glands in the skin. These sebaceous glands are more common in certain areas of the body—on the forehead, for exam-

ple, there are an estimated 2,000 glands per square inch.

Most of the excess oil produced by these glands reaches the surface of the skin through a series of tubes with small hairs, called hair follicles. Some oil, however, can clog tubes and form comedones.

Comedones that are open to the surface of the skin are called blackheads. These contain oil from the glands (sebum), bacteria, and skin tissue that builds up near the surface. If the comedone is closed at the surface, it is called a whitehead. These closed whiteheads can become inflamed and form pustules or pimples.

Acne is not caused by bacteria. Bacteria can, however, contribute to irritation of the surrounding skin as well as play a role in rupturing the follicular ducts, allowing oil to escape into the skin.

One of the more common beliefs about acne is that its severity can be affected by what a person eats. Authorities vary on the importance of diet in preventing acne, but almost all agree that following even the strictest diet will not cause the condition to disappear. However, some people find that their acne becomes worse when they eat certain foods, particularly chocolates and fats. These people should avoid the foods that seem to affect them.

Climate and exposure to sunlight also play a role in acne, with the condition often becoming less severe during the summer months when the skin is exposed to sunlight. In addition, emotional stress seems to aggravate acne in some people.

SYMPTOMS

Acne eruptions usually occur on the face, neck, back, chest, and shoulders. Soreness, pain, or itching may accompany the pimples. Severe acne may be characterized by pus-filled sacs which break open and discharge their contents.

Occasionally, an outbreak that looks like acne can actually be caused by reaction of the skin to substances like cosmetics, medications, grooming aids, or cleaning agents. A physician can usually diagnose the cause of the problem after an examination.

TREATMENT

Acne cannot be prevented or cured, but it can be treated. The most basic form of home treatment is to wash the affected areas at least twice a day with soap and warm water. Wash thoroughly but gently, to avoid irritating the skin. Overwashing should be avoided, as it can dry the skin and further irritate it. Frequent shampooing is also recommended, particularly if the hair is oily.

Many people turn to over-the-counter acne medications, usually in the form of lotions or creams available at drugstores. These preparations, particularly those containing benzoyl peroxide, can be of some benefit. Most of these preparations will cause dryness if used excessively, however, so it is important to follow the manufacturer's directions carefully. In addition, makeup should not be used regularly.

If acne persists, treatment by a physician is recommended. The doctor may prescribe preparations that can be applied directly to the skin, or oral antibiotics such as tetracycline or erythromycin. These antibiotics are designed to reduce the bacteria that may damage the follicular ducts which release the oil. Steroid drugs may also be used, usually by injection directly into the eruptions.

A newer drug, tretinoin (Vitamin A acid), has been shown in most studies to reduce the number of comedones by as much as 50 percent. It can also be effective when combined with antibiotic therapy, but its use is recommended only under the supervision of a physician.

Female sex hormones (estrogens) are also sometimes helpful in the treatment of acne, since they reduce the size of the sebaceous glands. When the glands are smaller, the amount of oil produced is lessened, and the acne has less "fuel." Estrogens are found in many birth control pills, and their use in the treatment of acne must be prescribed by a physician.

A doctor should also be consulted about the use of a sunlamp or an ultraviolet lamp.

One form of treatment which is not recommended is picking, scratching, popping, or squeezing the pimples, since more inflammation or scarring may result.

BOILS AND CARBUNCLES

A boil (also called a furuncle) is a bacterial infection and irritation of a hair follicle. The bacterial organism that causes the boil may be spread to other people. In most cases, however, the person coming in contact with the bacteria will not develop an infection.

Boils can appear on any part of the skin, although they most frequently occur on the neck, face, armpit, and back. Boils vary in size, but they commonly form white or yellow pustules as the infection progresses. A carbuncle is a group of boils which are interconnected, like a tunnel, below the surface of the skin.

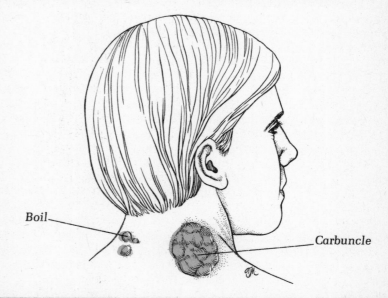

Boil

Carbuncle

A boil is a bacterial infection of a hair follicle. A carbuncle is a group of boils interconnected below the surface of the skin. Both frequently occur on the neck or back.

Boils must be taken seriously. Particularly if the infection has produced large or extensive boils, the affected person can experience fever, pain, and a generally weakened condition. It is possible for the infection to get into the bloodstream, causing infection throughout the body. Bacteria which causes the boil may also produce a toxin (poison) which causes blood clots, usually around the area of the boil.

If a boil does not seem to be healing, treatment by a physician is recommended. In addition, all boils near or on the nose, cheeks, or forehead and all carbuncles should be treated by a physician as soon as possible.

Boils are generally caused by a bacterium called *Staphylococcus aureus*. The bacteria get rubbed into a hair follicle, where there is moisture, warmth, and an ideal environment in which to multiply. As the bacteria grow, they produce substances that attack the surrounding cells, and the body's natural defenses respond. White blood cells (leukocytes) ooze through the walls of the blood vessels and cluster around the bacteria. As more and more leukocytes arrive, they eventually surround and digest the bacteria, killing the infection. This counterattack by the white blood cells is what produces the pustule at the center of the boil. Generally, the pustule will rupture, draining out the pus and the skin cells that were killed by the bacteria.

The staphylococci germs which cause the infection are common, often present in the nose and throat where washing cannot kill them. They can be transferred to a hair follicle from another site on the body, or by contact with another person or an infected article, such as a washcloth.

A person who gets boils frequently should be examined by a physician. Some people do seem more susceptible to boils, particularly those with anemia (a deficiency of red blood cells) or diabetes—diseases which weaken the body's natural defenses against the staphylococci bacteria.

Persons who are simply physically run-down also have more difficulty fighting off the infection.

Improper bathing or showering can also encourage the growth of the bacteria that produce boils. Boils are more common in the summertime, when sweaty skin helps provide the moisture for the bacteria to grow in.

People who frequently work with cutting oils, solvents, or grease are more likely to develop boils, since these substances trap the bacteria against the skin under a film of moisture. Persons with other localized infections, such as abscessed teeth or respiratory infections, are also more susceptible to boils.

SYMPTOMS

Boils can vary greatly in size. Usually, the boil pustule is a tender, hot, red mass. As the boil fills with pus, it causes pressure on the nerves underneath and results in soreness and pain.

A "blind boil" is one in which not much pus is formed, and the inflammation recedes slowly without rupturing; it sometimes leaves a small scar.

TREATMENT

One of the most important facts about treating boils is what *not* to do. *Boils should never be squeezed*, particularly if they are on the face. Squeezing can force the infection deeper into the skin, or even into the bloodstream. Boils should be opened only by a physician.

Many boils, however, will rupture and heal on their own. To encourage this, you can soak a soft cloth in warm water and hold it against the boil for 15 or 20 minutes at least four times a day. Such warm compresses increase the blood supply to the area and speed up the formulation of the pustule. Because the bacteria that cause boils can be transferred to other people, the cloth should not be used by other people until it has been washed in boiling water

for five minutes or in the hot cycle of a washing machine.

If the boil ruptures, the infected area should be washed thoroughly and covered with an antibiotic cream and sterile gauze. Once the boil has burst, it should heal rapidly. If it does not seem to be healing within a few days, a physician should be consulted.

All boils around the face and all carbuncles should be treated by a physician from the beginning. The physician may lance the boil to promote drainage and may also prescribe oral antibiotics such as penicillin or erythromycin to combat the infection.

Rest is also often prescribed, and the skin should be kept cool and dry if possible.

Boils may occur in several places at once, and treatment should also help prevent new eruptions. For this reason, a patient is often advised to wash the entire body with an antiseptic (germ-fighting) soap twice a day. If the boils recur frequently, underclothing and bed linen should be changed daily.

CANKER SORES AND FEVER BLISTERS

Canker sores are small, painful ulcers found in and around the mouth. They affect approximately one of every four people, but they are not contagious. They are more common in women, and they tend to recur, sometimes every few weeks or months.

Fever blisters (or cold sores) are caused by a virus, and usually appear as tiny, clear, fluid-filled blisters on the lips, on and around the nostrils, and in the mouth. The virus which causes cold sores is called the herpes simplex virus, and it is very common, having affected at one time or another at least 70 percent of the population. Cold sores are very contagious and can recur.

Canker sores do not cause cancer, but they can be extremely painful, often interfering with a

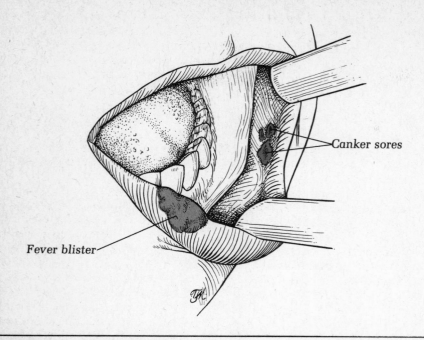

Canker sores

Fever blister

Canker sores are small painful ulcers usually found in the mouth. They are not contagious. Fever blisters, on the other hand, are caused by the herpes simplex virus and are very contagious. Fever blisters, or cold sores, are fluid-filled blisters that appear on the lips and around the mouth.

person's eating ability.

Complications from *fever blisters* are much more serious. One such complication is herpes simplex keratitis, a painful infection of the cornea (transparent covering) of the eye which can result in blindness. If an eye becomes inflamed when a *fever blister* is present, see a physician immediately. It is also important not to use a steroid medication or cream near the eyes during a herpes attack, as such preparations can make it easier for the virus to infect the eye.

Another complication from *fever blisters* afflicts those people who suffer, or have suffered, from eczema. Eczema is an inflammation of the skin characterized by redness, flakiness, and itching. The herpes virus can spread from the *fever blister* and cause sores over much of the body, even if the person is not suffering from eczema at the time. If this begins to occur, the individual should see a physician immediately.

In infants and in people who are severely ill, the herpes virus can have serious, even fatal, consequences. The infection can in-

volve the lungs, brain, and other internal organs. In addition, the herpes virus can be spread to the external sexual organs by the hands or through sexual contact.

There are many theories about the cause of *canker sores*, but researchers have not yet isolated any one factor. One theory suggests that the sores may be caused by an "autoimmune response," where the body develops an allergy or sensitivity to its own tissue, but no research has proven this to be the case.

Although no cause for *canker sores* has been established, physicians have suspected that a number of factors may help trigger an attack. These include fevers, menstruation, fatigue, tension, or allergies. Some people seem to have *canker sores* after eating certain foods, particularly chocolate, citrus fruits, spices, milk, and cola drinks. Poor dental hygiene, ill-fitting dentures, or injuries caused by stiff toothbrushes can also contribute to the eruption of *canker sores*.

The virus which causes *fever blisters* is much better understood. The herpes virus is found

almost everywhere in our environment. The infection begins when the virus enters the body through a small break in the skin. The virus most often appears in the genital region or around the mouth because the skin is easier to penetrate in these areas.

The first infection may produce the characteristic blisters or it may go unnoticed. After the initial infection, the virus retreats from the site on the skin to a nearby nerve, where it remains. The body's defenses keep the virus inactive inside the nerve until stress — for example, an illness — triggers a recurrence. The virus then overruns the body's protection system, travels along a branch of the infected nerve, and reappears on the skin in the same general area as the original infection. The factors which seem to cause recurring *fever blisters* include fever, colds, menstruation, injuries to the skin from dental work, exposure to the sun and wind, and emotional stress.

Some people, however, will have only one cold sore in a lifetime; others will have infections every few weeks for several years.

SYMPTOMS

Canker sores are small blisters, occurring singly or in groups, and are found almost anywhere in the mouth, including the inside of the cheek, the sides of the tongue, the gums, the lips, and elsewhere. The blisters break, and a small ulcer develops. This gradually enlarges until it becomes bright red around the margin and yellowish at the base of the ulcer. *Canker sores* usually heal themselves within ten days to two weeks, but they often recur. They do not leave scars.

As mentioned earlier, the initial infection which causes *fever blisters* may have no symptoms, and the person will be unaware of the infection. For those persons who do experience symptoms, the area may at first feel numb and tender. This is followed by the appearance of small blisters filled with a yellowish fluid. These blisters break, form a crust, and heal themselves within one to two weeks. Cold sores do not leave a scar. Occasionally, there is excessive pain, and the lymph glands in the neck may become swollen. This may indicate a secondary infection, and a physician may prescribe a medication to combat the infection.

TREATMENT

As yet, there is no cure for *canker sores* or *fever blisters*. There are many unproven folk cures for *canker sores*, including chewing a twig from a cherry tree. Persons who suffer recurrent attacks should see a physician or dentist. Recurrence may be lessened by improved dental hygiene or by avoiding certain foods and other substances such as chewing gum, lozenges, or mouthwashes.

Some physicians recommend a prescription antibiotic, tetracycline, for *canker sores*. This treatment involves dissolving a tetracycline tablet into an ounce of warm water, shaking the solution, and gargling with it for five or ten minutes every three hours. The doctor may recommend soaking a cotton wad in the solution and applying it directly to the sores.

There are a number of over-the-counter preparations which do not affect the disease itself, but are designed to relieve pain. These are often used for both *canker sores* and *fever blisters*. Application of tincture of benzoin or spirits of camphor can help dry the blisters. However, a topical corticosteroid cream should not be used unless recommended by a physician.

There are prescription preparations that can be helpful in shortening healing time for *fever blisters*, if applied early in the development of the disease. Applying rubbing alcohol or salt water compresses to the infected area four to six times a day are also sometimes recommended. Antibacterial ointments can help prevent a secondary, bacterial in-

fection of the blister. They do not, however, affect the herpes virus.

CORNS AND CALLUSES

Corns are small mounds of dead skin on or between the toes. They are firm on the surface, with a hard, waxy core extending about one quarter of an inch into the skin. This hard material presses on the sensitive skin underneath, causing pain. *Calluses* are thickened areas of skin, usually found on the ball of the foot, around the heel, or on the hands. They may be preceded by a blister, and are actually protective in nature. They do not have the regular, round shape of corns or the hard, waxy core.

Corns and calluses can be extremely painful, making participation in sports, or even walking, difficult and uncomfortable.

Sometimes the core, or "point," of a corn reaches all the way to the joint of the toe below the skin. This irritates the bursa, the fluid-filled sac which lubricates the joints, and bursitis can develop in the joint.

Both corns and calluses are usually caused by pressure and friction on the affected area. Often, poorly-fitting shoes are the culprit.

Corns are the body's attempt to protect an area from excessive pressure. As the pressure continues, dead skin cells accumulate and the skin thickens and swells. The swelling may go unnoticed until the mass presses on the underlying nerves, causing pain.

People with flat feet are more prone to calluses on the bottom of the foot. If the bone structure of the foot is abnormal, as in the case of hammertoes (toes that are permanently flexed) or some types of arthritis, corns are more likely to

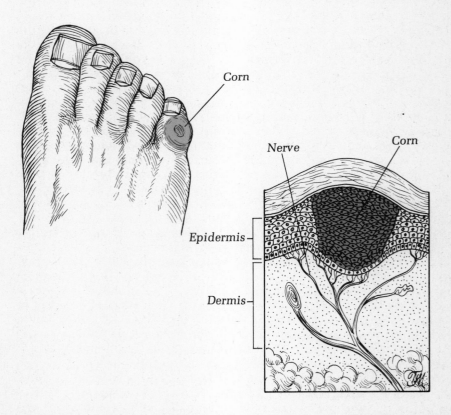

Corns are small, firm mounds of dead skin on the toes with a hard core extending down into the skin. This hard core presses on the nerves in the lower layer of skin, causing pain and tenderness. Corns develop as a reaction to and as a protection against excessive pressure on the toes.

develop. Wearing high heels, which puts more pressure on the ball of the foot, can also encourage the development of corns and calluses.

SYMPTOMS

Corns most often occur on the outside of the first and fifth toes, as a result of pressure from improperly fitting shoes. They are generally white, gray, or yellow in color. Corns which occur between the toes are called soft corns. The most common location is between the fourth and fifth toe. Soft corns are not as firm as those found on the outside of the toes, because of the moisture between the toes.

Calluses vary in size, but are usually found on the heel, the ball of the foot, or the hand—anyplace where there is repeated friction or pressure. Once a callus forms, it is not usually painful, unless it becomes so thick and inflexible that the skin cracks.

TREATMENT

The most effective treatment for corns and calluses is to relieve the pressure which caused them in the first place.

If corns and calluses are severe, or persist, examination by a doctor is recommended. In rare cases, surgery may be necessary to relieve the pressure and correct the problem. In milder cases, padding can sometimes help relieve the pain by reducing the friction on the affected area.

Many corns can be removed by using over-the-counter preparations which soften the tissue, making it easier to remove. These ointments generally contain agents which cause blistering. They usually take a week or more to work, and should be used according to the manufacturer's directions. They should be applied only to the affected area and should be discontinued if a rash develops. These preparations should not be applied to broken skin.

Other over-the-counter remedies include salicylic acid plasters, which come in medicated sheets. A small pad from the sheet can be placed over the corn or callus after bathing and held there with tape. The pad should not be removed until just before the next bath, when the softened layers of skin can be gently removed with a pumice stone or other rough surface. Once the corn or callus has ceased to be painful, the pad can be applied for 24 hours once every three days or so to maintain the improvement.

While these home remedies are often successful, persons who suffer from diabetes, atherosclerosis, or other circulatory disorders should never try to remove corns or calluses on their own. Because the risk of infection is greater in such cases, a physician should be consulted before any treatment is undertaken.

HEAT RASH

Heat rash, also known as prickly heat, is a generally mild skin condition most commonly found in infants and overweight adults. It produces an itching, burning sensation and usually occurs in areas where skin surfaces are close together.

The warm, moist areas where heat rash occurs are also ideal breeding grounds for microorganisms, and secondary infections. If heat rash is present and the affected person is exposed to high temperatures for a prolonged period of time, heat exhaustion leading to collapse can result. This is rare, however.

The medical term for heat rash is *miliaria*, and it is caused by a temporary obstruction of the sweat duct opening on the skin surface. In adults, this is usually caused by folds of fat which press together. When hot weather or exertion cause the affected person to sweat, the perspiration cannot reach the surface of the skin. The sweat may then break through the wall of its duct leading to the surface and become trapped in an internal layer of the skin, creating inflammation.

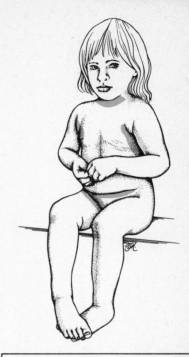

Heat rash usually occurs in areas of the body where skin surfaces are close together or overlap. For example, folds of fat press together and may temporarily obstruct the opening of the sweat gland.

In very young infants, heat rash may also be caused by immature sweat glands which cannot transport large amounts of perspiration to the surface of the skin. The sweat may, in this case, be retained in the skin, producing the same reaction.

Since the body's need to perspire triggers heat rash, it is more common during hot weather, although it can occur at any time. Tight fitting or heavy clothing may also contribute to the problem.

SYMPTOMS

Heat rash usually occurs on the upper portion of the body. It appears as tiny, pinhead-sized red pimples that itch and cause a burning or prickling sensation.

Chafing is another condition which produces a similar response, but it is caused by friction, not blocked sweat glands. Chafing can appear at any point where two skin surfaces rub together.

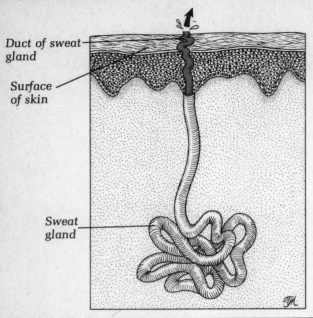
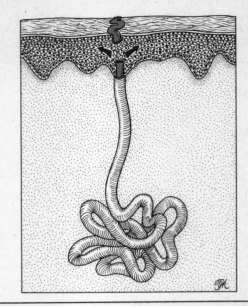

Duct of sweat
gland

Surface
of skin

Sweat
gland

Normally a sweat gland releases perspiration through a duct onto the surface of the skin, as illustrated on the left. Heat rash develops when perspiration cannot reach the skin's surface (perhaps because of folds of fat or tight clothing). As shown on the right, the sweat may then break through the wall of its duct and become trapped in an internal layer of skin, causing inflammation and rash.

TREATMENT

The most obvious form of treatment for heat rash is to remove the stimulus to sweat by keeping the affected person in a cool environment and avoiding unnecessary exertion. Once sweating stops, the rash may disappear within a few hours. Air-conditioned rooms where the skin's surface can be exposed are ideal. Cool showers followed by thorough drying and the use of dusting powder can also help. Affected persons should wear light, loose clothing.

Babies suffering from heat rash can be bathed in plain water and should be dried thoroughly. If the rash persists, or causes extreme discomfort, a physician should be consulted.

PSORIASIS

Psoriasis is a common, chronic skin disease which is not contagious. It appears as thickened, reddened patches of skin with silvery scales. These "plaques," as they are called, may be just a few small patches on the skin or they may cover large areas of the body.

Psoriasis often first appears between the ages of 15 and 30 and frequently requires lifelong treatment.

Although psoriasis does not threaten general health, in rare cases the condition can become so severe that there are chills, a painful reddening of the entire skin, cracking of the skin around joints, and shedding of large areas of scaling skin. Physicians call this "exfoliative psoriasis," and sufferers often need to be hospitalized for intensive treatment.

Researchers have not yet discovered the cause of psoriasis, but they believe it may be related to a problem with the way the skin grows and replaces itself. All body cells have a life span, growing and dying within a specific period of time. Normally, for example, the cells that form the outer layer of skin flake off and die about a month after they are formed in the deep layers of the skin. In psoriasis, however, the rate of cell growth is abnormally high, and the skin cells may move to the surface and die in as little as four or five days.

Psoriasis appears to be an inherited disease. Not all persons

with psoriasis can recall a relative who suffered from the condition, but at least one third of psoriasis patients are able to give a family history of the disease.

In addition to this genetic tendency, other factors may trigger an outbreak of psoriasis. An injury to the skin, such as a cut or burn, may be followed by an outbreak of psoriasis, usually eight to 18 days following the injury. A change in the seasons often has an effect, with psoriasis usually worsening during the winter months. Serious infections, such as upper respiratory infections or severe strep throat, appear to aggravate psoriasis. And many patients notice flare-ups of the disease during periods of physical and emotional stress.

SYMPTOMS

The red patches of skin, or plaques, most commonly appear on the elbows, knees, trunk, or scalp. The underarm and genital areas may also be involved. The borders between the plaques and normal skin are sharply outlined, and the patches may itch. The patches on the scalp usually are visible at the hairline, and they shed large, silvery-white scales that may resemble severe dandruff. The patches in moist areas, such as the underarms, are usually less scaly and red.

If the fingernails are involved, they may appear less shiny, discolored, or pitted. The nails may separate from the nail bed.

TREATMENT

There is no known cure for psoriasis, and all of the various treatment methods offer only temporary relief from the symptoms. Nevertheless, advances within the last 15 years have greatly diminished the symptoms of the disease.

Often, regular and controlled exposure to sunlight is the best treatment available, particularly during the summer. Some patients find that use of a sunlamp is helpful, although care must be taken to use such equipment safely, following instructions from the manufacturer and from the physician.

Keeping the skin clean is also important, and there are several over-the-counter lotions and creams which can provide relief. These usually contain a small amount of coal tar, along with ingredients which are designed to remove scales. If such preparations cause irritation to the skin, they should be discontinued.

In recent years, cortisone and the newer steroid drugs have been applied to the skin with good results, clearing the psoriasis patches in about 50 percent of the cases. When using the corticosteroid creams, you may be told by your physician to cover the treated areas with a thin plastic wrapping. This is called "occlusive" therapy.

Scientists are investigating a new group of drugs that slow the growth rate of cells. The most commonly used of these drugs is methotrexate, and it has been helpful in certain severe cases of psoriasis. Because its effects are still not fully known, however, the drug is used only under close

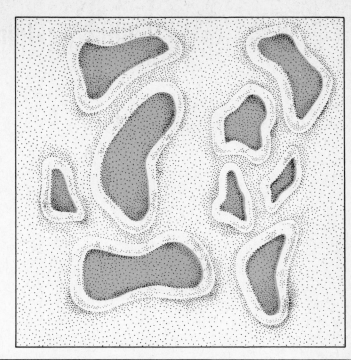

Psoriasis is characterized by plaques—clearly defined, red, raised patches of skin topped by silvery scales.

supervision of a physician.

A new form of treatment for psoriasis is called PUVA therapy. In this treatment, a patient is given a measured dose of the drug methoxsalen, followed two hours later by a measured dose of long-wave ultraviolet light. This is repeated about twice weekly until the psoriasis clears (usually about 20 to 25 treatments) and then is continued less frequently thereafter. More than 80 percent of the psoriasis patients who have been given this therapy have experienced at least partial clearing of their disease. This type of therapy is not without its risks, however. Both the patient and physician must carefully weigh the benefits of PUVA therapy against the long-term risks of premature aging of the skin and skin cancer. Any physician undertaking PUVA therapy must have special training and competence.

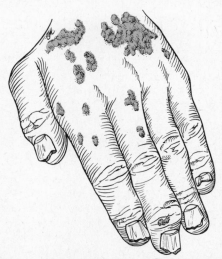

Psoriasis may be accompanied by pitted and discolored fingernails.

JOINTS, BONES, AND MUSCLES

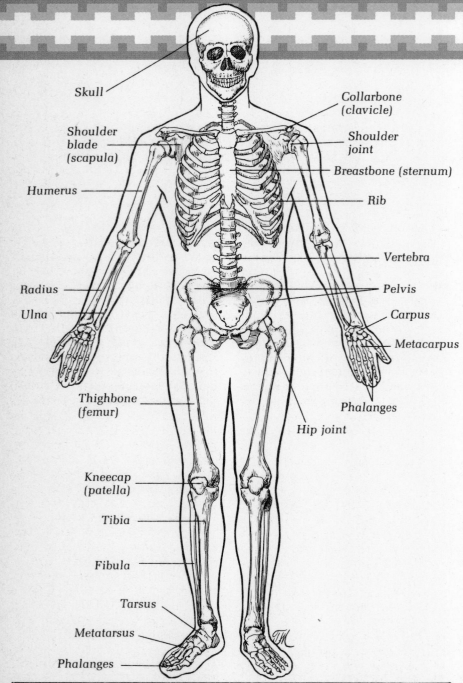

Skull

Shoulder blade (scapula)

Humerus

Radius

Ulna

Thighbone (femur)

Kneecap (patella)

Tibia

Fibula

Tarsus

Metatarsus

Phalanges

Collarbone (clavicle)

Shoulder joint

Breastbone (sternum)

Rib

Vertebra

Pelvis

Carpus

Metacarpus

Phalanges

Hip joint

The skeleton is the framework of the body.

The skeleton, the bony framework of our bodies, is comprised of 206 bones. The skeleton provides structure and form for our bodies. It also protects our internal organs. For example, the skull surrounds the brain, the ribs encircle the lungs and heart, and the pelvis provides a protective basin for the abdominal organs.

Bone, like the rest of the body, is living tissue. In addition, the center of the bone contains marrow, the factory that produces multitudes of red and white blood cells. Bone is also the storehouse of calcium for the body—99 percent of the calcium in the body is found in the skeleton, and it is this mineral that keeps our bones firm and strong.

A joint is the juncture of two bones. Most of the joints in our body are movable, but their movement is controlled by tough bands of tissue called ligaments which are attached to the bones. Ligaments connect the bones one to another. Cartilage, a somewhat transparent, elastic tissue, lines the ends of the bones in a joint. Cartilage, together with various joint fluids and the bursae (small sacs within the joints containing lubricating fluid), cushions and protects the bones. The bones are connected to the muscles by tendons, bands of fibrous connective tissue. Movement occurs when a muscle contracts and pulls its tendon and attached bone.

Muscle comprises about 50 percent of our total body weight. It is composed of tissue that has the ability to contract, and it is classified into three types: striated, smooth, and cardiac.

Striated muscle is the muscle attached to the skeleton. It is under our conscious control. When we bend an arm, take a step, or sit down, striated muscle contracts. Under a microscope, striated muscle looks striped.

Smooth muscle is not striated; it lines most of the hollow organs of the body and is controlled by the autonomic nervous system. Smooth muscle aids in circulating blood and fluids through the body; it moves material through the digestive tract; it helps in respiration by moving the diaphragm (the partition that separates the chest cavity and the abdominal cavity), abdomen, and rib case. In short, smooth muscle is responsible for most of the internal functions of the body.

Cardiac muscle is the muscle of the heart. Cardiac muscle has the ability to contract spontaneously but it also is regulated by the autonomic nervous system.

Our body's frame is an intricate structure of interconnecting parts. Every voluntary movement we make is the result of bones, ligaments, tendons, and muscles working together in a smooth, coordinated way. And every involuntary movement we make — our automatic internal processes — occurs within the protective enclosure of our musculoskeletal structure.

ARTHRITIS

Arthritis means "inflammation of the joints." There are two forms of arthritis. *Osteoarthritis* is a deteriorative disorder resulting in the wearing down of the cartilage in the joints. *Rheumatoid* arthritis is a systemic inflammatory disease affecting all the connective tissues in the body. Osteoarthritis affects almost everyone who lives beyond the age of 50, simply because of long-term wear and tear of the joints. It commonly strikes

sometime after the age of 55. Rheumatoid arthritis, on the other hand, can strike at any age, including infancy.

Left untreated, osteoarthritis can lead to permanent damage to the joints, and rheumatoid arthritis can lead to damage of the heart, lungs, nerves, and eyes.

Osteoarthritis is usually caused by a gradual wearing away of the cartilage, the elastic tissue that cushions joints (the points where two bones meet) and prevents the bones from actually touching. When this cartilage wears away, the bones rub together causing swelling and pain. In some cases, the disease is brought on by a direct injury to the joint.

The precise cause of rheumatoid arthritis is unknown, although researchers believe that it is an autoimmune disease, that is, one in which the body attacks its own tissues. A virus may be the underlying cause, although there is no conclusive evidence for this. In rheumatoid arthritis, the synovium, a thin membrane that lines the joint and produces lubricating fluid, becomes inflamed. As the inflammation continues, it destroys the cartilage. Eventually the damaged cartilage is replaced by scar tissue, making the joint rigid and altering its shape.

For some reason, women are more likely to be affected by arthritis than men. Overweight may cause osteoarthritis to occur at an earlier age because of the increased burden on the joints. Although damp weather may make the symptoms of arthritis worse, it does not cause the disease; similarly, moving to a dry climate will not prevent it.

Although the constant joint abuse brought on by the continued exertion and strain of certain sports or occupations can make arthritis more likely to develop, inactivity can be just as risky. Moderate exercise throughout life is the best way to keep joints in good health.

Arthritis itself is not an inherited disease. Nevertheless, a tendency to develop it may occur within a family.

SYMPTOMS

The symptoms of arthritis are pain, tenderness, swelling, stiffness, or redness in one or more joints. Often the pain is worse in the morning and improves as the patient moves about during the day. Damp weather and emotional stress can make the symptoms of arthritis worse. In rheumatoid arthritis these symptoms may be accompanied by a general feeling of fatigue and a fever.

Rheumatoid arthritis victims often enter long periods of remission when they experience no symptoms at all, but arthritis is a chronic (long-term) disease and never just disappears. When the symptoms return, they are likely to be even more severe.

Arthritis is diagnosed by a physical examination and observation of symptoms. In addition, your doctor may request X rays and laboratory tests to confirm the diagnosis.

TREATMENT

Treatment for arthritis should not be delayed, as permanent damage can be prevented if therapy begins soon enough. The best results occur with a program of drug therapy, exercise, and rest.

Several drugs are used to treat arthritis, aspirin being the foremost among them. Two to three tablets taken several times a day may be prescribed not merely to relieve pain, but also to reduce inflammation. Aspirin should be taken after meals or in a coated tablet form to help prevent stomach irritation.

Nonaspirin pain relievers and nonsteroid anti-inflammatory drugs (such as ibuprofen, naproxen, tolmetin, sulindac) may be prescribed. Other drugs, including indomethacin, gold salts, and penicillamine may also be used for arthritis. Your doctor may try several different drugs before finding one that works effectively without producing side effects in your particular case. Corticosteroids are also sometimes prescribed, although their side effects limit their usefulness.

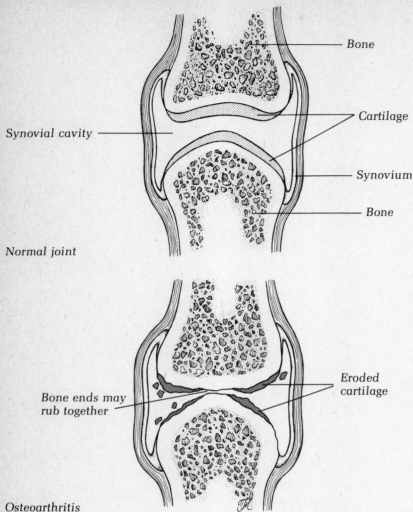

Normal joint

Osteoarthritis

Osteoarthritis is the wearing away or erosion of the cushioning cartilage at the ends of bone. As the cartilage wears away, the bones may rub together causing swelling and pain.

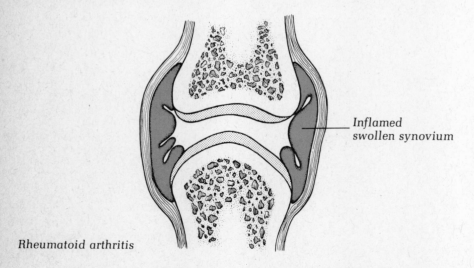

Rheumatoid arthritis

In rheumatoid arthritis, the synovium, a thin membrane lining the joint that produces lubricating fluid, becomes inflamed and swollen.

Daily exercise such as swimming, walking, or perhaps working with a physical or occupational therapist is essential to maintaining mobility in arthritic joints. However, exercise must be balanced with rest to reduce inflammation of joints. Your doctor will design the proper routine to be followed.

Maintaining correct posture and body weight are also important in alleviating the burden on painful joints. Moist heat can help to lessen pain and ease the motion of stiff joints.

In some severe cases, surgery may be required to remove inflamed synovial tissue. Artificial joints may also be implanted to replace those that have been damaged beyond repair by arthritis.

BACKACHE

Backache is one of the most common physical complaints, experienced by millions of people every day. It is estimated that eight out of every ten people will suffer from this universal affliction at some point in their lives.

Many victims of lower back pain — spasmodic pain near the inward curve of the back above the base of the spine—are stricken while simply reaching to pick something up. The pain may disappear as spontaneously as it came, or last for days, and commonly it will reappear periodically.

Almost anything can cause pain in the back, from a sudden stop in a car, to athletic overexertions, to a reflex action like sneezing. The lower portion of the spine is the site of most back pain which may simply develop from overworked or underexercised muscles. Strains are especially common when tired or weak back muscles are called upon to do more than they are capable of doing. The muscles will then suddenly go into spasm—an involuntary contraction — and become a knotty mass while the body sends out a signal of sharp pain. Other muscles nearby will also go into spasm in an effort to protect the strained muscles and prevent further damage.

Obesity may be one of the most common causes of backache because the extra weight greatly increases the stress on the back muscles and the spine.

Women sometimes have back pain because of menstrual disturbances or pregnancy—usually because of the weight of the unborn baby.

Backache can also come with age, as joint tissues deteriorate or shift. It is also believed that back pain can be caused by a response to psychological tension, stress, and anxiety related to the problems of everyday life.

Occasionally, a backache is associated with a congenital (present from birth) abnormality. The pain is not due to the deformity itself, but rather to unusual stresses imposed by it on surrounding structures, especially the muscles. For example, a slight variation of more than an inch in the length of the legs or curvatures of the spine may force the surrounding muscles out of normal alignment and cause back pain. In such cases, surgery may be required to correct the problem, but often braces, corsets, or lifts in the shoes can be helpful. Exercises to help strengthen participating muscles can be performed to counter the unusual stress on the back from some of these abnormalities.

Back pain can also stem from conditions that have nothing to do with the back itself — from diseases of the heart, lungs, intestinal tract, or reproductive organs.

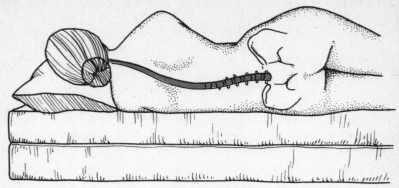

Rigid mattress

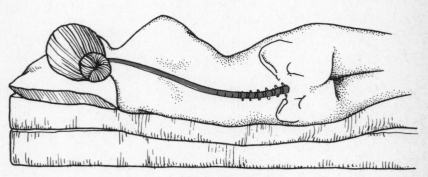

Soft mattress

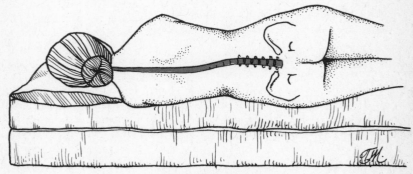

Semi-rigid mattress

The appropriate mattress is necessary to prevent backache. A hard, rigid mattress with little "give" may distort the alignment of the spine and its surrounding muscles as much as a soft, sagging mattress. A semi-rigid mattress which allows the spine and back structures to remain straight may be the best choice.

SYMPTOMS

The onset of pain after physical activity may be abrupt or slow. In its severe form, the pain may be so piercing that a person who is bending over will not be able to straighten up. The pain itself may be felt as a stabbing or aching sensation. Acute back pain may also be accompanied by pain or numbness radiating down the leg.

Ninety percent of low back pains disappear within two months after they occur, but the pain will probably return unless preventive steps are taken.

A victim of chronic back pain should first consult a doctor to determine if there are any disorders, for example, kidney or heart problems, that may be causing the backache. When other medical factors have been excluded, the next step may be to see an orthopedic physician who specializes in bone and muscle treatment. If it is confirmed that the bad back is due to strain or arthritis, the doctor may prescribe an exercise program that can provide significant relief of symptoms.

An initial examination for back pains will include a questioning session in which the doctor determines when the pain began, what type of pain it is, and where it is located. The doctor will inquire closely about general health, past illnesses, and physical activities. The patient will also be observed as he or she walks, sits, stands, and performs certain exercises.

During a physical examination the doctor may check the lowest four vertebrae, the bony segments of the spinal column. An X ray may reveal some deteriorating changes in the spine, but for many people with back problems nothing will show up. This does not, however, indicate that their pain is imaginary.

TREATMENT

Because backache is so common, many who suffer from it tend to accept it and just live with it. Proper treatment, however, can relieve the immediate symptoms. Hot pads on the site of pain will bring some relief as will mild painkillers such as aspirin. Medicines containing methyl salicylate (oil of wintergreen) and other similar ingredients in the form of a rub may be recommended because they produce warmth at the site of application, and the rubbing is soothing. Muscle relaxant drugs may also be prescribed.

In some cases, the best healer is time. For all types of back pain the patient should avoid further strain and rest in bed to allow the muscles to relax. In addition, preventive measures are helpful. When picking up objects from the floor, kneel rather than bend from the waist; be sure to bear the weight of the object with the legs, keeping the back straight. Avoid sitting for long periods of time at a desk looking downward without moving the head, or lying on the floor to watch TV with the head jutted forward or the chin propped on the chest.

Correct posture is also important to help prevent back pain. Properly fitting shoes are necessary to maintain good posture as is a firm bed. In fact, selecting the proper mattress is probably one of the most important considerations since so much time is spent in bed. Contrary to proper belief, a rigid, hard mattress is not always the best choice. A hard mattress with little "give" may distort the alignment of the spine and its surrounding muscles as much as a soft sagging mattress. Often a semi-rigid mattress is the most appropriate selection.

If there are no physical causes, backache can be relieved by a program of exercise designed specifically to strengthen weak muscles. Losing weight, especially if a potbelly has developed, will also relieve unnecessary pressure on the spine.

BUNION

A bunion is a thickened swelling usually found on the side of the foot at the joint of the big toe. Often there is a bony protuberance at the joint of the big toe where the bunion is located.

Bunions can be the result of inherited structural problems in the foot, but more commonly they are caused by ill-fitting footwear. In a healthy foot the two major bones of the big toe, the metatarsal of the foot and the phalanx of the toe, must be in a straight line and fit together properly. A person with an inherited tendency toward bunions will usually have loose bone joints in the foot and a big toe that tends to point outward toward the other foot. In pointed-toed or tight shoes the big toe is forced inward and the big toe joint is pushed out so that it rubs against the inner surface of the shoe. This produces a bunion. A normal foot may develop a bunion in a similar way, but its normal structure makes it more resistant.

A bunion can be acute or chronic. Acute bunions are a form of bursitis. The bursa is a sac containing a thick fluid that acts as a protective lubricant between the bone and surrounding skin and tendons. In an acute bunion, the bursa protecting the big toe joint becomes inflamed from continued pressure on the joint, often because of the deforming effects of the ill-fitting shoe. This swelling can be very painful.

In the chronic, or long-term, form of the disorder, the continued friction on the joint causes the bone to become hardened and inflexible. A bony protuberance develops at the joint.

Bunions are three times as common in women as in men. In fact, almost all women show some sign of big toe displacement, which is the beginning of a bunion. This is probably because women's shoes often have narrow insteps, pointed toes, and high heels, all of which force the big toe joint outward. However, there is evidence that the preference for cowboy boots among men is increasing the incidence of bunions among males.

Since bunions can result from inherited problems of bone structure, your chance of developing them may be increased if someone in your family has suffered from bunions.

SYMPTOMS

The main symptom of a bunion is swelling at the big toe joint accompanied by tenderness and pain. If the bunion grows large, it may force the other toes to overlap because of the pressure from the big toe. Other problems, for example, corns, may develop because of friction on the skin of the overlapped or distorted toes.

Bunions are diagnosed by physical examination. If surgical correction is contemplated, X rays may be taken.

TREATMENT

The only permanent cure for a bunion is surgery. In cases where only the bony protuberance needs to be removed, surgery can sometimes be performed in the doctor's office under local anesthesia. The incision will probably be no more than an inch long. The patient can be sent home with only minor pain medication. However, it will be about six weeks before full use

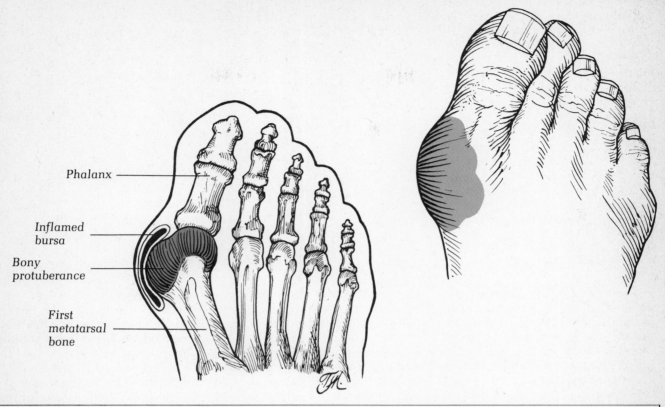

Phalanx

Inflamed
bursa

Bony
protuberance

First
metatarsal
bone

A bunion is a swelling on the foot at the joint of the big toe caused by pressure or friction on the joint. The bursa, a fluid-filled sac that acts as a cushion in the joint, may become inflamed. A chronic bunion may also cause a bony protuberance to develop at the joint.

of the foot is regained. Until recently all such surgery required a week's hospitalization.

Sometimes a doctor will decide to realign the bones, muscles, or tendons which led to the formation of the bunion. This involves far more complex surgery than simple removal of the excess bone. It must be performed in a hospital, usually by an orthopedic surgeon.

If surgery is not determined to be necessary, certain devices can be used to relieve the pain and discomfort of bunions. Padding is available that works to shift the weight of the foot in the shoe. There are also protective shields that prevent the bunion from coming into contact with the inside of the shoe.

Proper footwear can prevent the development of bunions. It is particularly important that children's shoes fit well, since this is the time of life when most foot problems begin. A shoe should have a sturdy sole and be wide enough to fit all the toes without cramping them. The heel should be about an inch in height. Women who want to wear high-heeled or pointed-toes shoes should look for less extreme designs. If a high-heeled shoe is chosen, open-toed styles are least damaging. Similarly, if a narrow-toed shoe is chosen, the heel should be low.

When buying shoes, be certain that the width and length of each foot is measured separately. If one foot is longer or wider than the other, buy for the larger foot. Allow one inch between the big toe and the tip of the shoe—even more space in pointy-toed shoes. Make sure the heel does not slip when you walk. Well-fitting shoes should not require a break-in period—they should be comfortable from the first wearing.

Nothing is better for feet than walking barefoot on unlittered grass or sand. If this is seldom possible, sandals are almost as effective. Some doctors recommend the wearing of Japanese thongs in the home to ease the cramping effects of shoes. Wooden-soled clogs can also provide relief for the feet.

BURSITIS

Bursitis is an inflammation of the bursae, the sacs or pouches containing lubricating fluid that are located at the ends of bones in the joints. The bursae help muscles move smoothly across places where bones are prominent.

When the inflammation occurs, it is usually within a specific area and is the result of excessive pressure on that area. Although the shoulder, elbow, and knee are the most commonly affected spots, almost any joint in the body can be the site of bursitis. An attack can be very disabling because of the severe pain which makes it almost impossible to move the joint.

Bursitis is usually caused by deposits of calcium from the

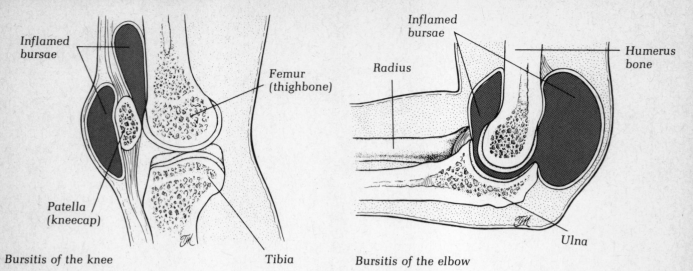

Bursitis of the knee

Bursitis of the elbow

bones or by continual stress on a given joint, or a combination of the two. This produces inflammation of the bursae. An acute form of bursitis may come on suddenly and can be set off by a chill or a draft.

Workers in occupations that require constant use of certain joints are subject to acute or chronic bursa trouble. "Typist's shoulder" and "housemaid's knee," for example, are forms of chronic bursitis, and even baseball pitchers can develop such an inflammation in the shoulder, the upper arm, or the elbow.

SYMPTOMS

The inflamed bursa produces a tender swelling near the affected joint. In an acute attack, the pain can be severe enough to immobilize that area.

An X ray of the joints of a bursitis patient may reveal calcium deposits in one of the important bursae around the joints. If the bursitis is caused by stress on the joint, however, the X ray will only reveal swollen bursae.

TREATMENT

Sometimes an acute attack of bursitis will heal by itself if the joint is immobilized in a sling or if the patient stays in bed. In addition, moist heat applied directly on the problem spot frequently helps, whereas dry heat may cause more pain. However, some patients find that cold applications are more effective. A short period of experimentation will determine which method is the best to relieve your pain. Aspirin and other pain relievers may also alleviate the initial symptoms. In severe cases or to speed healing, anti-inflammatory corticosteroids may be injected directly into the painful area.

If none of these procedures relieve the condition, surgery may be required to remove the deposits of calcium salts or free the area of chronic inflammation. Such an operation should be performed only by an orthopedic surgeon.

OSTEOPOROSIS

Osteoporosis is a decrease in bone tissue, causing the bones to become weak and break easily. It is one of the most common bone disorders, particularly in older people.

Osteoporosis is not life-threatening, but it can lead to fractures—often of the hip—and thus can be disabling. Crush fractures of the vertebrae (bony segments of the backbone) are also common because of the normal pressure of the body's weight on the thinned vertebrae.

The causes of osteoporosis are unknown, although the disease does seem to occur more often in women and most commonly in middle life or beyond. One widely held theory is that the disorder arises from the loss of the female hormone estrogen, without which bones become abnormally thin. The victims of this form of osteoporosis are most often women who have passed menopause when the body decreases its production of estrogen. In fact, about one third of all women over the age of 60 have the disease in some degree.

Lack of physical activity, for example, if a person is confined to bed for a long period of time, and low intake or poor absorption of various nutrients (particularly calcium which promotes bone formation) are other causes.

Osteoporosis is more common among women than men, in older persons than in middle-aged, and in Orientals and whites than in blacks. Other conditions which may lead to disabling osteoporosis include early surgical removal of both ovaries (female sex glands which produce estrogen); an inactive life style; bones already affected by chronic arthritis; steroid drugs; or Paget's disease, a disorder of unknown cause which results in bone destruction.

SYMPTOMS

The disease may have no symptoms or it may cause pain. The most common symptom of osteoporosis is a sudden back pain immediately following a minor injury that causes a vertebral fracture. The pain of the fracture may gradually disappear, but it may also increase if additional vertebrae collapse. A vicious cycle may develop; the pain leads to inactivity which in turn contributes to the progression of osteoporosis.

When the vertebrae fracture, they become compressed, and the patient, in fact, becomes shorter as the spinal bones are reduced in size. In addition, there may be an increased curvature of the spine. As fractured bones in the spine heal, they also become distorted resulting in back deformities often called "widow's hump" or "dowager's hump."

Osteoporosis may proceed silently until a fracture of the hip or wrist or a vertebra occurs. At this point, X rays may show some thinning of the bone, and a diagnosis of osteoporosis may be confirmed.

TREATMENT

Osteoporosis can sometimes be controlled by administering the female hormone estrogen or steroids which appear to decrease bone loss. A woman receiving such treatments should have regular physical examinations and a Pap test every six months because estrogen therapy has been linked to cancer of the uterus. (A Pap test is the standard test for detecting cancer of the cervix, the lower end of the uterus.) The male hormone testosterone, which stimulates growth of body tissue, may also be used to treat osteoporosis in men.

A balanced diet rich in nutrients, combined with vitamin and mineral supplements, is important for those susceptible to the disease. Milk and other foods rich in calcium and Vitamin D appear to enhance bone formation. Often, calcium supplements are prescribed.

Patients are also urged to exercise to strengthen the muscles that support the weakened bones. The doctor can usually suggest an exercise program that will be helpful. In an advanced case of osteoporosis, a back brace may be necessary if sitting or standing upright becomes difficult. Additionally, a cane, crutches, or a walker can be used to aid walking. Most important of all, an individual with osteoporosis should avoid lifting heavy objects in order to protect the bones in the spinal column.

SLIPPED DISC

The backbone, or spine, is a column made up of many small bones which are held together by bands of tissue called ligaments. Between each layer of bone lie discs of cartilage, elastic tissue that cushions the friction between those bones. Because of the way the bones and discs are loosely strung together, the backbone is very flexible and allows for bending and other body movements. However, this structure can also cause problems, especially when strain and overexertion are factors.

Actually, a spinal disc does not slip, as is commonly believed; rather the rim of the disc weakens and tears causing part of the gelatinous center of the disc to be pushed out or extruded. This extruded material presses on the

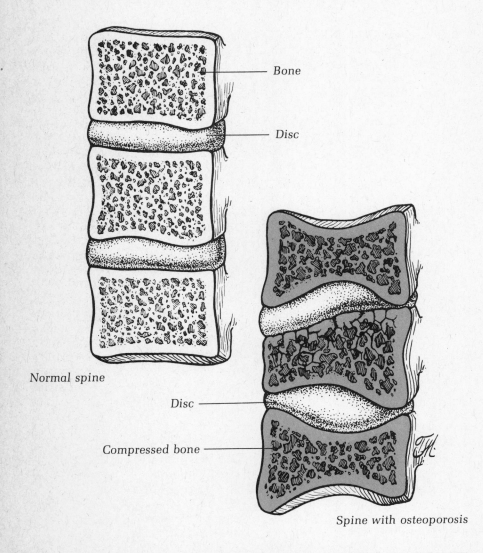

Bone

Disc

Normal spine

Disc

Compressed bone

Spine with osteoporosis

Osteoporosis is a reduction in bone tissue, causing the bones to become weak and break easily. Compression of the vertebrae—the bones in the spine—may occur because of the pressure of the body's weight on the thinned vertebrae.

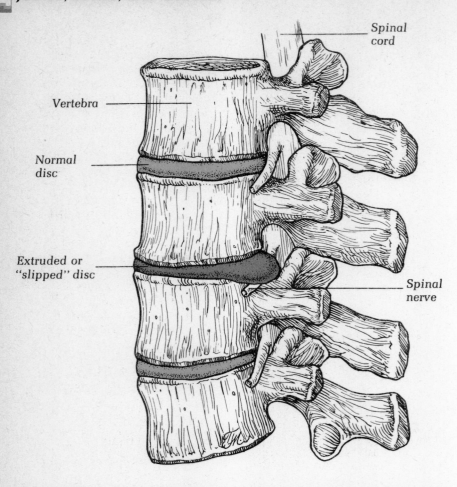

Vertebra

Normal disc

Extruded or "slipped" disc

Spinal cord

Spinal nerve

Between the vertebrae, or bones in the backbone, lie discs of cartilage that cushion the friction between the bones. If the rim of a disc weakens or tears, part of the jelly-like center of the disc becomes pushed out or extruded. This extruded material presses on the nearby spinal nerve causing pain along the path of the nerve. This is commonly referred to as a "slipped disc."

adjacent nerve root emerging from the spinal cord, causing pain along the path of the affected nerve. The disc most often involved is the lowest movable disc in the small of the back—the one that bears the most pressure. An injury to this disc causes pain which runs down the thigh and into the outer part of the lower leg and the foot. This is the course of the sciatic nerve, and the pain is often called "sciatica." This pain can be so great as to be disabling.

With age, the discs also tend to disintegrate, becoming less jelly-like and more compressed. Such degeneration, however, usually causes no more than mild, intermittent backache and stiffness.

A slipped disc is a condition usually caused by strain or injury in the discs as a result of bending and straightening the back to lift heavy objects. Most people with this problem seem to have some history of past damage to the affected part of the back.

SYMPTOMS

Often damage from a slipped disc will not be felt until months or years after the injury, and symptoms may vary with the location of the disc. A person with such a problem may stand more upright than usual and curve the back toward the side opposite the pain. Tenderness and pain may be felt along the path of the sciatic nerve and there may be weakness in the foot or toe or the muscles of the arm. Such pain will be aggra-

vated by moving, coughing, or straining in any way. Additionally, numbness or tingling may be felt in various parts of the legs, feet, or arms.

To determine the exact cause of back pain, a physician will listen carefully to the patient's explanation of when and where the pain is felt. During an examination, the doctor will observe the patient sitting, walking, and bending. Then the doctor will probe for sensitive areas by placing the patient's legs in various positions, by checking reflexes in the ankle and knee, and by testing muscle strength. Structural changes in the bones and joints and collapsed discs can be shown on standard back X rays.

Special studies may be required to locate the problem discs, and these tests are considered a requirement before surgery is performed. A myelogram may be done. This is an injection of dye into the space surrounding the spinal cord and nerve roots. A protruding disc will distort or block the flow of dye as seen on X rays. Discography is an additional type of X ray study done after the injection of dye directly into the discs. Another test that may be performed is called "conduction nerve velocity." This test measures the speed of nerve impulses to muscles and can be used to assess nerve damage.

TREATMENT

When a protruding disc is pressing on a nerve and causing trouble, it is sometimes possible to relieve the pressure by strict bed rest with a firm mattress. Rest may also cause the shrinkage of the protruded tissue.

Although many people undergo surgery to remove slipped discs, most doctors will first try nonsurgical treatment — bed rest, pain relievers, some form of back support, and gradually increased exercises to strengthen muscles.

The majority of people affected with disc problems seem to respond partially or completely to nonsurgical treatment and thus may avoid an operation to remove a disc.

TENDONITIS

Tendonitis is an inflammation of a tendon, a fibrous cord which connects muscle to bone. In strenuous physical activity of long duration there is a tendency for the muscles, strengthened by exercise, to increase tension on the somewhat inelastic tendons. This tension may cause the tendon to rub against bones or other tendons and thereby become inflamed.

Continued stress to the tendon from minor injuries may become a serious problem if, for example, an inflamed tendon later ruptures.

Many people may develop tendonitis as a result of improper or poor athletic training. This especially occurs among nonathletes who suddenly become long distance runners or joggers, or among athletes who resume a strenuous sport after an interval of inactivity.

Improper activity or poor equipment may also result in tendonitis. For example, running the wrong way or wearing shoes with a rundown heel may put needless strain on the Achilles tendons, the heel cords which join two major muscles of the back of the legs to the back of the heel bones. Incidentally, women may have an increased problem with inflamed Achilles tendons because their tendons may be greatly shortened as a result of wearing high-heeled shoes.

SYMPTOMS

During an attack of tendonitis, the muscles attached to the affected tendon may hurt when they are used. The tendon may be tender to the touch and is usually thicker than normal. Sometimes, the tendon is excruciatingly painful.

The first step in the diagnosis of sports-related problems is to provide an exercise and sports history, so that the physician can see what activities the patient has participated in and if there have been any changes in routine. During a general physical examination, the doctor will also check muscle lengths in search of unusually short or inflexible muscles which may be causing the problems.

TREATMENT

The best treatment for tendonitis is prevention, and the way to prevent tendonitis is to take plenty of time for an adequate warmup before beginning an activity. Stretching out the leg and calf muscles before and after running, for example, can help prevent inflammation of the Achilles tendon. Supports in shoes and sneakers worn during physical activity can correct any instability in the foot. If an attack of tendonitis occurs, such devices can also make walking and running less painful.

Drugs cannot solve the problem of tendonitis, which often returns as soon as the activity is resumed. However, your doctor may prescribe pain relievers or anti-inflammatory drugs to relieve the immediate symptoms. Resting the affected part of the body is usually recommended.

A very small number of tendonitis patients may need surgery to remove the tendons. There is new hope for people who have severely injured a tendon or who have had tendons removed — a process that may allow the human body to regenerate or recreate destroyed connective tissue.

In the past, surgical repair of tendonitis was often difficult and artificial tissues never had the strength and flexibility of real tissues. But today, a new treatment is being investigated which involves surgical implantation of a carbon filament material to replace the damaged tendon. The filament provides a framework that will eventually be surrounded by newly developed tissue, produced naturally by the body. As a result the new tendon can be as strong and as flexible as the original.

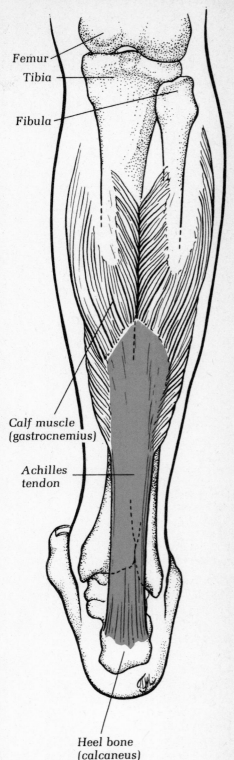

Femur
Tibia
Fibula
Calf muscle (gastrocnemius)
Achilles tendon
Heel bone (calcaneus)

Tendonitis is an inflammation of a tendon, a fibrous cord that connects muscle to bone. This illustration shows the Achilles tendon which joins the major muscle (gastrocnemius) of the back of the leg to the back of the heel bone.

EYE DISORDERS

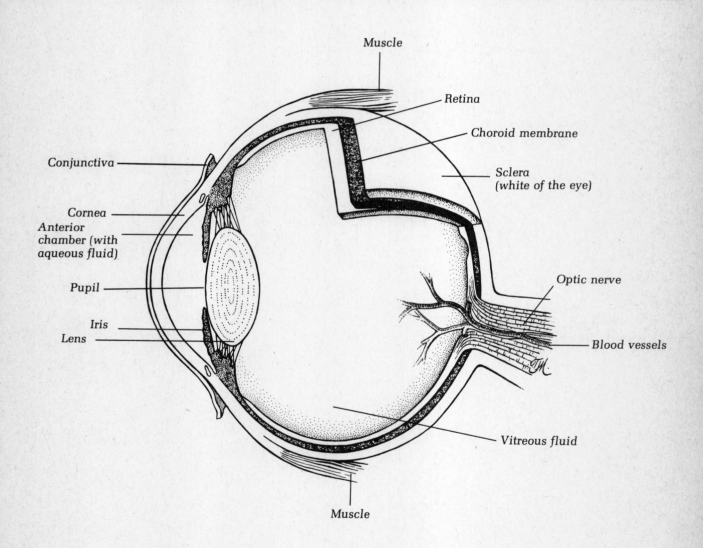

Muscle

Retina

Choroid membrane

Sclera (white of the eye)

Conjunctiva

Optic nerve

Cornea

Anterior chamber (with aqueous fluid)

Blood vessels

Pupil

Iris

Lens

Vitreous fluid

Muscle

The human eye is a complex sensory organ.

The human eye is the sensory organ most individuals depend upon for much of their information about the world. It is designed to capture light and transform it into impulses that the brain can interpret as images.

Because the eye is a direct continuation of the brain, it is well protected. It rests in a bony socket, cushioned by a layer of fat, and is guarded by the eyebrow, eyelashes, and eyelid. The conjunctiva, a thin membrane, lines the inner surface of each eyelid and continues over the exposed surface of the eyeball. Lacrimal (tear) glands above the eye within the socket continuously release tears to keep the eyeball moist and clean.

The cornea is the transparent covering across the front of the eyeball, and it helps focus light. Behind the cornea is the iris, the colored part of the eye. In the center of the iris is an opening, the pupil, whose size determines the amount of light admitted to the eye. In back of the iris is the lens, held in place by muscles that change the lens' shape to enable the eye to focus on objects at various distances.

Between the cornea and the lens is a space, the anterior chamber, which is filled with fluid called aqueous fluid. The aqueous fluid contains nutrients that nourish both the cornea and lens. The clear, jelly-like fluid filling the eyeball behind the lens is called the vitreous fluid.

The eyeball has three outer layers: the sclera, or white of the eye; the choroid membrane, containing blood vessels that nourish the eye; and the retina, the light-sensitive innermost layer. The retina is rich in nerve endings which convert light, focused through the lens onto the retina's surface, into electrical impulses. These impulses are then transmitted to the brain through the optic nerve. The optic nerve is directly connected to the brain through the rear of the eyeball.

Like the rest of the body, the eyes are subject to injury and disease. Because eyes are so important to the quality of life, they deserve expert care.

CATARACT

Cataract is a clouding of the lens of the eye. A healthy lens is clear, and its function is to focus light entering the eye so that objects are seen clearly. As the lens becomes progressively more cloudy, the incoming light is scattered instead of focused and vision becomes blurred. Persons with cataracts see the world as if they were looking through a waterfall—the name cataract is from the ancient Greek word for waterfall.

Although cataract is curable in most cases, it can cause blindness. Furthermore, since the lens is the window to the eye, a clouded lens can obstruct a clear picture of the interior of the eye. A doctor, therefore, may not be able to look into the eye to diagnose other potentially serious eye disorders, such as changes in the retina or damage to the optic nerve.

The development of cataracts most often accompanies aging. However, it can occur in young persons and in newborns whose mothers contracted German measles during pregnancy. Although the exact cause is unknown, it is thought that such diseases as diabetes, glaucoma, or uveitis (inflammation of the colored portion of the eye) may lead to cataracts. In addition, research suggests that cataracts may be triggered by injuries penetrating the lens, by long-term use of certain drugs, or by high doses of radiation (such as X rays and microwaves).

SYMPTOMS

Gradual and usually painless blurring of vision is the primary symptom of cataract. Often only one eye is affected. Because the clouded lens scatters rather than

Gradual blurring of vision accompanies the development of cataract. Vision with early cataract may be close to normal (left drawing). As cataract becomes more advanced, vision begins to blur (center drawing), and as cataract continues to develop, vision may become extremely blurred (right drawing).

focuses incoming light, persons afflicted with early cataract may experience glare in bright light. As the condition advances, the progressively clouding lens becomes milky white accompanied by a growing loss of vision.

TREATMENT

Cataract is a condition that can be successfully treated. Vision can usually be restored by having the affected lens surgically removed and then by wearing special eyeglasses or contact lenses.

Operating with the aid of a microscope, the surgeon opens the front of the eye and withdraws the lens. The procedure is painless because the patient has been given anesthetic eyedrops. After a few weeks of recuperation while the eye heals, the eye specialist will prescribe special cataract eyeglasses or a contact lens which takes over the job of the removed lens. In recent years many surgeons have recommended an IOL, intraocular lens (intra — inside, ocular — eye). This tiny, lightweight plastic lens is implanted in the eye after the cataractal lens is removed. Because the IOL is inserted into the position formerly occupied by the natural lens, vision is free from distortion and is closer to normal than it would be with eyeglasses or a contact lens. An intraocular lens, however, is not suitable for everyone; those patients with glaucoma, a detached retina, or eye disorders caused by diabetes, are generally not considered for lens implantation. In these cases, eyeglasses or contacts can restore their vision to almost normal.

Restoration or substantial improvement of vision, in fact, occurs in about 95 percent of the cases after surgery. If vision is not restored, the cause may be from other disorders which were undetected because the cataract blocked the view of the interior of the eye. In general, though, cataracts can be successfully remedied, and most people can resume the lives they led before cataracts diminished their vision.

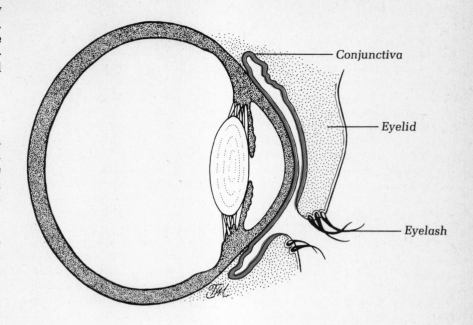

The conjunctiva is a delicate membrane that lines the eyelids and covers the exposed surface of the eye.

CONJUNCTIVITIS

Conjunctivitis, often called pinkeye, is an infection or an inflammation of the conjunctiva, the delicate membrane that lines the eyelids and continues over the exposed surface of the eye.

Although conjunctivitis will generally run its course in about two weeks and not cause permanent damage, some untreated cases of conjunctivitis may lead to more serious eye problems. Such complications may include ulcers on the cornea, the transparent covering across the front of the eye. A corneal ulcer is an eroded area of the cornea, which if untreated, may leave a scar which interferes with vision.

Most cases of conjunctivitis are caused by bacteria, viruses, or fungi. Allergies, chemicals, dust, smoke, or foreign objects may also irritate the conjunctiva and lead to conjunctivitis. Occasionally, a sexually transmitted disease may cause conjunctivitis if the eyes come into contact with secretions from the sexual organs — for example, if a person with a sexually transmitted disease rubs the eyes after handling the genital organs.

Children are most often affected by conjunctivitis, especially infectious conjunctivitis. Measles, a childhood illness, is often accompanied by conjunctivitis. In addition, both children and adults who swim a great deal may contract conjunctivitis — either from chlorine in the pool or from contaminated water. People with allergies, such as hay fever, are prone to conjunctivitis, and those whose occupations or living conditions expose them to chemicals, fumes, or other irritants may also develop conjunctivitis.

SYMPTOMS

The symptoms of conjunctivitis include redness (pinkeye), burning, itching, tearing, discharge (sometimes containing pus), and perhaps pain or sensitivity to light. Sometimes the symptoms last a few days; at other times a severe case may linger for two weeks.

TREATMENT

Treatment can range from symptom-relieving measures to medication. Rest and shielding the eyes from bright light are often helpful. If the conjunctivitis is caused by environmental irritants, eliminating such factors may be sufficient. If there is a discharge that glues the eyes shut, you can bathe the eyes with warm water and wipe with a clean cloth. Antibiotic or antiseptic (germ-killing) eyedrops may be prescribed, and you should use them as directed, usually several times a day since the natural cleansing action of the eyes' tears will wash away the drops in a few hours.

In treating conjunctivitis, you should remember one essential fact: infectious conjunctivitis is extremely contagious or catching. Therefore, someone with this ailment should not share hankerchiefs, towels, or washcloths and should avoid close contact with other family members.

GLAUCOMA

Glaucoma is an eye disorder characterized by increased pressure within the eyeball. The pressure builds up because the fluids within the eye do not circulate and drain properly.

Normally, the healthy eye maintains the aqueous fluid in the anterior chamber of the eyeball under gentle pressure. However, when the fluid-regulating mechanism fails, internal pressure rises in the eye. This in turn causes damage to the sensitive nerve endings and delicate structures within the eye.

Glaucoma is one of the most frequent but unnecessary causes of blindness. Untreated, it can lead to partial or complete permanent loss of vision. Because of this danger and because chronic glaucoma usually gives no warning signals, it is vital that testing for this disease should be done on a regular basis, especially after the age of 40. Early diagnosis and treatment can usually halt vision loss and prevent blindness.

The cause of glaucoma is unknown, although obviously the eye's fluid-regulating mechanism is defective in some way. There are two types of glaucoma, and each results from a different type of defect in the fluid-regulating system. *Acute,* or *closed angle, glaucoma* often develops when the pressure suddenly elevates and pushes the iris (the colored portion of the eye) into the angle of the eye where the iris joins the cornea. The iris thus "closes" the angle of the eye and blocks drainage of aqueous fluid from the anterior chamber. *Chronic,* or *open angle, glaucoma* does not usually result from a sudden block of the angle of the eye. Rather, it is thought to be caused by the gradual obstruction of the eye's system for draining of eye fluid.

Glaucoma occurs most commonly after the age of 40, although it can develop in infancy

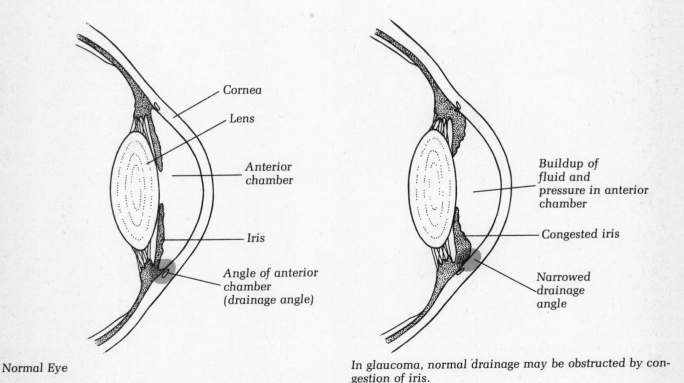

Cornea

Lens

Anterior chamber

Iris

Angle of anterior chamber (drainage angle)

Buildup of fluid and pressure in anterior chamber

Congested iris

Narrowed drainage angle

Normal Eye

In glaucoma, normal drainage may be obstructed by congestion of iris.

Glaucoma—one type of which is illustrated here—is one of the most frequent causes of blindness unless diagnosed and treated.

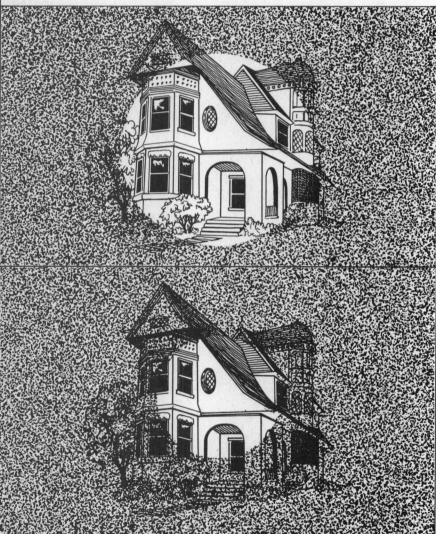

Untreated glaucoma can cause progressive loss of vision. The view on the top is what is seen if glaucoma is properly treated and there is no vision loss. The center view shows some loss of side vision that occurs with untreated glaucoma. The bottom view shows serious loss of side vision with advanced untreated glaucoma.

or childhood, too. It has not been proved that glaucoma is inherited. However, statistics seem to show that people with glaucoma in their families are often at a higher risk. Sometimes glaucoma follows other eye disorders, such as injuries, infections, or cataracts. And there is some evidence that may link glaucoma to long-term use of certain drugs, particularly steroids.

SYMPTOMS

Chronic glaucoma is often called the "sneak thief of sight" because frequently in the beginning there are no noticeable symptoms — vision deterioration is gradual and painless. Sometimes there is a slow, and unnoticed, loss of peripheral or side vision while central vision remains normal. As the disease progresses, there may also be other visual disturbances such as foggy, misty, blurred vision, often intermittent rather than constant. There may be difficulty adjusting to brightness and darkness. Occasionally, slight pain in or around the eye, usually on one side and again intermittent, will occur. But the symptom most indicative of chronic glaucoma is the halo—the perception of a faint, white circle surrounding a light. This is most visibly noticeable in the dark while looking at a distant light.

Acute glaucoma, on the other hand, is characterized by sudden and quite severe symptoms: abrupt blurring of vision and severe eye pain. Oftentimes the pain can be strong enough to cause nausea and vomiting. Acute glaucoma is an emergency situation, since permanent blindness can result in a matter of days. However, the symptoms are usually so dramatic that medical attention is sought immediately. Fortunately, this condition is not very common.

Early diagnosis of glaucoma is crucial; it is the key to preventing blindness. Most physicians recommend that persons over 40 be tested every two to three years for glaucoma. Those with a family history of the disease are urged to be screened every year and perhaps before the age of 40.

Glaucoma is usually diagnosed by a simple procedure. After applying anesthetic eyedrops, the doctor places a pressure gauge directly on the front surface of the eye. This device measures the amount of pressure within the eye. The doctor will also want to inspect the interior of the eye by looking into the eye with a special instrument. The physician will be looking at the eye's angle (where the iris and cornea meet) for a blockage in the normal drainage system and at the optic nerve for signs of damage. And since the loss of peripheral vision may be an early sign of glaucoma, the doctor may want to use a side vision test along with the standard central vision examination.

TREATMENT

Acute glaucoma is a medical emergency and is treated by surgery to quickly reestablish the eye's drainage system. Most cases of chronic glaucoma, however, are treated successfully with medication which either increases fluid drainage or decreases the amount of fluid produced. Eyedrops that are administered daily promote fluid drainage. Since some of the prescribed eyedrops constrict the pupil of the eye to pull the iris away from the angle of the eye and open up the drainage area, many glaucoma patients find it advantageous to carry an identification card with this pertinent medication information. Therefore, if they are unexpectedly admitted to a hospital while unconscious, the doctor on duty will understand why the pupils are constricted and will not be concerned about a possible drug overdose which is often indicated by constricted pupils.

There are also drugs taken orally (by mouth) that work by decreasing the production of eye fluid. In addition, there is a new type of eyedrop, beta blocker drops, that is believed to reduce the production of eye fluid. Unlike the other eyedrops, the new beta blocker drops do not alter the size of the pupil or affect vision. However, since beta blocker drugs can affect the heart rate and narrow breathing passages, these eyedrops may not be suitable for those with heart or lung disease.

Although the usual treatment for chronic glaucoma is medication, surgery is occasionally recommended for those persons who do not respond to the drugs. While less than 5 percent of patients will require surgery for chronic glaucoma, there are several surgical procedures used today, all of which attempt to create new pathways for drainage of the fluid. Laser therapy is a surgical technique currently under investigation and it has indeed proven successful in many cases. The laser, an intense light beam, generates heat which can alter tissues and cells in order to promote better fluid drainage.

The treatment available for glaucoma is effective and, if the condition is discovered early, the loss of vision can be halted. The keys to preventing loss of vision are periodic screening and careful attention to treatment if glaucoma is diagnosed. Glaucoma need not be the sneak thief of sight.

STY

A sty is an infection or inflamed swelling of the sebaceous (oil-secreting) glands of the upper or lower eyelid. A sty is usually caused by staphylococcus bacteria. It can be external, occurring on the edge of the lid at the base of an eyelash, or internal, located on the inside surface of the eyelid.

Although a sty is usually not serious, it may often lead to a recurrent inflammation of the eyelids.

SYMPTOMS

The first symptom is usually a feeling of having a foreign object in the eye. There may be pain, tearing, redness, swelling, and the appearance of small, tender areas. The eye may be sensitive to touch and light. Eventually small yellowish boils filled with pus appear. When they burst, releasing the pus, the pain subsides and healing begins.

TREATMENT

A sty is often treated with antibiotic eye solutions and ointments. Applying warm, moist heat three or four times a day for about ten minutes at a time may help to bring the sty to a head so that it will spontaneously burst. A sty should never be opened by anyone but a doctor.

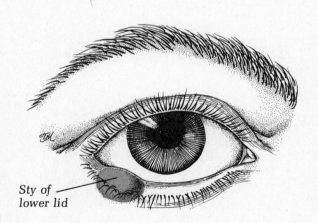

Sty of lower lid

A sty is an inflamed swelling of the oil-secreting glands of the eyelid.

EAR, NOSE, AND THROAT

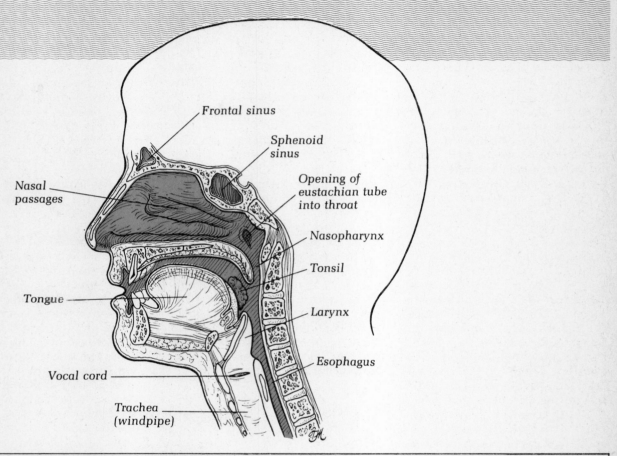

Frontal sinus

Sphenoid sinus

Opening of eustachian tube into throat

Nasal passages

Nasopharynx

Tonsil

Tongue

Larynx

Esophagus

Vocal cord

Trachea (windpipe)

The ear, nose, and throat are all interconnected.

In medicine, the ears, nose, and throat are often grouped together, just as they are joined in the body. The eustachian tubes connect the ears to the nasopharynx, the upper part of the throat which opens into the nose. Because they are joined, infection in one structure often spreads into one of the others.

Ear. The ear has three parts — the external ear, the middle ear, and the inner ear. The external ear, called the pinna, collects sound waves and transmits them through the eardrum to the middle ear. The middle ear transmits these sound waves through a series of tiny bones—the hammer, anvil, and stirrup — to the inner ear. The cochlea in the inner ear changes the vibrations to nerve impulses that are sent to the brain through the auditory nerve. Also within the inner ear are the semicircular canals that detect motion as the head is moved. These canals tell the brain about the position of the head and body.

The eustachian tubes, which extend from the middle ear to the nasopharynx, allow the air pressure in the middle ear to equalize with that outside the body, thus protecting the eardrum from rupturing. However, these same tubes also pose a threat, for they serve as a passageway for infecting microorganisms. Microorganisms from a respiratory infection can enter the middle ear from the nose and throat through the eustachian tubes. This results in middle ear infections.

Nose. Air can enter the respiratory system through the nose or mouth, but only the nose warms and moisturizes the air and filters out dust and other particles. The lining of the nose contains glands which secrete mucus, a sticky substance which coats and lubricates the walls of the nose as well as the other parts of the throat. The mucus helps moisturize the incoming air, but it also has a protective function in that it traps foreign matter entering the nose. The mucus even contains a special substance which can dissolve bacteria. Propelled by tiny hairs, called cilia, the mucus with its trapped bacteria and particles moves to the entrance of the throat where it is swallowed. The stomach produces acids which then destroy any bacteria which may have survived the anti-bacteria substance in the mucus. This is an extremely efficient line of defense against the billions of bacteria constantly entering the nose.

Located in the facial bones next to and connected with the nose are the sinuses. The sinuses are air-filled cavities that are also lined with mucous-secreting glands. There are four different groups of sinuses — frontal, ethmoidal, sphenoidal, and maxillary. Their purpose is to reduce the weight of the skull and to add resonance to the voice.

The nose is also the site of our sense of smell. It contains specialized nerve receptors that detect odor and transmit signals to the brain. Our sense of smell is far more delicate and specialized than our sense of taste. Many of the tastes that we experience are actually discerned by our sense of smell. Thus, when we have a cold or stuffy nose, foods often seem bland and tasteless.

Throat. The throat, or pharynx, is a tube approximately five inches long extending from the back end of the nasal passages to the esophagus (the passageway from the mouth to the stomach). The throat is divided into three parts: the nasopharynx, which opens into the nose; the oropharynx, which opens into the mouth;

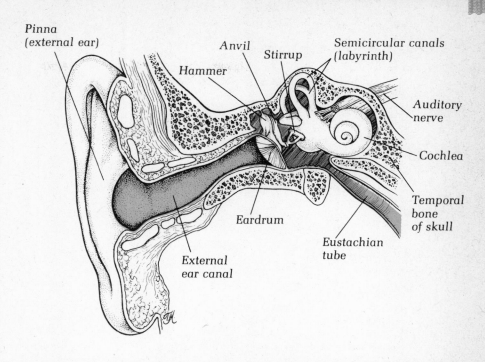

The ear is a complex structure encased in the temporal bone at the base of the skull.

and the laryngopharynx, which includes the larynx, or voice box. The throat also contains the tonsils, small lumps of tissue that fight disease and help protect the body. Air and food pass through the throat, which is therefore part of both the respiratory and the digestive systems.

COMMON COLD

The group of symptoms known as the common cold are caused by viruses. Colds affect the upper respiratory tract, which includes the nose, throat, and sinuses. Everyone gets colds at some time. Adults have an average of two to four colds each year, while children have six to eight. This mild disease is a major reason for visits to doctors and for lost days both at schools and in business and industry.

In general, colds are self-limiting diseases. That is, they last a certain length of time and then the symptoms disappear, without leaving lasting ill effects. However, a simple cold can be complicated by more serious illnesses. The most dangerous complication of colds is pneumonia, or infection of the lungs. Other possible complications are ear infections, sinus infections, and bronchitis — infection of the tubes that lead into the lungs. These secondary infections are usually caused by bacteria and can be treated with antibiotics.

In children, croup is a possible complication of colds. In croup, the airway to the lungs becomes blocked, which makes breathing difficult and causes a barking cough. This condition sometimes requires immediate medical care.

Colds are not dangerous, except in rare cases where extreme complications develop. However, colds are more uncomfortable and last longer in smokers and in persons who have long-term respiratory illnesses such as emphysema and chronic bronchitis. Such persons are also likely to have complications.

Children are especially susceptible to colds, and in general they develop complications more often than adults. Children get more colds because they have not developed immunity, or resistance,

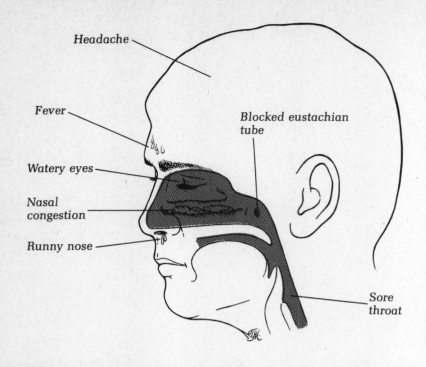

Headache

Fever

Watery eyes

Nasal congestion

Runny nose

Blocked eustachian tube

Sore throat

The symptoms of a common cold are caused by viruses.

to the viruses in their environment. Generally, small children build up immunity gradually to viruses at home, then have to begin again when they go to school and encounter many new viruses from their classmates. Adults who have small children at home are likely to have more colds than those who do not. Also, persons who travel or who have many contacts from outside their usual community are likely to encounter cold viruses to which they are not immune.

There are at least five major groups of viruses that cause colds. One of those groups, the rhinoviruses, has at least 100 different viruses within it. Each group causes a somewhat different pattern of symptoms and may lead to different complications. It is not known exactly how the viruses spread from person to person, but researchers believe it is a combination of physical contact (hand to hand, for example), airborne particles, and airborne moisture. The viruses are apparently present in the infected person's nasal passages and throat and get into the air or onto the skin when the cold sufferer coughs, sneezes, and blows the nose.

SYMPTOMS

Colds have an incubation period of 48 to 72 hours. That is, it takes two to three days to develop symptoms after the virus enters the body. Symptoms and severity vary, probably depending on the virus. Typical symptoms include stuffy nose, runny nose, sneezing, sore or scratchy throat, and/or coughing. Fever seldom occurs with an ordinary cold; but if it does, it usually is mild. The initial symptoms can lead to others such as burning or watering of the eyes, temporary loss of the senses of taste and smell, a feeling of pressure in the ears or the sinuses, nasal voice, and tenderness around the nose.

A cold can begin with any of the symptoms and proceed in any order. Colds usually last about a week, but about one in four lasts up to two weeks.

In diagnosing a cold, the physician looks for signs that the illness is *not* a simple cold. This may require taking material from the patient's throat or nasal passages to be tested for bacterial infection. A blood test may also be done in certain circumstances, for instance, when a persistent sore throat and swollen glands suggest the possibility of infectious mononucleosis. If sinusitis (inflammation of the air-filled cavities within the facial bone structure) is suspected, the doctor may want an X ray of the sinuses.

TREATMENT

There is no cure for the common cold and no treatment that will make recovery faster. The only action that can be taken is to try to make the symptoms less severe. There are thousands of medicines available without a prescription to treat cold symptoms. Many physicians recommend using specific remedies for the symptoms rather than a combined medication, because it is generally safer and more effective to treat only the symptoms that you actually have.

Be sure to follow the directions on cold medicines carefully. Overuse of cold remedies can make symptoms worse. For example, regular use—more than three days — of some types of nasal decongestants can have a rebound effect and actually cause worse irritation and more congestion. These products work by constricting the blood vessels in the nose. Their repeated use tires the constricting vessels which then relax, making the nose even more congested. Also, use of antihistamines and other drying agents for nasal congestion can make a cough more uncomfortable. Anyone who has a chronic disease or is pregnant should check with a physician before using even nonprescription cold remedies. Generally, it is a good idea to find out what is in the medicine and what it is supposed to do before taking it. Consult a physician or pharmacist if you have questions.

Simply getting plenty of rest, drinking extra liquids, and using a vaporizer to add moisture to the air can also be helpful.

There is no known way to prevent the common cold. Although many people believe Vitamin C is a preventative, studies have shown that it does not have any measurable effect. Colds are mild illnesses, and medical science has concentrated on preventing and curing more dangerous diseases. However, as more is learned about viruses and how they work, a cure for this universal and irritating disease may yet be found.

CROUP

Croup is the term for the harsh, barking cough that results from an acute viral infection of the larynx (voice box) in very young children. It is most commonly found in children below the age of two and most often occurs in cold weather.

Croup is not usually a serious problem, despite the fact that it appears and sounds very frightening. It may not even reappear after the first attack. However, if the infection that causes it is widespread, croup may become more dangerous. Sometimes the windpipe and the bronchi leading into the lungs become blocked. In these cases, croup attacks may recur, or may be quite severe with serious breathing difficulties.

The passageway for air in a child is very narrow. Infections that result in inflammation and swelling of the larynx can seriously limit the child's breathing ability. It is the air forcing its way through the swollen larynx that produces the characteristic cough.

SYMPTOMS

An attack of croup will usually occur toward evening, generally after the child has been suffering from a cold and perhaps a fever for several days. Sometimes the child wakes from sleep with the rasping, barking cough and breathing difficulties. Hoarseness and fever may also be present. The coughing spells usually last less than an hour. In some cases, a

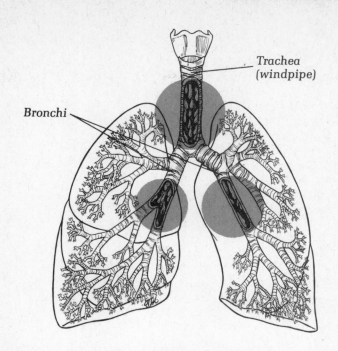

Trachea (windpipe)

Bronchi

The most serious form of croup occurs when mucus blocks the windpipe and the bronchi leading into the lungs. This may result in serious breathing problems and is considered a medical emergency.

child will gag while coughing, causing vomiting which usually relieves the cough.

If a child has a fever of 101°F. or more, or if there is real difficulty breathing, a doctor must be consulted. Because croup can unexpectedly worsen, a child must be carefully monitored for several days following an attack.

TREATMENT

The treatment of croup usually involves relieving the cough, which is done by reducing the inflammation and swelling in the larynx. However, the first step in treatment should be to calm the child. An attack of croup, especially if accompanied by difficult breathing, can seriously frighten a child, aggravating the symptoms. It is important to inform the child of steps that are being taken to ease the discomfort. The child should be told to attempt to breathe slowly and evenly. It may help to have the child visualize the illness: tell the child to picture the tubes to the lungs gradually opening for the passage of air. Or the child can simply be told to

imagine a very relaxing scene, like listening to a bedtime story. Sometimes a doctor may administer a sedative, but this must be done cautiously because it will also slow down the breathing of the child.

Treatment in the home consists of introducing moist air into the child's environment. Moist air reduces inflammation and makes breathing easier. A humidifier or vaporizer may be placed close to the child. Extreme caution must be taken to prevent scalding that can result if the child accidentally touches the vaporizer. For similar reasons, boiling water is not recommended for use in treatment.

If a vaporizer is not available, or if it seems to be ineffective, the child can be placed in a bathroom with a hot shower running. You can also position the child over a basin of hot water, possibly with a towel draped over the head to trap the moist air. The steam from the hot water will often bring relief. While these procedures are being attempted, the child should never be left alone, especially in a hot steamy bathroom.

Never put a spoon or any other

object in the child's mouth during an attack of croup to aid breathing. This could obstruct the airway further. Cough syrup is also not an effective treatment for a croup attack. A vaporizer should be left in the child's room for several days following the attack of croup. An increased intake of fluids (not milk or orange juice) at room temperature will also help.

The warning signs of a worsening condition include blue skin and lips, drooling, and extreme exhaustion. When the croaking sound produced while inhaling continues after the child is calmed, it is known as *stridor*. If stridor is present, a doctor should be called.

In an emergency a doctor can control the inflammation in the throat with drugs. Sometimes hospitalization is necessary, and in very rare cases a breathing tube or even surgery may be required. Antibiotics will sometimes be prescribed to control infections connected with croup.

EAR INFECTIONS

The ear is a complex organ that provides both hearing and the sense of balance. It has three parts. The outer ear includes the pinna, or the visible ear, and the outer ear canal. The middle ear begins at the eardrum and includes the hammer, anvil, and stirrup—tiny bones that vibrate and convey sound into the inner ear. The inner ear has two parts, the semicircular canals (labyrinth) and the cochlea. The cochlea translates sound into nerve impulses and sends them to the brain, and the labyrinth is the organ of balance.

All three parts of the ear can become infected, but middle ear infections are the most common. The medical term for middle ear infections is *otitis media*.

Outer ear infections are essentially skin infections. They are seldom serious and are usually treated by cleaning and sometimes with antibiotic or steroid ointments or drops. Inner ear infections are rare, but they may be a

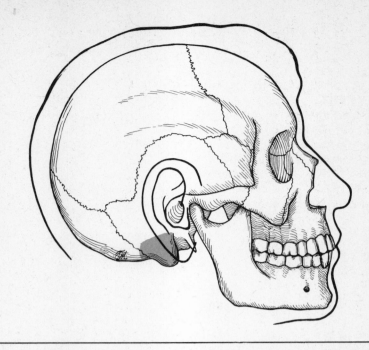

The mastoid bone is a projection of the temporal bone behind the ear. Occasionally, the mastoid bone becomes infected as a complication of a middle ear infection.

complication of middle ear infections and can cause permanent damage to hearing and balance.

Middle ear infections usually clear up quickly with treatment. However, stubborn or untreated infections can lead to serious complications. These include temporary or permanent hearing loss, infection of the semicircular canals, facial paralysis, brain abscess, and meningitis (infection of the covering of the brain). Another possible complication is infection of the mastoid bone, located behind the pinna.

Infections of the nose and throat may lead to middle ear infections, especially in children. The organisms causing the infection may be either bacteria or viruses. The organisms may travel to the middle ear through the eustachian tube, which connects the middle ear to the throat. Infection can also enter the middle ear from the outer ear if the eardrum is damaged by either an injury or a severe outer ear infection.

Children are more likely to have ear infections than adults. Almost every child has had at least one ear infection serious enough to

cause a temporary hearing loss by the age of eight. The most susceptible ages are from six months to two years and from four to six years. Children who have infections in their first year are most at risk for chronic, or long-term, ear infection.

SYMPTOMS

The symptoms of a middle ear infection are severe, throbbing pain in the ear, temperatures of up to 104° or 105°F. (101° or 102°F. in adults), and hearing loss. Some patients also have dizziness, nausea, and vomiting. Occasionally, there may be a sore throat. These symptoms may worsen over a period of hours or days. The eardrum may bulge out, or even burst. If it bursts, blood and pus ooze into the outer ear canal, and the pain is relieved.

A small child who cannot talk may have an ear infection if he or she seems ill or feverish and pulls on an ear.

A physician will diagnose an ear infection from a description of the symptoms and an examination of the eardrum. If the eardrum is red and swollen, and especially if

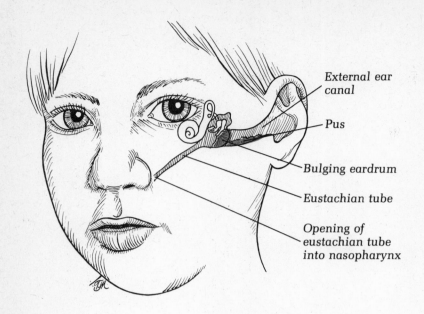

External ear
canal

Pus

Bulging eardrum

Eustachian tube

Opening of
eustachian tube
into nasopharynx

In a middle ear infection, the eardrum may bulge out or even burst. If the eardrum ruptures, pus may ooze into the outer ear canal. A middle ear infection often follows a nose or throat infection which travels to the middle ear through the eustachian tube.

it is bulging outward, the middle ear is probably infected.

TREATMENT

If the physician suspects a bacterial infection in the middle ear, an antibiotic will be prescribed, usually a form of penicillin, along with decongestants and possibly mild painkillers. Antibiotics are not used for virus infections. If the eardrum is bulging and the pain is intense, the physician may make a small cut called a myringotomy in the eardrum to relieve the pressure. The eardrum usually heals naturally. If the eardrum bursts, it is important to keep the outer ear canal clean to prevent infection from spreading.

If an ear infection does not respond to treatment, surgery may be necessary to remove the infected tissue. The hammer, anvil, and stirrup may be damaged, but they can sometimes be reconstructed or replaced with artificial bones. If infection spreads to the mastoid bone, it may have to be removed as well. This procedure is called a mastoidectomy. However, these procedures are seldom done today because of improved antibiotics.

SINUSITIS

The sinuses are cavities within the facial bone structure that are connected to the nose and are part of the respiratory system. They are filled with air and lined with mucous membrane. There are four different groups of sinuses, called the frontal, ethmoidal, sphenoidal, and maxillary sinuses.

Normally, the sinuses are constantly kept clean by the drainage of mucus from the sinuses into the nasal passages. During a cold, the flu, or some other respiratory system illness, the sinuses may not be able to drain properly because of congestion in the nose. However, according to most experts, this in itself is not sinusitis. Sinusitis occurs when an infection, usually caused by bacteria, actually enters one or more of the sinuses.

Sinusitis can become a chronic, or long-term, problem. The infection may spread from the sinuses to the brain and cause meningitis (inflammation of the membranes that surround the brain), but this seldom happens. Osteomyelitis, or infection of the bone, is another rare but possible complication.

A number of different bacteria can cause sinus infection. Some of these bacteria may also cause pneumonia, laryngitis, and middle ear infections. Some cases of sinusitis occur when an abscess (an inflamed pocket of pus) in the root of a tooth penetrates into the sinuses, releasing bacteria into the cavities.

Anything that prevents the mucus in the sinuses from draining into the nasal passages can promote infection. Swimming and diving, injury, and abnormalities in the bone structure are some of the factors, other than congestion from colds or flu, that can cause blockage. Sometimes symptoms that resemble sinusitis are caused by an allergy such as hay fever.

Anyone who has frequent colds has an increased chance of getting a sinus infection. The problem is more common in adults than in children, and there is also some evidence that sinusitis may occur more frequently in smokers than in nonsmokers.

SYMPTOMS

The most usual symptom of sinusitis is pain and tenderness in the face, usually above the infected sinus. The pain can be felt in the forehead, behind the eyes, in the eyes, or near the upper part of the nose. Sometimes the pain seems to be in the upper teeth (not in a single tooth). Sinusitis may also cause headache, slight fever, chills, sore throat, and nasal obstruction. Depending on which sinuses are affected, the pain may seem to go away in the morning and worsen as the day progresses, or may change in intensity as the patient changes position. There may also be pus in the discharge from the nose. The infection usually lasts about two weeks.

Sinusitis is difficult to diagnose because the physician cannot see directly into the sinuses. The

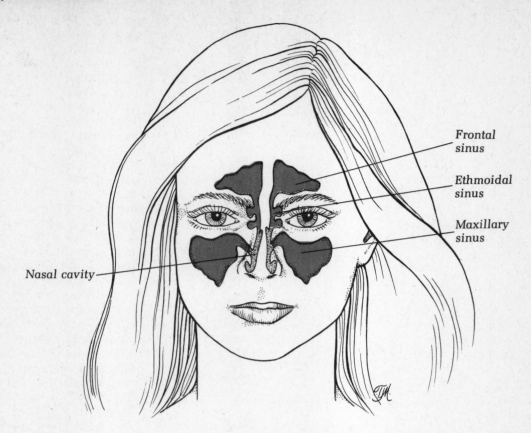

Frontal sinus

Ethmoidal sinus

Maxillary sinus

Nasal cavity

The sinuses are air-filled cavities within the facial bone structure that are connected with the nasal passages. The sinuses are called frontal, ethmoidal, maxillary, and sphenoidal. The sphenoidal sinuses are located behind the ethmoidal sinuses.

doctor will look for typical symptoms and try to make sure they are not caused by some other problem such as a tooth abscess or an allergy. If sinusitis seems to be the cause, the doctor may want to take X rays to see if there is fluid and/or some abnormality in the sinuses. X rays may also be needed to find out exactly which sinuses are involved. A technique called sinus puncture, in which a needle is inserted into the sinus through the upper jaw above the molar teeth, may be done to take a sample of the material in a sinus for laboratory tests. This is the only way the bacteria that are causing the infection can be identified with certainty, since a nasal discharge may contain a completely different infectious agent.

TREATMENT

Nasal decongestants can be used initially to unblock the sinuses to allow them to drain. Hot compresses or dry heat may also help. Codeine, a narcotic painkiller, may be prescribed if the condition is very painful.

Most physicians will prescribe an antibiotic that will kill either of the two most common bacteria causing the infection. If this is not effective, sinus puncture may be necessary to determine what is causing the infection. Once the infectious agent has been identified, the physician may try a different antibiotic. In very severe cases of sinusitis, the doctor may "wash out" the sinuses to remove the bacteria. Salt water is usually injected into the infected sinus through the nose, and the solution then drains out through the nose. It may have to be done several times.

In rare cases of recurrent or chronic sinusitis, surgery may be necessary. Occasionally, the removal of a nasal polyp (a mass of swollen tissue) or the repair of structural abnormalities in the nose may relieve the obstruction of the sinus and allow normal drainage. In rare cases, surgical removal of infected and damaged sinus tissue may be necessary to cure the problem.

TONSILLITIS

The tonsils are small, almond-shaped lumps of tissue located in the throat at the back of the mouth. The tonsils become infected periodically, especially during childhood, and this condition is called tonsillitis.

It is not known exactly what the tonsils do or how they function, but scientists believe they have two important roles in the immune system, the system that protects the body from infection. The first of these is to release a kind of antibody, or protective substance, into the throat to prevent the spread of infection from the nose and throat to the lungs. This function is important in young children, who are susceptible to many types of ear, nose, and throat infections. Another function the tonsils may have is to attract bacterial infection, which then stimulates the production of antibodies. Antibodies ordinarily do not develop unless infection is present. These antibodies build up in the body to prevent future infections that may be far more serious than tonsillitis. If this theory is correct, each episode of tonsillitis in a child actually increases his or her resistance to disease as an adult. Once resistance is developed, the function of the tonsils is completed. In fact, the tonsils are barely visible in infants, increase in size in the preschool and early school years, and shrink again in adulthood.

Tonsillitis can be caused by many different infectious agents, but in young children the most common cause is streptococcus bacteria. There are two types of tonsillitis. One is called "acute" tonsillitis, which means the condition flares up and then disappears in a short time. Acute tonsillitis is usually a "strep" infection. It is also possible to have "chronic" tonsillitis. This form of the disease recurs over and over again, or never really goes away. The tonsils seem to become permanently enlarged, and abscesses, or pus-filled sores, may develop on them. It is not known why this occurs in some individuals or what causes it.

Infections caused by streptococcus bacteria can lead to rheumatic fever, a heart disease that usually affects the heart valves and may cause life-long health problems. Other complications may include infections of the sinuses, ears, and kidneys. However, these complications are uncommon today, because antibiotics are effective against strep infections, and the problem can usually be cleared up before complications develop.

Tonsillitis can occur at any age, but it is most common between the ages of five and 15 years. It seldom occurs in children under two.

SYMPTOMS

Acute tonsillitis begins with a sore throat. Other symptoms are fever up to about 101°F., chills, headache, and muscle aches. These symptoms may get worse for one to three days, then gradually subside. The lymph glands in the neck — whose job it is to trap and destroy disease-causing microorganisms — may become swollen as well. In children, nausea, vomiting, and stomachaches may also occur. The symptoms usually last about a week.

In chronic tonsillitis, there is a recurrent or persistent sore throat, difficulty with swallowing or with breathing, and unpleasant-smelling breath.

To diagnose tonsillitis, the physician looks at the throat and tonsils for redness and swelling. The tonsils may have gray material on them. In chronic tonsillitis the tonsils may be covered with a yellowish material. To find out what is causing the infection, the doctor may take a sample of the material on the throat and tonsils with a cotton swab to examine in a laboratory test.

TREATMENT

For ordinary causes of tonsillitis, most physicians prescribe an antibiotic. Penicillin is often used, because it works well against streptococcus bacteria. Even if the symptoms improve, the patient should take the entire prescription to make sure the infection is completely gone. Bed rest or at least reduced activity is usually helpful, and sore throat pain can be relieved by gargling with warm salt water — one-half teaspoonful of table salt in a cup of warm water every two to four hours.

Tonsillectomy, or surgical removal of the tonsils, is seldom done today. A physician may recommend it when the tonsils enlarge enough to block the air passages or when the tonsils are abscessed (filled with pus). Recent studies, however, have found that even when the tonsils appear to be greatly enlarged they almost always shrink with time. Also, it has been found that removing the tonsils does not prevent recurrent sore throats and colds as was once believed. Research on the possible role of the tonsils in building immunity has also made physicians hesitate to remove them.

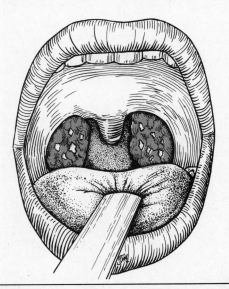

Tonsillitis is an infection of the tonsils, small lumps of tissue in the throat. Infected tonsils may be enlarged and may also have gray or yellow patches of infection on them.

RESPIRATORY DISEASES

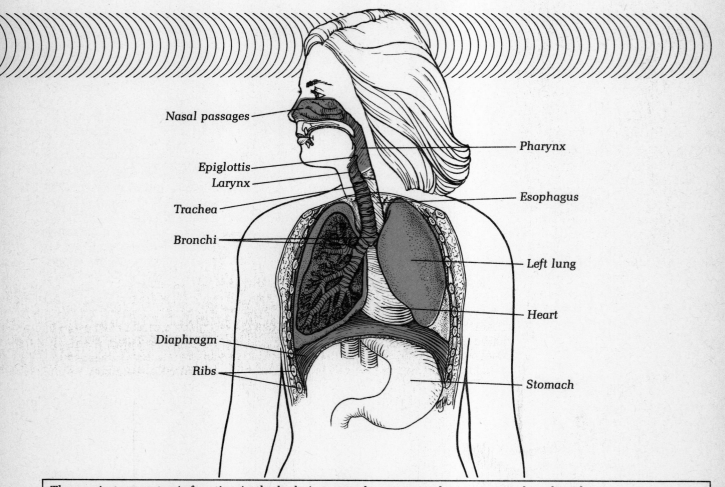

Nasal passages

Pharynx

Epiglottis

Larynx

Esophagus

Trachea

Bronchi

Left lung

Heart

Diaphragm

Ribs

Stomach

The respiratory system's function in the body is to supply oxygen and to remove carbon dioxide.

Respiration is the process by which body cells are supplied with necessary oxygen and relieved of waste carbon dioxide. In simple animals, this exchange may take place across a membrane, air ducts, or gills. But in humans, the process is complex, involving two body systems, the respiratory and the circulatory.

The respiratory tract includes the nose, the pharynx (throat), the larynx (voice box), the trachea, the bronchi, and the lungs. Breathing is the process by which air flows through these structures to the lungs (inhalation) and by which waste gases exit from the body (exhalation).

The nose warms, moistens, and filters air entering the respiratory tract. Both air and food pass through the throat, but the epiglottis, a thin flap of tissue, prevents food from passing into the larynx, which is a tubular passage containing the vocal cords and joined to the lower end of the trachea, or windpipe. The trachea divides into the two bronchi, one passageway leading into each lung. The bronchi divide and subdivide like the roots of a tree; hence, the term bronchial tree.

Every tube of the bronchial tree is lined with membranes that produce mucus — a clear, flowing substance that keeps the tubes moist and protected. The linings also contain cilia — tiny, hairlike projections that sweep excess mucus, dust particles, and other foreign matter up out of the lungs and air passages.

The very smallest bronchial tubes end in cup-shaped air sacs, called alveoli. It is in the alveoli that vital gases, oxygen and carbon dioxide, are exchanged. Each alveolus is richly supplied with tiny blood vessels called capillaries. Oxygen crosses the alveolar and capillary walls and enters the blood, while carbon dioxide passes from the blood through the capillary walls into the alveoli. The blood then carries the oxygen to the body's cells, while the carbon dioxide is released from the alveoli into the outside atmosphere upon exhalation.

The lungs are divided into sections called lobes. The left lung has two lobes, and the right lung has three. Furthermore, each lung is covered by a thin, moist membrane called the pleura, which also lines the chest cavity. The two pleural surfaces slide and glide past each other as the lungs expand and contract.

Although the lungs do expand and contract, they have no muscle tissue. They are flexible, passive organs, expanded and contracted by the movement of the ribs and diaphragm—the large muscle that divides the cavity of the chest and the cavity of the abdomen. During inhalation, the diaphragm contracts, which causes it to descend. The chest cavity in turn expands which causes the air pressure inside the chest cavity to be less than that of the air outside the body. As a consequence, air from the outside rushes into the lungs. During exhalation, the diaphragm relaxes and moves up, chest capacity is reduced, and air is pushed out of the body, taking with it waste gases.

ASTHMA

Asthma is a respiratory disease characterized by periods of breathlessness that result when the bronchioles (small respiratory tubes) constrict (narrow), or become clogged with mucus or when the membranes that line these tubes become swollen. The flow of air both into and out of the lungs is reduced. Stale air which cannot be completely exhaled becomes trapped in the air sacs of the lungs, thus preventing fresh air from being inhaled. The wheezing that is characteristic of asthma is caused by the effort to push air through the constricted bronchioles.

Asthma comes on in acute, or sudden, attacks. The disease is extremely unpredictable: attacks may be only hours apart, or several years may elapse between them. Once the disease develops, it can never be entirely cured, although it may be quite effectively controlled. Children never truly "outgrow" asthma, but the attacks may become less severe and less frequent. Asthma is rarely fatal; however, it can be very danger-

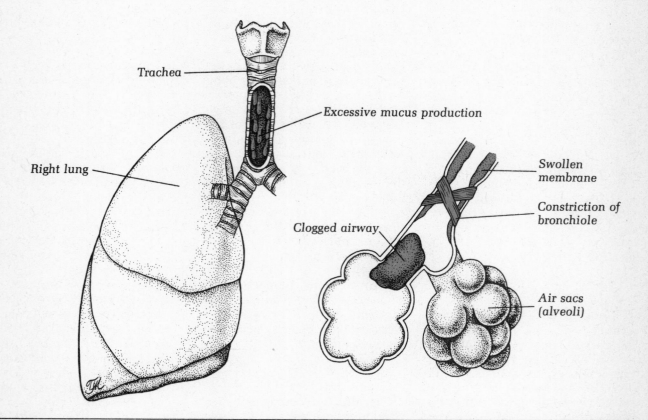

Trachea

Excessive mucus production

Right lung

Swollen membrane

Constriction of bronchiole

Clogged airway

Air sacs (alveoli)

Asthma is a disease characterized by periods of breathlessness that result when the bronchioles constrict or become clogged with mucus, or when the membranes that line the tubes become swollen. The wheezing that is a common symptom of asthma is caused by the effort to push air through the constricted or blocked bronchioles.

ous, especially in very young children.

The bronchial system of persons with asthma is overly sensitive to substances or conditions that would not normally bother a nonasthmatic person. In about one half of the cases of asthma, this sensitivity is thought to be caused by allergies. The other half consists of those persons whose asthma occurs in response to nonallergic agents or environmental changes. Substances that precipitate allergic asthma attacks include household dust, smoke, pollen, feathers, pet hair, insects, and mold spores. Additionally, allergies to specific foods or medications can trigger asthma. Nonallergic agents or environmental changes that can cause an asthma attack include infections of the ear, nose, and throat, as well as strenuous exercise or breathing cold air.

Although asthma is in no way a psychosomatic disease (a physical disease caused by psychological factors), emotional stress can make an attack worse or even set one off. In addition, asthmatic children are often so overprotected by their parents that they develop emotional problems. In some instances, they may manipulate their families by purposely behaving in a way that they know will trigger an attack.

The susceptibility to asthma may be hereditary. If both parents are asthmatic or have many allergies, there is a 50 percent chance that their child will develop asthma. In addition, people who have hay fever are more likely to develop asthma.

SYMPTOMS

The word "asthma" comes from a Greek word meaning "panting," which is a primary symptom of an attack. Often the first symptom noted before an attack is a feeling of tightness in the chest. The asthmatic experiences difficulty in breathing, and wheezes and coughs, possibly bringing up a thick mucus. Neck veins stand out; the face becomes flushed or pale. The attacks may come at any time, even during sleep. They may last less than an hour or as long as a week or more. Despite the severity, few are fatal.

During an asthma attack, the muscles around the tiny bronchioles (air tubes) tighten and narrow, making air passage difficult. Mucus collects. The asthmatic finds it difficult to breathe.

The severity of a case of asthma is determined by the suddenness of the attacks and the amount of time between attacks. Mild asthma may be marked by an almost constant wheezing and coughing with very little shortness of breath, while a severe attack may cause the patient to turn blue from lack of oxygen. Untreated, the attacks can last from minutes to hours to days.

Diagnosis of asthma is made by a thorough medical history, physical examination, and chest X ray. Additionally, other tests may be performed to insure that asthma is not misdiagnosed as chronic bronchitis or recurrent colds.

Since many cases of asthma are triggered by some sort of allergy, a battery of allergy tests may have to be done if the patient does not already know to what substances he or she is allergic. A food allergen (allergen is the substance or food thought to be causing the allergic reaction) is generally determined by going on a very restricted diet, then gradually introducing more foods — one at a time — until the one that triggers an allergic reaction is identified. Allergies to environmental substances are generally determined by a skin scratch test, in which small amounts of the suspected substances are introduced just under the skin. A positive reaction is characterized by a swollen, red bump at the application site.

TREATMENT

If an allergy is discovered, every effort must be made to eliminate the offending substance from the asthma patient's environment. Additionally, there are many different types of asthma medications, each working in a slightly different manner. Therefore, all medications are not right for each case of asthma. Generally, your doctor will start treatment with the mildest medication with the fewest side effects, changing to more potent preparations until one is proven to be very effective. No matter which drug is prescribed, asthma patients should drink plenty of water to keep the respiratory passages moist and to replace fluids depleted by the drugs.

During an acute asthma attack patients are usually given an injection of epinephrine (adrenaline) or an adrenaline aerosol to dilate (enlarge) the bronchial tubes and allow free breathing. However, this therapy cannot be used constantly since adrenaline also overstimulates the heart. These treatments, in conjunction with oxygen, therefore are usually given during a visit to the doctor's office or emergency room during an attack. However, older children and adults can be taught to use the aerosol forms of these drugs during an emergency attack in their own homes.

Newer adrenaline-like drugs that affect only the muscles of the airways have been developed. They can be taken orally and are longer-lasting without the side effect of heart overstimulation. Usually these drugs are prescribed to be taken for a few days after an attack, since round-the-clock use may cause the patient to build up a tolerance to the drug that makes the disease more difficult to treat during an attack.

There are other drugs used in the treatment of asthma. Many forms of the drug theophylline are prescribed for asthma patients who need constant medication to keep their bronchial tubes dilated. The patient using this drug must be monitored closely; some persons eliminate the drug so quickly that it has almost no effect, while in others the drug accumulates, at times to toxic levels. Diet, smoking, and liver disease can all affect the rate at which theophylline is absorbed. Nausea, vomiting, and agitation are common side effects of this drug.

Corticosteroids, which are hormonal drugs, can be extremely effective in controlling asthma attacks. However, patients may become dependent on them, and they have undesirable side effects such as weight gain, diabetes, ulcers, and high blood pressure. In children, steroid therapy may stunt growth and development. However, for severe cases of asthma, steroid therapy may be the only effective treatment.

For an asthma patient whose attacks are triggered by a specific allergy, allergy shots to reduce the patient's sensitivity to the specific irritant may be helpful. Similarly, antihistamines may offer some relief, although they tend to dry out mucous membranes excessively.

Cromolyn is the only drug available that actually prevents asthma attacks by inhibiting the release of histamines, chemicals released by body cells as part of the allergy reaction. Cromolyn, which is inhaled, is usually only effective in mild cases of asthma and cannot relieve an attack that has already begun.

There are other preventive measures that may be helpful. Since the tendency toward developing asthma is inherited, babies born into asthmatic families should be fed breast milk or soy protein formula to prevent the possibility of triggering an allergic reaction that can bring with it an attack of asthma. Breast milk and soy formula have been shown to cause fewer allergic reactions than cow's milk. Completely eliminating from the home any irritants such as smoke and pet hair, as well as rugs, drapes, and overstuffed furniture that trap dust, can also reduce the likelihood of an asthma attack. Furthermore, although strenuous exercise may precipitate an asthma attack, moderate exercise can be quite beneficial. Each asthma patient should learn exactly how much he or she can do without triggering an attack.

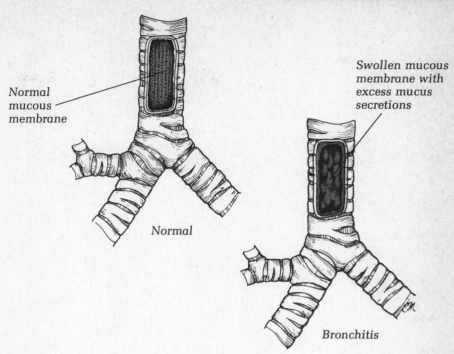

Normal mucous membrane

Swollen mucous membrane with excess mucus secretions

Normal

Bronchitis

Bronchitis is an inflammation of the inner linings—or mucous membranes— of the bronchial tubes. As the membranes become swollen, more mucus is secreted. The result is narrowed, clogged bronchial tubes causing a reduction of air flow into the lungs.

BRONCHITIS

Bronchitis is an inflammation of the inner linings, or membranes, of the bronchi. The bronchi are the major breathing tubes through which air travels from the windpipe into the lungs. When the bronchi are inflamed and swollen, mucus glands embedded in the membranes expand and secrete more mucus. The bronchial tubes, already narrowed from the swelling, begin to get clogged, and the mucus must be coughed up to restore air flow into the lungs.

The combination of mucus production and coughing is called a productive cough; it ceases when the source of inflammation has been removed or overcome and the bronchial lining heals. A short-lived period of productive coughing is called *acute* bronchitis. When the cough lingers for about three months a year and for two years in a row, or when it persists for six months during one year, the condition is termed *chronic,* or long-term, bronchitis.

It is a signal that the membranes of the bronchi are being continually inflamed. In time, this causes them to deteriorate, leaving the lungs susceptible to serious infection and damage.

Bronchitis may be a cause of death but it more often leads to death from other causes. For example, bronchitis-damaged lungs can deprive the heart of adequate oxygen, leading to death from heart failure. Or a person whose weakened lungs are no longer able to resist infection may die of pneumonia.

Chronic bronchitis is linked with emphysema and several similar diseases in a category called chronic obstructive pulmonary (lung) disease (COPD). Two or even three of the COPD conditions frequently occur in the same person, and one may lead to another. More than nine million people are believed to have COPD, and it is responsible for about 45,000 deaths a year.

Inflammation of the bronchial tubes is a reaction to irritation or infection. Many people get acute bronchitis (which they call a chest cold) with a cold, flu, or strep throat (a sore throat caused by *Streptococcus* bacteria). Chronic bronchitis may get started from such infections if they are very frequent, but more often the cause is constant irritation from smoke and other air pollutants.

By far the most significant cause of chronic bronchitis is cigarette smoking. Inhaled tobacco smoke stops the action of the cilia, tiny hairlike projections all along the bronchial lining that sweep mucus up and out of the lungs. Normally, the mucus collects dust particles and bacteria along the way, but when the cilia are paralyzed, these particles aggravate delicate bronchial tissue while the stagnant mucus becomes a breeding ground for infection.

Of all victims of chronic bronchitis, 75 percent are smokers. People who give up smoking begin to reduce their risk immediately. About 90 percent of the people who smoke and also live in polluted environments, or are exposed to occupational dusts, have a persistent cough; they are at great risk of developing serious cases of the disease by the time they are 50 to 60 years old. Chronic bronchitis is about three times more prevalent among men, but women are beginning to catch up as long-term women smokers come down with the disease.

Babies and young children who have chronic bronchitis usually overcome it, but they are at higher risk than others of developing it again as adults. Bronchitis also tends to cluster in families. This is only partly explained by sharing the same conditions; some unknown predisposing factor seems to be present. People are also at greater risk if they are undernourished, inadequately housed and clothed, and frequently fatigued.

SYMPTOMS

The main symptom of bronchitis is a persistent, mucus-laden cough. In acute bronchial infections, typical accompanying symptoms may be hoarseness, chest discomfort, and a low-grade fever. Wheezing and shortness of breath may also be present. In children, the productive cough may "settle in" after a series of short-term infections, signaling chronic bronchitis. In adults, chronic bronchitis tends to start with a slight amount of coughing and throat-clearing upon awakening in the morning. Other symptoms appear gradually and become more pronounced as the disease progresses. Coughing becomes more vigorous and mucus is thicker. Chest infections occur more often and last longer. Wheezing and shortness of breath become noticeable, and physical exertion begins to cause heavy panting. In time, perhaps 15 to 20 years after the early signs have appeared, more and more of the smaller bronchial tubes may become obstructed, and breathing capacity is irreversibly reduced. To get sufficient oxygen, the heart pumps more blood into the lungs and becomes enlarged. Heart pounding and chest pain may be felt. A poor supply of oxygen may also cause the lips, nails, and skin to develop a bluish tinge.

The physician will probably take a medical history to learn whether the lungs are being exposed to irritating substances and to understand the patient's pattern of coughing and respiratory infections. The physical examination includes listening to the chest with the stethoscope for the rumbling and wheezing chest sounds made by mucus-filled air tubes. Also, several machines are available to test how well air moves in and out of the lungs. In another common test, the patient walks on a treadmill for awhile and then blood is drawn from an artery to measure how efficiently oxygen gets from the lungs to the bloodstream during exercise. The doctor may also take a chest X ray; if the disease has advanced, the X ray may show dilated bronchial tubes, clogged airways, or other signs of obstruction or damage.

TREATMENT

Treatment of bronchitis is aimed at removing irritants, clearing the lungs of mucus, and fighting infections. The most important measure is to stop smoking and avoid exposure to air pollution and occupational dusts. Breathing warmed and humidified air helps to loosen mucus, and drinking lots of water helps to thin it. Drinking and inhaling steam from hot liquids, like chicken soup — a favorite home remedy — are beneficial, as are vaporizers and humidifiers. Cough suppressants or drugs that dry the respiratory passages should not be used to treat bronchitis; it is important that the passages remain moist and that mucus is coughed up.

The physician may recommend the use of a bronchodilator, a drug that relaxes constricted airways. This may be combined with steam inhalation. Airways drain more easily when the head is lower than the chest; sometimes lying across a bed with the head hanging over the edge may help drainage.

Persons with chronic bronchitis should maintain good nutrition and good health habits to build resistance to respiratory infection. To help overcome infections, the doctor will prescribe antibiotics. The doctor may also advise the patient to get an influenza vaccine every fall and an inoculation against pneumonia. (A vaccine or inoculation is a preparation containing the microorganism that causes the disease. When the vaccine is introduced into the body, it stimulates the body to produce its own protective substances to fight and prevent the disease.)

CYSTIC FIBROSIS

Cystic fibrosis is an inherited disorder marked by abnormal mucus, sweat, and other secretions of the exocrine glands. These are the glands in the body that secrete their products through ducts and across membranes to keep the linings moist and to get needed chemicals to their destinations. The worst complications of cystic fibrosis occur because of faulty mucous glands, which produce a thick and gummy mucus instead of clear, free-flowing fluid. This thick mucus clogs up ducts in various parts of the body and accumulates in the glands, causing swellings. Often, cysts form; these are abnormal membrane-enclosed sacs that are filled with blocked secretions.

The most serious effects of abnormal mucus secretion and blocked ducts occur in the lungs. There the thick, sticky mucus, instead of helping to clear the lungs of infectious bacteria and viruses, becomes a breeding ground for them. Infections produce more mucus, and the lung's airways, already narrowed by swollen membranes, become obstructed. After recurrent infections, breathing becomes more difficult and the distress becomes chronic, or long-term. The effects on the respiratory system are similar to those in chronic bronchitis and other chronic obstructive pulmonary diseases, but the outcome is swifter and more devastating. Many patients may die while still young of respiratory failure caused by infection.

Another complication of cystic fibrosis results from abnormal secretions in the pancreas. The pancreas is a long, thin organ behind the stomach; it secretes digestive juices through a series of ducts into a main duct that connects with the small intestine. Thickened secretions can block the smaller ducts and prevent the passage into the small intestine from the pancreas of digestive enzymes, vital chemicals that are needed in the small intestine to dissolve food and digest fats. The trapped enzymes may injure the pancreas itself, causing fibrous scar tissue to form.

An additional problem is the loss of salt because of abnormal sweat, which leaves victims of the disease susceptible to heat exhaustion. Reproductive tract secretions are also thick. In fe-

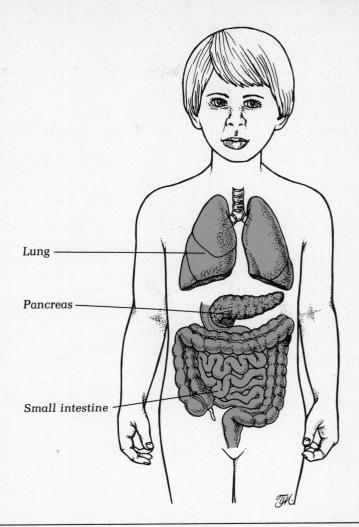

Cystic fibrosis is a hereditary disease in which abnormal secretions affect many parts of the body. Symptoms primarily involve the lungs, the pancreas, and the digestive tract. Thick mucus in the lungs hinders breathing and leads to infections. Thickened secretions can block ducts in the pancreas and prevent pancreatic digestive enzymes from passing into the small intestine.

males, mucus may plug the pathway to the ovum, or egg, and make it more difficult to become pregnant. About 98 percent of males are sterile (unable to reproduce) because of blockage of the duct that conducts sperm. On the other hand, tears seem to be normal, and saliva, although altered in composition, causes no discomfort or medical problems.

Cystic fibrosis is still often described as a disease of childhood because until the 1960s few patients lived beyond the age of ten. But with continuing advances in managing the disorder, it is not unusual today for afflicted persons to live into their 30s and

even beyond. The sooner treatment can begin, the brighter is the outlook. Unfortunately, the symptoms of cystic fibrosis are often the same as those of less serious disorders. Of those persons with the disease today, perhaps 40 to 50 percent go undetected or are misdiagnosed as having upset stomach, allergies, bronchitis, and other common disorders. That is why it is important that diagnosis be as accurate as possible.

Cystic fibrosis is caused by a defective gene. (A gene is a unit of heredity in the cell that determines a body characteristic such as blue eyes or curly hair.) The gene involved in the faulty exocrine gland secretions is recessive, which means that it must be inherited from both parents. If only one parent transmits the gene, their child may be a carrier but will not get the disease. How the gene acts in the body's exocrine gland cells to make the secretions abnormal is still a mystery. The altered composition of the secretions seems to be related to a lack of sufficient water in the fluids. In the case of the sweat glands, some unidentified substance in the sweat gland ducts seems to prevent the salt in the sweat from being reabsorbed into the body tissues.

One person in 20 among the white population is a carrier of the defective gene that causes cystic fibrosis. Among black people and Orientals the incidence is much lower. The United States has about ten million carriers, and about one in every 400 marriages takes place between carriers. A child born of two carriers has one chance in four of getting the disease, one chance in two of being healthy but becoming a carrier of the disease, and only one chance in four of being completely free of the defective gene.

Researchers have been looking for a biological marker, some difference in a cell or in any of the body's chemicals, that would enable them to identify carriers. There is hope now for a new test that measures certain chemicals in the amniotic fluid — the fluid that surrounds an unborn baby. Studies are showing that this test may detect the disease before birth.

SYMPTOMS

The first signs of cystic fibrosis may be apparent at birth or may not show up until adolescence. Some babies, about one in ten, are born with a putty-like plug in their intestinal tract and require surgery, but this condition is not completely exclusive to cystic fibrosis. In typical cases of cystic fibrosis, children eat well but gain weight slowly and show signs of

malnutrition because much of the fat in their food leaves the body unused. (The fat is not used because the pancreatic enzymes necessary to digest fats are prevented from leaving the pancreas.) For this reason, the stools are large, frequent, and foul-smelling, and digestive upsets are common.

Cystic fibrosis patients are typically subject to respiratory distress from repeated infections. In time, a chronic, heavily mucus-laden cough develops, with rapid and labored breathing. The chest often is barrel-shaped from over-inflated lungs. Sinusitis (inflammation of the air-filled cavities in the facial bones) is very common, as are nasal polyps — growths in the nose caused by persistently swollen nasal membranes. Fatigue and muscle cramps from loss of salt are also common symptoms.

The symptoms and severity of cystic fibrosis vary from person to person, some having greater respiratory difficulties and some having more impaired digestion. Evaluation of the symptoms can be confusing. But almost all cystic fibrosis patients seem to have excessively salty sweat, and parents are advised to call it to a doctor's attention if their child's skin persistently tastes salty.

The doctor will perform a physical examination and take a careful medical history of symptoms and ailments. A family history is also taken to see if the disease has appeared in relatives. If cystic fibrosis is suspected, the doctor will perform a sweat test. A drug that increases fluid outflow is applied with a weak electric current to a patch of skin on the forearm. This causes the sweat glands to release their sweat, which is collected on a gauze pad for salt analysis. A salt level considerably higher than average is usually an indicator of cystic fibrosis. But the salt level has nothing at all to do with the *severity* of the disease; a person may have high salt content in the sweat and yet have a very mild case.

The doctor may take a chest X ray to check the lungs for airway obstruction, pockets of infection, and other damage. The stool and a sample of the digestive juices from the small intestine may be analyzed to see how efficiently the pancreatic enzymes are moving through the pancreatic duct.

TREATMENT

Although there is no way to prevent or cure cystic fibrosis, a great deal can be done to relieve symptoms and prolong life. Cystic fibrosis patients with an affected pancreas may take the replacement enzyme tablets pancreatin or pancrelipase before meals to digest food effectively. However, many persons still need to reduce their fat intake. Doctors also have found that patients need very nourishing food with extra vitamins and minerals for reserve energy to carry them through times of infection and illness. In addition, physicians can fight respiratory infections more aggressively with antibiotic drugs, sometimes in aerosol mists, and they may switch antibiotics to prevent bacteria from developing resistance to one type of drug. Vaccination against specific respiratory illnesses and other preventive measures are taken as well. (A vaccine is a preparation containing the microorganism that causes the disease. When the vaccine is introduced into the body, it stimulates the body to produce its own protective substance to fight and prevent the disease.)

Mucus is kept from collecting in the lungs by various means. Physical exercise helps. So does frequent "postural drainage," placing the body in various head-down positions and pushing on the chest with cupped hands to help loosen mucus. Mist tents are also used. Salt loss from sweating poses little threat once the patient is aware of the need to take salt tablets.

Cystic fibrosis centers have been established at many hospitals and medical centers, where a team approach is used. Usually the team includes a physician-specialist, a psychologist, a nutritionist, and a physical therapist. Half of all patients now live 20 to 25 years, and some much longer. While research goes on to find the cause of the disease and to develop new drugs, patients and their families are learning to live well and productively in the face of the disease.

EMPHYSEMA

Emphysema is a chronic progressive disease in which the air sacs (alveoli) of the lungs become overinflated with trapped air. The word *emphysema* itself is the Greek word for "inflated."

When the lungs are frequently exposed to irritants such as cigarette smoke, polluted air, or toxic fumes, the bronchi (air passages) into each lung become inflamed. To combat the inflammation, the linings of the bronchi produce mucus which clogs the airways. As the clogged bronchi narrow, air is trapped in the alveoli, the tiny, cup-shaped air sacs at the end of the smallest bronchial tubes. Eventually, the trapped air breaks down the walls of the alveoli, and they lose their elasticity. As a consequence, the waste carbon dioxide waiting in the alveoli to be expelled cannot be exhaled nor can it be replaced with oxygen.

As the disease progresses, there are fewer functioning air sacs, and the resulting lack of oxygen places a heavy burden on the heart. The oxygen starvation may lead to heart strain, high blood pressure in the lungs, and, ultimately, to heart failure.

The exact cause of emphysema has not been determined. However, research has indicated that most cases are linked to cigarette smoking. On the other hand, while external factors such as cigarette smoke and air pollution are generally held to be major contributors to the development of emphysema, in a few cases

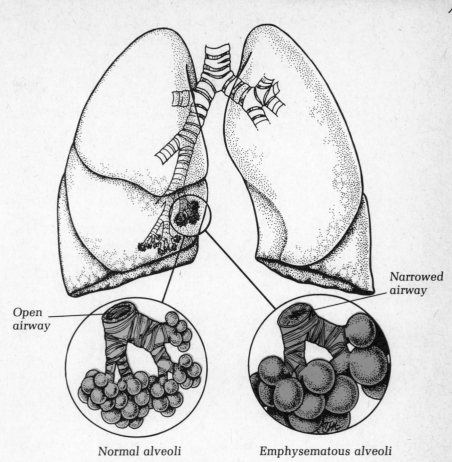

Narrowed
airway

Open
airway

Normal alveoli   *Emphysematous alveoli*

Emphysema is a chronic disease in which the air sacs, or alveoli, of the lungs become overinflated with trapped air. When the lungs are frequently exposed to irritants, the bronchial linings secrete mucus which narrows and clogs the airways to the alveoli. Air becomes trapped in the alveoli, and eventually they lose their elasticity and become overinflated.

---

there may be a genetic component —something that is inherited. Research has shown that these few persons have an inherited deficiency or lack of a blood protein that may lead to loss of elasticity in lung tissue.

Emphysema is not caused by bacteria or viruses, and it is not contagious (catching). However, it is often preceded by chronic bronchitis — inflammation of the bronchial passages — which may be caused by a bacterial or viral infection. Both emphysema and bronchitis are categorized as chronic obstructive pulmonary (lung) diseases (COPD). Often more than one of these diseases occur in the same person at the same time. In addition, while tuberculosis occurs much less fre-

quently than it did two or three decades ago, this disease, too, may cause lung damage that may lead to emphysema.

Age and sex are also factors in the disease. Emphysema primarily affects white men over the age of 50. However, more and more women over age 50 are now at risk because of the increase in the number of women who smoke.

In addition to these risk factors, a number of work environments may contribute to the development of the disease. This is particularly true in such occupations as mining or chemical manufacturing in which unprotected workers may inhale dust or irritating fumes on a continual basis. Smoking, of course, compounds the risk for such persons.

SYMPTOMS

Shortness of breath is usually the primary symptom. At first, the patient may experience only slight breathlessness. This may be combined with steady, persistent, racking coughs that either bring up large amounts of mucus or are painfully dry.

As the disease progresses, the patient begins to struggle for every breath and has trouble performing even simple tasks because of difficulty in breathing. The body must work harder to get an adequate supply of fresh air; so instead of the normal 15 breaths a minute, the emphysema patient may breathe twice as often and still not get enough air. The person with advanced emphysema may spend up to 80 percent of his or her energy breathing instead of the 5 percent normally required. Some people develop a "barrel chest"—a rounded chest caused by both overdistension of the lungs by trapped air and enlargement of certain muscles of the chest wall used in normal breathing.

In addition, the emphysema sufferer may also develop a blue tinge on the lips, ear lobes, skin, and fingernail beds because of the lack of oxygen to these parts of the body. The fingertips may become "clubbed" or thickened. With the beginning of heart failure, the ankles usually swell.

No single test has been developed to diagnose emphysema. However, your doctor may use several procedures to aid the diagnosis. Breathing tests to measure volume of air inhaled and exhaled and the speed with which the lungs are emptied may indicate that emphysema is present. However, the breathing function test will not reveal very early emphysema. A blood test may also be taken. The emphysema patient's red blood cell count may increase to compensate for the reduced oxygen. The red blood cells carry oxygen throughout the body, and a greater number of red blood cells means that more oxygen can be delivered.

Chest X rays will not help diagnose early emphysema, but the doctor may use an X ray to confirm the presence of other lung conditions that may lead to emphysema. Chest X rays, however, will reveal certain lung changes associated with the later stages of emphysema.

TREATMENT

Although there is no cure for emphysema at present, the progress of the disease can be slowed. Furthermore, people with emphysema can be helped to lead more comfortable and productive lives.

Physicians can prescribe drugs that loosen mucus secretions so that they may be coughed up, as well as drugs that relax and expand the air passages to ease breathing. Medications to eliminate or to prevent lung infections are also used. However, emphysema patients are usually advised to avoid medications with sedatives that can slow down an already laboring system and perhaps result in respiratory failure.

Drinking extra fluids can help thin out the secretions blocking the air passages. Vaporizers and humidifiers are used to ease breathing. Home air conditioners to filter dust and other particles from the air may be beneficial. Adequate rest and a balanced diet, along with exercise, also are essential. In fact, moderate regular exercise is often recommended. To ease breathlessness during exercise or any activity, a patient may work with a physical therapist to learn to use chest and abdominal muscles in such a way as to increase breathing capability. Occasionally, when the disease is advanced, oxygen may be administered under the supervision of a physician.

PLEURISY

Pleurisy is a general term for any inflammation of the pleura, the membrane that covers the outside of the lungs and lines the chest cavity. The more common simple inflammation of the pleura is called dry pleurisy. When the inflamed pleura also has fluid oozing from it, the condition is called wet pleurisy. The fluid produced in wet pleurisy often compresses the lungs.

Pleurisy may be a complication of other diseases such as an upper respiratory tract infection, pneumonia, tuberculosis, or a tumor.

Dry pleurisy can be caused by any type of infection of the lungs; however, it most often follows viral or bacterial pneumonia. It may also accompany simple, acute bronchitis, or be a complication of tuberculosis or a tumor.

Wet pleurisy can also be caused by infection, tuberculosis, or tumor, as well as by injury or liver disease. Certain liver diseases may inflame the diaphragm (the muscle dividing the chest and abdominal cavities) and thus inflame that part of the pleura that covers the diaphragm.

There is no way to determine when or why a lung infection will lead to pleurisy. Generally, people who are susceptible to upper respiratory infections and pneumonia are more likely to develop pleurisy.

SYMPTOMS

The primary symptom of dry pleurisy is a sharp, stabbing pain that is aggravated by breathing, coughing, or any other work of the chest muscles. The pain is usually located toward the side and lower front of the chest, although it may also be felt around the shoulders and neck and as low as the abdomen. The discomfort interferes with breathing and may make the patient feel short of breath. A fever and an irritating dry cough may also develop.

Wet pleurisy generally has the same symptoms, along with chills and increased difficulty in breathing because of the fluid pressing on the lungs. The patient's coughing will bring up phlegm, or mucus discharge, which may be tinged with blood.

PNEUMONIA

Pneumonia is an inflammation of the air sacs in the lungs where blood exchanges the waste product carbon dioxide for oxygen. When pneumonia is present, the air sacs become filled with fluid and white blood cells trying to fight the infection.

Pneumonia is sometimes classified by its location in the lung. Thus, pneumonia that affects just one section, or lobe, of one lung is referred to as lobar pneumonia. When the disease strikes a lobe or lobes in both lungs, it is referred to as double pneumonia. When it affects the part of the lung adjacent to the bronchi (the passageways into the lung from the windpipe) as a complication of acute bronchitis, it is referred to as bronchial pneumonia. "Walking pneumonia" is a nonmedical term that refers to someone who has pneumonia without knowing it and who has not sought treatment or stayed in bed.

Although pneumonia is very common and fairly easily treated, it still causes many deaths. Perhaps this is because it most frequently occurs in those who are least able to resist it — the very young, the very old, and the chronically ill.

Pneumonia can be caused by viruses, bacteria, fungi, other microorganisms, or by inhaling certain chemicals. If food, vomit, or some foreign object goes down the trachea (windpipe) instead of the esophagus (passageway from the mouth to the stomach) and settles in the lung, this too can cause pneumonia. However, everyone who is exposed to pneumonia-causing organisms or who swallows something the wrong way will not develop the disease. Pneumonia most frequently develops in a person with lowered resistance. Thus, pneumonia is often preceded by some other upper respiratory tract infection or systemic disease.

Pneumonia is more likely to strike those persons whose respiratory defense mechanisms are not working adequately. Upper

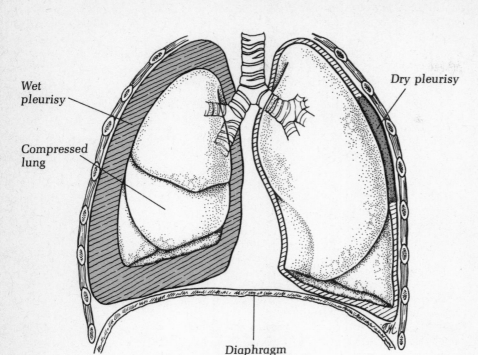

Wet pleurisy

Compressed lung

Dry pleurisy

Diaphragm

Pleurisy is an inflammation of the pleura, the membrane that covers the outside of the lungs and lines the chest cavity. A simple inflammation of the pleura is called dry pleurisy. If the inflamed pleura produces fluid, the condition is called wet pleurisy. The fluid produced in wet pleurisy may compress the lungs.

Pleurisy is diagnosed through physical examination and observation of symptoms. The doctor will listen to your chest through a stethoscope. Pleurisy is characterized by a low-pitched, grating sound during breathing. The doctor will also look for signs of tenderness when the affected area is pressed.

Diagnosis of wet pleurisy may require an analysis of the fluid that is oozing from the pleura. A tuberculin skin test may be performed to rule out the possibility of tuberculosis. If the pleurisy is not obviously caused by an upper respiratory tract infection or by pneumonia, X rays will be taken to determine if there is some other underlying cause.

TREATMENT

Treatment is aimed at the underlying disease causing the pleurisy. Antibiotics are often prescribed to eliminate the primary infection. Once the initial disease is under control, the pleurisy begins to clear up.

Treating pleurisy itself usually means relieving the symptoms until the pleurisy has run its course. Bed rest is usually recommended. Painkillers may be prescribed not only to relieve the pain while breathing but also to permit coughing (which the patient may try to stifle if the pain is too great). A humidifier or vaporizer may also make breathing easier by adding moisture to the air. Although strapping the chest with a tight elastic bandage will relieve some of the pain of breathing, it is not always recommended since this treatment may cause respiratory secretions to collect by preventing deep breathing and coughing.

In the case of wet pleurisy, the excess fluid in the chest cavity may be drained if the breathing is severely affected.

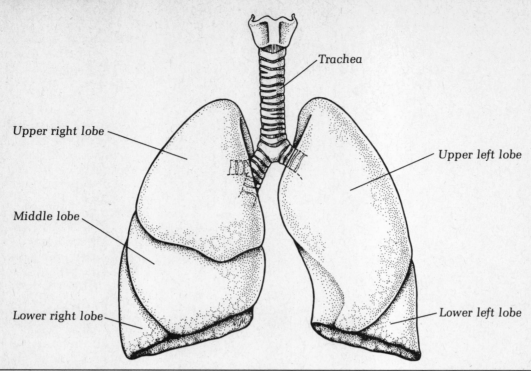

Trachea

Upper right lobe

Upper left lobe

Middle lobe

Lower right lobe

Lower left lobe

There are five lobes, or sections, in the lungs. Pneumonia that affects just one lobe is called lobar pneumonia. If the disease strikes a lobe or lobes in both lungs, it is referred to as double pneumonia.

respiratory tract infections such as cold and flu, as well as smoking, excessive drinking, prolonged bed rest, anesthesia, sedatives, and immune-suppressing drugs can all increase the body's susceptibility to pneumonia. Additionally, chronic or long-term health problems like chronic bronchitis, emphysema, asthma, diabetes, cancer, and sickle-cell anemia can make a person susceptible to pneumonia. Infants and the elderly are at a higher risk for developing and dying from this disease.

Pneumonia is most common during the winter months when people are indoors and germs can be easily spread; however, the disease can strike at any time. It is extremely common during flu epidemics, since pneumonia can occur as a secondary infection as the body struggles to rid itself of the primary infection.

SYMPTOMS

Viral pneumonia is more common and generally less severe than the other varieties. It is marked by coughing and other cold symptoms and a general feeling of fatigue. Fever, chest pain, and difficulty in breathing may also be present.

Bacterial pneumonia, on the other hand, has a sudden and dramatic onset characterized by shaking chills and a rapid and steep rise in temperature. Coughing will often bring up bloody, dark yellow, or rust-colored sputum (or discharge) from the lungs, and breathing will be rapid and shallow. Signs of oxygen shortage in bacterial pneumonia include hot, dry skin, headache, nausea, and vomiting.

Generally, the four signs of all types of pneumonia are sudden rise in fever, chest pain, coughing, and difficulty in breathing.

Pneumonia is diagnosed by observation of symptoms and physical examination. Your doctor will be able to detect the presence of fluid in the lungs by listening to your chest through a stethoscope as you breathe and by tapping your chest and back. To determine the precise nature and extent of the disease, chest X rays may be taken and an analysis of sputum performed.

TREATMENT

Treatment of pneumonia depends upon what has caused the disease. For viral pneumonia, bed rest, ingestion of fluids, a light diet, pain relievers, and oxygen may be prescribed. The body normally can fight off this viral infection, except in cases where the patient is already weakened by another disease or by age.

Bacterial pneumonia and most other forms of the disease are treated with antibiotics. Penicillin is most commonly prescribed, but the analysis of sputum may reveal the presence of a bacterium that responds better to some other type of antibiotic. Bed rest is always necessary, and some severe cases may even require hospitalization. Oxygen may be administered if difficulty in breathing becomes serious.

A vaccine that is effective against most forms of bacterial pneumonia is available and is recommended for the elderly and for persons with chronic illnesses. The likelihood of contracting viral pneumonia can be lessened in persons who are considered highly susceptible by a vaccination against influenza A, one of the viruses commonly responsible for viral pneumonia. (A vaccine is a preparation containing the microorganism that causes the disease. When the vaccine is introduced into the body, it stimulates the body to produce its own protective substances to fight and prevent the disease.)

TUBERCULOSIS

Tuberculosis is a bacterial infection that commonly strikes the lungs, although it can travel through the blood and lymph systems and cause disease in other parts of the body such as the spine, kidneys, digestive tract, and lining of the heart. The infection causes the formation of small nodules or masses called tubercles at the site of infection. These tubercles break down healthy tissue and form pus. The disease may be complicated by a streptococcal (another kind of bacteria) infection.

The tuberculosis bacteria can often infect a person and lie inactive for many years until some other disease weakens the body's defenses and causes active symptoms of tuberculosis to emerge. Only one in ten infected persons becomes sick within three months of the bacterial invasion. Another 10 percent of infected persons will become sick from the disease at some point in their lives. Thus, the majority of people who harbor the tuberculosis bacteria in their body never contracts an active case of the disease. In these instances, the body acts to wall off the bacteria within cysts (closed sacs) to prevent the bacteria from spreading. However, the body cannot kill these bacteria.

Tuberculosis is caused by the organism *Mycobacterium tuberculosis*. It is spread when healthy persons breathe in fine bacteria-containing droplets coughed or sneezed into the air by infected persons.

For this reason, tuberculosis is far more contagious (or catching) in crowded living conditions. Persons in close proximity to an actively infected, untreated person are much more susceptible to becoming infected themselves. Persons who are undernourished or who are generally in poor health are more likely to develop an active case of the disease after becoming infected. Young children, the elderly, the urban poor, and people in the medical profession are at the highest risk for contracting TB.

SYMPTOMS

Symptoms usually do not appear until the later stages of the disease. The first signs of tuberculosis often include fever (particularly in the afternoon), fatigue, loss of appetite, and weight loss. These symptoms may develop long before the appearance of the characteristic coughing, blood-tinged sputum (coughed-up discharge), shortness of breath, and chest pain.

Tuberculosis mimics the symptoms of many other diseases, and persons with respiratory problems are often treated unsuccessfully for other conditions before the testing for tuberculosis (since the incidence of tuberculosis has been steadily declining). The tuberculin skin test, in which tiny amounts of dead tuberculosis bacteria are introduced under the skin, is used to reveal whether a person has been infected with the TB bacteria. A reaction (usually a swelling at the test site) to the painless scratch test indicates the presence of the tuberculosis bacteria, regardless of whether the disease is active or inactive. Everyone who has been in close contact with a patient with active TB should be tested for the disease.

In more advanced cases of active TB, chest X rays are taken to determine the presence of the cysts on the lungs, while a sputum analysis may show the presence of the bacteria.

TREATMENT

If tuberculosis is diagnosed early enough and the patient follows the prescribed drug program carefully, the disease is now rarely fatal. The most common reason for a patient's continuing infection with tuberculosis, as well as for the disease's spread, is the patient's failure to take the medication for the entire course of treatment.

Tuberculosis is treated with a variety of antibacterial drugs simultaneously to prevent the bacteria from becoming resistant to one particular medication. The drugs must be taken for anywhere from nine to 18 months. After the first two weeks of treatment, the patient is no longer considered contagious and may return to normal activities. Although the discovery of effective anti-tuberculosis drugs has eliminated the disease as a major cause of death, the drugs themselves can have serious side effects, especially liver or hearing damage. Therefore, persons taking these medications should be examined periodically for any signs of side effects.

In some high risk cases, persons who have a positive skin test but who are not actively ill will be given anti-tuberculosis drugs as a preventive measure. High risk cases include persons under 35, especially children, and those with other chronic diseases that would make them more susceptible to tuberculosis. Liver damage from the drugs is more likely in persons over 35, so these drugs are not routinely prescribed to this age group as a preventive measure.

HEART AND CIRCULATORY CONDITIONS

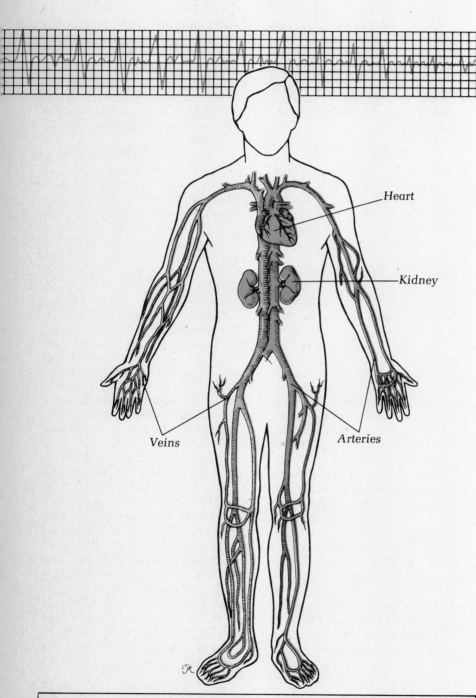

This illustration of the circulatory system shows the heart, the kidneys, and the major arteries (right side of the body) and major veins (left side of the body).

The circulatory system, including the heart, the blood vessels, and the blood nourishes every part of the body. Blood is the mixture of fluid and cells that carries nourishment to the body's tissues.

Blood. Blood consists of formed elements (red blood cells, white blood cells, and platelets) and plasma (a straw-colored solution of protein and water that makes up more than half the volume of blood). The formed elements are produced in the bone marrow, the soft tissue in the center of bones.

In a teaspoon of blood, there are about 27 million red blood cells. They carry oxygen from the lungs to the body's tissues. (Carbon dioxide, the waste product of the cells, is transported from the cells back to the lungs where it can be dispersed by the lungs into the outside air.) The oxygen is carried by hemoglobin, an iron-containing substance in the red blood cells. Any reduction in hemoglobin or in the total number of red blood cells below a certain limit is termed anemia.

White blood cells are scavengers and defenders. Whenever the body has a wound or damaged tissue or is fighting off an infection, white blood cells invade the affected area and destroy bacteria or any debris and help the damaged area heal. White blood cells also produce antibodies, protective substances that destroy or neutralize undesirable invaders of the body. A symptom of many diseases is a change in the number of white blood cells. The normal quantity of white blood cells ranges from 25,000 to 50,000 per teaspoon of blood. This number may rise greatly in persons with leukemia, while it may drop in some viral diseases.

The platelets are small, colorless bodies whose job is to help blood clot. There are 750,000 to 1,750,000 per teaspoon of blood.

Heart. The heart is a large, hollow, muscular organ containing four chambers. The movement of blood among the chambers is controlled by valves between these compartments. The heart lies between the lungs and directly behind the sternum or breastbone. An average adult heart is about the size of a clenched fish and beats 60 to 90 times a minute.

The upper right chamber, called the right atrium, receives blood from the veins of the body. From the right atrium, the blood flows into the right lower chamber, called the right ventricle. The right ventricle pumps the blood to the lungs to exchange carbon dioxide for oxygen. This newly refreshed blood then returns to the left atrium, or upper left chamber of the heart, which pumps it into the left ventricle, or lower left chamber. The left ventricle has the responsiblity for pumping blood through the aorta, the great trunk artery that carries blood to the rest of the body.

Blood vessels. Blood vessels are classified according to their size, function, and physical makeup. Thus, there are large or elastic arteries, medium-sized or muscular arteries, small arteries or arterioles, capillaries, small veins or venules, and veins. Arteries receive the blood from the heart and circulate it to body tissues. Arteries subdivide into smaller vessels, and ultimately into numerous tiny vessels called capillaries. It is through the capillary walls that nutrients pass to the tissues and waste products from the tissues and cells enter the blood. The venules and veins then carry this "used" blood back to the heart to

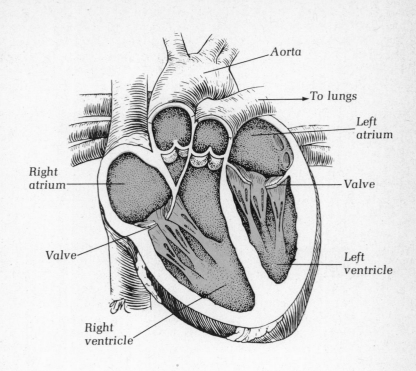

The heart is a large, hollow muscular organ that acts as a pump to maintain the circulation of blood. The heart is divided into four chambers, and the movement of blood among the chambers is controlled by valves between the chambers.

be recycled through the lungs for rejuvenation and subsequent recirculation through the body. Only in the pulmonary system (which carries used blood from the heart to the lungs and then back to the heart) does a vein carry oxygenated blood and an artery carry deoxygenated blood.

This entire system of circulation transports body fluids from one region of the body to another. These fluids not only carry nutrients to and remove waste products from the body cells, but they also help maintain the fluid balance of the body. In addition, the bloodstream carries hormones — chemical messengers, produced by glands, that have specific effects on the function of body cells far away from the hormone's point of origin. Thus, the circulatory system is a complex network — reaching into every cell of the body—that is absolutely essential to the normal working of the body.

ANEMIA

Anemia is a reduction in the number of red blood cells or in their hemoglobin content below a certain limit. Hemoglobin is the pigment (coloring material) in blood responsible for the transport of oxygen, so a deficiency ultimately leads to an inability to circulate enough oxygen in the blood to meet the body's demands. There are many different types of anemia, all with different causes. In general, however, anemia is caused by excessive loss or destruction of red blood cells or inadequate production of red blood cells.

Although most people may suffer from a mild form of anemia at some point in their lives, severe anemia can cause unusual weakness and may even be fatal.

Women are at a greater risk for iron deficiency anemia because of blood loss through menstruation and the increased demand for iron brought on by pregnancy. Anyone with a poor diet and a history of alcoholism is more susceptible to the anemias caused by vitamin deficiencies.

Heredity is the largest risk factor in developing sickle-cell anemia, since one in every 11 blacks is a carrier of the disease. Carriers experience no symptoms themselves, but if both parents are carriers there is a very high risk that their children will actually have the disease. Testing for the trait and genetic counseling are generally advised.

SYMPTOMS

The symptoms of anemia vary with the seriousness of the disease. For example, a mild case may result in nothing more noticeable than a general lack of pep, while a very severe case may be marked by swollen ankles and other signs of heart failure, extreme abdominal pain, and shock. Generally, however, the signs of anemia are paleness in the palms, fingernails, and inner eyelid; fatigue; shortness of breath; a sense of the heart pounding and increased heart rate; headaches; loss of appetite; dizziness; ringing in the ears; and faintness.

Diagnosis for all forms of anemia is made through a laboratory testing of the blood and, at times, the bone marrow, in conjunction with a physical exam.

TREATMENT

Each type of anemia has its own specific treatment based on its specific cause.

Iron deficiency anemia, one of the most common types, is caused by a shortage of the mineral iron which is necessary to produce hemoglobin. This can result from a drastic blood loss, as from an accident, or a chronic blood loss, as from a bleeding ulcer or excessive menstrual flow. Chronic diarrhea and hookworm decrease the body's ability to absorb iron, while pregnancy may divert a woman's iron supply to the unborn baby. A diet lacking enough

dark green vegetables and organ meats — both of which are good sources of iron — will result in an insufficient supply of iron. This form of anemia can be treated by simply taking iron supplements in the form of ferrous sulfate or ferrous gluconate tablets.

Folic acid deficiency anemia is linked to an insufficient dietary supply of this nutrient which is also necessary to produce hemoglobin. Since Vitamin C is required for the body to use folic acid, malnourishment and alcoholism contribute to this disease by depleting Vitamin C reserves. It is treated with the administration of folic acid and other vitamin supplements.

Pernicious anemia results from the body's inability to absorb Vitamin B12, a necessary component of red cell production in the bone marrow. Persons suffering from pernicious anemia lack a substance found in the stomach called intrinsic factor which helps in absorption of Vitamin B12. This type of anemia is treated with injections of Vitamin B12 which are taken directly into the bloodstream, thus bypassing the stomach altogether.

Hemolytic anemias, caused by the destruction of red blood cells, can be either congenital (present from birth) or acquired. The acquired type may stem from mismatched blood transfusions, a drug allergy, or the presence of a widespread cancer or severe infection. The source must be located and treated, although blood transfusions may help the problem temporarily.

Congenital forms of hemolytic anemia, such as sickle-cell anemia, result from an inherited abnormality in the red blood cells. Sickle-cell anemia, which affects primarily blacks, is the most prevalent form of congenital hemolytic anemia. In this disease the red blood cells are sickle-shaped rather than round and are unable to transport sufficient oxygen. Sickle-cell anemia is marked by periods of crisis in which the patient experiences severe joint and abdominal pain. Its complica-

tions, such as kidney disease, gallstones, and enlarged heart, can be fatal. Although research is being done on this disease there is no cure, and treatment is aimed mainly at alleviating symptoms by administering painkillers and monitoring the acid-base balance of the body to help reduce the likelihood of crises.

Aplastic anemia is caused by an impairment in the ability of the bone marrow to manufacture blood cells, thus affecting the production of platelets (the type of blood cell that helps coagulate or clot the blood) and white blood cells as well as red blood cells. The marrow can be invaded by cancer or a tumor, or it can be destroyed by exposure to radioactivity or certain chemicals. This disease is treated with blood transfusions and bone marrow transplants.

ANGINA PECTORIS

Angina pectoris, usually referred to simply as angina, means literally "pain in the chest." It is a warning signal short of an actual heart attack that the heart is not receiving enough oxygen-rich blood. When angina occurs, it is a sign that the heart is working ahead of its supply of nourishment and that the body must slow down to allow the heart to catch up.

You may experience angina for years and never have a heart attack or, on the other hand, you may suffer a heart attack without ever feeling the symptoms of angina. However, angina patients are considered to be at a greater risk for heart attack than the general population, even though angina does not lead directly and inevitably to a breakdown of the heart muscle.

Anything that prevents the heart from getting enough blood from the circulatory system to satisfy its need for oxygen can cause angina. Thus, activities as simple as running for the bus or climbing stairs increase the heart's demand for oxygen and can bring on an attack of angina. Stress, cold weather, and smoking also contribute to angina. (Smoking narrows the arteries, thus slowing the flow of blood.) If arteries are already obstructed by the cholesterol and calcium deposits characteristic of atherosclerosis, or by a blood clot, the supply of blood to the heart is further reduced. Overeating can also cause angina, since a full stomach draws blood away from the heart to be used instead in the digestive process.

High blood cholesterol levels increase the risk of atherosclerosis, and thereby the risk of angina. Anything that constantly puts extra demands on the heart such as obesity, smoking, or high blood pressure also increases the chance of developing angina.

SYMPTOMS

Pain which comes on after physical exertion or emotional stress is the foremost symptom of angina. The pain lasts only three to five minutes and usually is relieved by resting and relaxing. If the pain does not go away in a few minutes, it is most likely not angina, but instead a symptom of some problem entirely unrelated to the heart. On the other hand, it may, in fact, be a heart attack. Although the sensation of angina is very similar to that felt during a heart attack, angina is neither as severe nor as long-lasting as a heart attack. Angina indicates only that the heart is overworked, and unlike a heart attack, causes no physical damage to the muscle tissue of the heart.

The pain of angina is not sharp and stabbing; rather, it is described as a dull discomfort and a feeling of pressure, squeezing, or burning in the center of the chest behind the breastbone. Many angina patients liken it to acute indigestion or a sensation of fullness. Although it is most often felt in the chest, angina can also produce pain in the neck and abdomen, and a numbness may radiate along the arm to the wrist and lit-

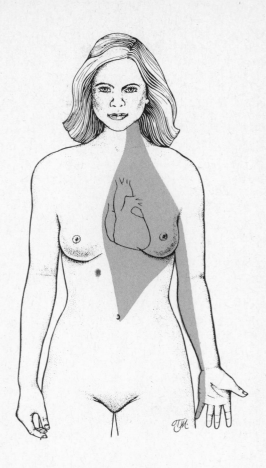

Angina pain is most often felt in the chest, but it can also be felt in the neck and the abdomen, and a numbness may radiate down the arm to the wrist and little finger.

tle finger. The pattern of pain may vary widely among different people, but generally remains consistent with each episode experienced by the same person. The severity of the pain also varies among different people — it may be serious enough to seem life-threatening or so mild as to go unnoticed and untreated for years.

The first step in diagnosing angina is to rule out all other possible causes for the pain, such as pleurisy (an inflammation of the covering of the lung), gall bladder disease, rib injury, or muscle strain — all of which produce symptoms that may be confused with angina. Therefore, your doctor will take a complete medical history, ask you to describe your pain very specifically,

and will perform a thorough physical exam.

To make the most accurate diagnosis, you may be asked to perform an exercise or stress test, using an electrocardiograph (EKG) which records electrical impulses generated by the heart. The EKG monitors are placed on the body while you are exercising on a treadmill or stationary bicycle, and the machine makes a visual record of your heart activity. Changes on the EKG reading imply that abnormalities may exist in the arteries that are preventing sections of the heart from receiving enough oxygen. The test also indicates the level of activity at which angina pain may begin.

In certain cases, radioactive isotopes or X-ray opaque fluid are injected into the bloodstream so that special devices may be used to monitor the flow of blood through the heart. If there are spots in the heart that these substances do not reach, the coronary arteries are generally considered to be abnormal.

TREATMENT

Angina is treated by a combination of reducing strain on the heart and improving its supply of blood. A change in lifestyle is required for the first; medication is needed for the second.

Angina patients who are overweight will be asked to reduce, and those who smoke will be advised to quit. Although overexertion may bring on a bout of angina, exercise should not be avoided since it improves collateral circulation — the natural development of a system of smaller blood vessels that feeds the heart directly by detouring arterial obstructions. However, since certain types of exercise — weight lifting, for instance — can be quite damaging, a doctor should devise and supervise any exercise program.

Nitroglycerin, which works by dilating or expanding the blood vessels to increase blood flow, is still the most effective medication to relieve angina. When a tablet is dissolved under the tongue — not swallowed — pain should cease within three to four minutes; if it does not, the pain may not be angina. Nitroglycerin can be taken as often as angina occurs since it is not toxic or habit-forming, although it may cause headaches when first taken.

Nitrates and calcium antagonists, types of drugs which work in a manner similar to that of nitroglycerin, are also prescribed for angina. Their effect is less dramatic immediately but more long-lasting, so they may be taken on a regular basis to prevent attacks of angina. A newer family of drugs called beta blockers, which work by decreasing the heart muscles' demand for blood, are even more effective in preventing

angina. However, these drugs should be used with great caution by persons with asthma, since they may cause spasms in the bronchi and consequently difficulty in breathing.

Surgery to bypass the major arterial narrowings or obstructions is only recommended for those patients whose angina cannot be controlled by medication or for those with progressively more severe pain, which may indicate an impending heart attack.

ATHEROSCLEROSIS

Atherosclerosis occurs when the normally smooth, firm linings of the arteries become thickened and roughened by deposits of fat, fibrin (a clotting material), calcium, and cellular debris. Atherosclerosis is a slow, progressive

disease that begins when small nodules of fatty deposits (cholesterol) project out from an artery wall. Then fibrous scar tissue grows under the fatty mass, followed by calcium deposits that develop into a hard, chalky plaque or film that cannot be removed. This buildup lessens the artery's ability to expand and contract and slows the blood's movement through the narrowed channels. These conditions make it easier for clots to form, blocking the artery and stopping blood flow completely.

If an artery leading to the heart is blocked in this manner, a heart attack is the immediate result. If an artery is only partially blocked, angina (chest pain) may result because the heart is unable to receive enough oxygen-rich blood. A blocked artery leading to the brain causes stroke, while similar

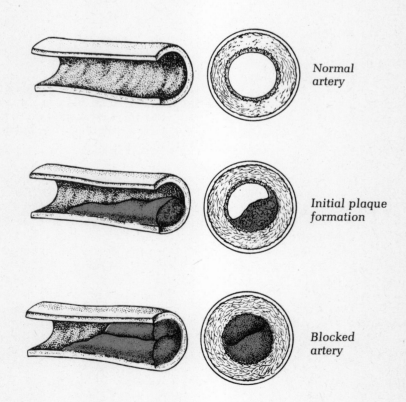

Normal artery

Initial plaque formation

Blocked artery

Atherosclerosis is a progressive disease that occurs when the normally smooth walls of an artery become thickened by deposits of fat, calcium, and fibrous material. These deposits grow into a hardened film called plaque, and eventually this buildup may block the artery.

obstructions in the arteries supplying the kidneys can cause kidney disease. Atherosclerosis can also contribute to blindness and diseases of the extremities by reducing blood flow to these areas.

Fats (called lipids) necessary for the production of certain hormones and tissues are constantly circulating in the blood. However, when the level of these fats is elevated, fatty streaks form along the walls of the arteries. While these streaks are not dangerous in themselves, they can lead to the formation of nodules and other buildup. Exactly what triggers this process is unclear; however, a diet high in saturated fats combined with an inability to absorb them correctly are probably contributing factors. (Saturated fats are usually solid at room temperature and include all forms of animal fat like butter and meat.)

Men are at a greater risk for developing atherosclerosis than women because estrogen, the female sex hormone produced by the ovaries, seems to provide some natural protection from this disease. However, women whose ovaries have been removed, or those who have already passed through menopause when the ovaries cease functioning, lose this protection. Hypertension (high blood pressure) contributes to atherosclerosis because it speeds up the artery-hardening process by subjecting the arteries to constant strain. In addition, smoking increases the risk of atherosclerosis by constricting the arteries and reducing blood flow.

SYMPTOMS

Atherosclerosis in itself produces no symptoms; in fact, it may be present in some degree from a very early age and go unnoticed until it becomes so severe that it begins to affect the function of a major organ. Once this happens, the symptoms of strain or damage to that organ will be felt. For example, if atherosclerosis strikes the arteries nourishing the heart, chest pain will occur; if it affects a cerebral (head) artery,

dizziness, blurry vision, and faintness may be felt.

Several procedures are used to determine the presence of atherosclerosis and to assess the extent of damage to the arteries. An exercise tolerance or stress test uses the electrocardiograph (EKG), which produces a visual record of the electrical impulses generated by the heart. EKG monitors are attached to the body while the patient exercises on a treadmill or a stationary bicycle. A normal heart will emit steady electrical impulses to produce a regular pattern on the graph; dead heart tissue or blocked arteries will cause the impulses to vary as they bypass the damaged area, producing an irregular EKG pattern.

Ultrasound is a newer diagnostic method that is helpful in detecting blockage of arteries caused by atherosclerosis. It may also be used to detect abnormalities of the heart chambers and valves. Movement of blood can be recorded as it moves through the heart.

Radioactive isotopes or X-ray opaque fluid may also be injected into the bloodstream. Their progress through the heart will be tracked by special devices, allowing doctors to visualize any obstructions or areas receiving insufficient blood supply.

TREATMENT

Since the deposits that cause the narrowing and thickening of the arteries cannot be removed or dissolved, treatment of this disease centers on reducing strain on the heart and trying to prevent the worsening of the condition. Different types of medications may be prescribed, depending on the complications present in each particular case; however, certain lifestyle changes will almost always be recommended for all patients suffering from atherosclerosis.

You will be asked to stop smoking and reduce the amount of cholesterol in your diet, as well as to lose weight, since obesity in itself increases the demands

placed on the heart. Exercise is also important because it helps develop the collateral circulation, a system of smaller blood vessels which can bypass a partially blocked artery and increase the supply of blood to the area that the damaged artery serves. However, an exercise program under a doctor's supervision should be followed slowly and carefully so that the heart is not unduly burdened.

If atherosclerosis has led to angina (chest pain) the drugs nitroglycerin, nitrates, or calcium antagonists, all of which expand the arteries and increase blood flow, may be prescribed. Anticoagulants, which thin the blood and protect against clotting, may also be helpful in the treatment of atherosclerosis. If hypertension is a contributing factor, drugs which reduce the demands of the heart, such as the beta blockers, or which lower the resistance in the blood vessels, such as diuretics, may be recommended. (Beta blockers should be used with care in those persons with asthma, since these drugs may cause spasms in the bronchi — tubes leading into the lungs—and consequently difficulty in breathing.)

If the artery is almost completely blocked by atherosclerosis and drug therapy has not been effective, surgery to bypass the major obstructions may be the only recourse. The coronary artery bypass graft uses a vein taken from the leg to create a detour around the blockage in the coronary artery. Partial replacement with artificial arteries is also possible.

HEART ATTACK

A heart attack, or myocardial infarction, is the damage to or death of an area of the heart muscle resulting from a reduction in the blood and oxygen supply to that area. The portion of the heart muscle that dies is replaced by scar tissue which affects the future performance of the heart. The disorder occurs when a coronary artery is blocked.

Although the chances of surviving a heart attack are better today than ever before, heart attack or some other form of circulatory disease is still the number one killer. More deaths could be prevented if people who suspect they may be having a heart attack sought medical attention sooner. Studies have shown that most heart attack victims wait three hours before receiving a doctor's attention.

Nonfatal heart attacks may result in shock; cardiac arrhythmia, in which the heart beats irregularly; and congestive heart failure, in which the heart is unable to pump out enough blood to meet the circulation demands of the body's other tissues resulting in accumulation of fluid in the lower parts of the body. Although complete recovery from a heart attack is very common, all persons who have experienced one have to change their living habits to avoid aggravating their condition.

Heart attack is caused by the complete blockage of a coronary artery by a blood clot (thrombus) or by advanced atherosclerosis, a disease which thickens and roughens the artery walls with deposits of fat, fibrin (a clotting material), cellular debris, and calcium. As the deposits continue to build, they narrow the artery until finally they shut off the flow of blood altogether. Narrow but unclogged coronary arteries may not be able to deliver the extra oxygen required when the heart is strained by physical or emotional stress.

Many physical and environmental factors can increase the likelihood of suffering a heart attack. Hypertension (high blood pressure) increases the heart's work by raising the resistance in the blood vessels against which the heart must pump. High levels of serum cholesterol in the blood increase the chances of atherosclerosis and thus of heart attack. Birth control pills, especially when taken by women over the age of 35 or by women who smoke, have been associated with an increased incidence of heart

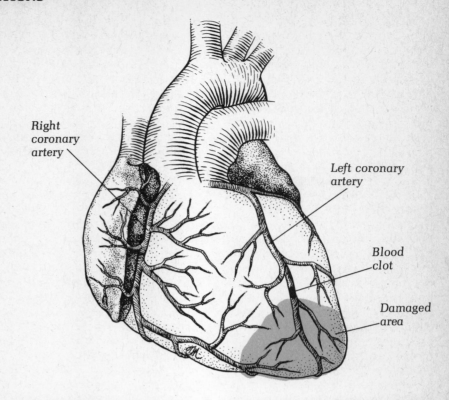

attacks. All these risk factors should be closely monitored by a physician.

Some risk factors, however, cannot be changed. These include heredity, age, sex, and race. A tendency toward circulatory disease can be inherited. Persons whose close relatives have suffered a heart attack, especially at an early age, should be on guard against the development of the disease in themselves. Young women are at the lowest risk for heart attack; after menopause the risk increases for women but never catches up to that of men. Blacks are generally at a higher risk for heart attack than whites because they are twice as likely to have high blood pressure, for reasons that remain unclear.

Many risk factors that are caused by the environment or your lifestyle can be changed. Cigarette smoking, stress, improper diet, and lack of exercise all may contribute to heart attack. Cigarette smoking constricts the arteries and reduces the flow of

A heart attack is the damage to an area of the heart that results from a reduction in the blood supply to that area. The blood supply is reduced when a coronary artery is blocked by a blood clot or by advanced atherosclerosis.

blood to the heart. However, some studies show that persons who quit smoking lower their risk for heart attack until they are at the same risk for attack within a year after stopping as those who never smoked.

A diet low in saturated fats (saturated fats are usually solid at room temperature and include all forms of animal fat like butter and meat) and cholesterol, as well as calories, will reduce the level of serum cholesterol in the blood and prevent obesity, which places a strain on the heart. Furthermore, an exercise plan undertaken on the advice of your doctor will help maintain your proper body weight, in addition to improving circulation.

SYMPTOMS

The primary symptom of a heart attack is a crushing pain in the middle of the chest behind the breastbone. The pain may radiate down one or both arms and will probably be accompanied by fa-

The image labels: Right coronary artery, Left coronary artery, Blood clot, Damaged area

tigue and sweating. Persons who have experienced angina pectoris (chest pain), a warning signal that the heart is under stress, will recognize the symptoms as similar, but more intense. Unlike angina, the pain will not be relieved by the drug nitroglycerin and will not subside quickly. A heart attack may also occur when the person is at rest, which is quite rare in cases of angina. Dizziness and difficulty in breathing may also be present. Occasionally, there is fever.

A heart attack may be so mild that no symptoms other than a vague feeling of nausea and faintness may be felt, and the damage will only show up later on an electrocardiograph (EKG) reading. On the other hand, a severe heart attack may be accompanied by cardiac arrest, in which the heart stops beating altogether; or ventricular fibrillation, in which the heart's normal, steady beat is reduced to useless quivering that prevents blood from being pumped to the body.

The electrocardiograph (EKG) is the primary diagnostic tool to check for heart damage caused by myocardial infarction. The EKG measures the electrical impulses emitted by the heart and makes a visual record of them. A normal heart produces steady impulses, making a regular, even pattern on the EKG reading. A diseased heart shows disturbed patterns because the impulses must travel around the damaged area.

If your doctor is uncertain whether you have suffered a heart attack, he or she may test for an increased white blood cell count, which may indicate that the body's immune system is working to carry away the dead tissue in the heart. (The body's immune system produces white blood cells to fight disease and injury.) The physician may also perform other blood tests that will measure the levels of certain proteins in the blood that may indicate damage to the heart muscle. Often, these blood tests will be done once a day for several days since the tests may not become positive until 24

to 72 hours after the heart attack. If there is no doubt that you have suffered a heart attack, your doctor may carry out any one of several other tests to determine the presence of advanced atherosclerosis or some abnormality of the heart.

TREATMENT

Anyone who suspects he or she is having a heart attack should rush to the nearest emergency room for immediate medical treatment. Hospitalization is almost always required if the physician suspects a heart attack. The length of hospitalization will depend upon the severity of the heart attack and the development of complications such as heart failure. In general, the patient will be hospitalized for about two weeks. In some cases, several weeks of hospitalization may be required to insure complete physical rest and close medical monitoring.

For the first few days in the hospital, you will probably be in the cardiac care unit (CCU) where a highly trained staff is always on hand to watch your progress and deal with any complications. At first, your physical activities will be severely limited, but gradually you will be permitted to return to a normal schedule.

Many different drugs can be prescribed, depending on the severity and the complications of the heart attack: anticoagulants to thin the blood and prevent the formation of clots; digitalis to insure a steady, strong heartbeat; antiarrhythmics to prevent heartbeat irregularities; diuretics to reduce strain on the heart by eliminating excess fluids in the tissues; sedatives to relax the body and relieve tension; antianginals to alleviate chest pain; and beta blockers to decrease the heart's work. Beta blocker drugs have been found to be particularly effective in preventing death and additional heart attacks in those who have survived the first heart attack. (However, beta blockers should be used only with great

care in persons with asthma, since they may cause spasms in the airways that lead into the lungs.)

In some severe cases, surgery may be necessary to bypass the major narrowings or obstructions in the arteries in order to supply more blood to deprived areas of the heart. In this bypass operation a vein from the leg is grafted onto the coronary artery to carry blood around the obstruction.

Persons who have suffered a heart attack will certainly be advised to stop smoking, lose weight, and undertake a moderate exercise plan.

HEARTBEAT IRREGULARITIES

A normal heart beats at regular intervals, maintaining steady circulation of blood throughout the body. Any variation from the normal rhythm of the heart is called "arrhythmia" or a heartbeat irregularity. The beating of the heart is controlled primarily by the sinus node, a small mass of specialized tissue in the heart, and any damage to that node, or to the heart muscle itself, can cause heartbeat irregularities.

Although minor irregularities are common (everyone's heart "misses a beat" at times), more serious arrhythmias can cause fainting, angina (chest pain), or even a sudden heart attack. Ventricular fibrillation, the most serious heartbeat irregularity, occurs during a heart attack or after some other severe damage to the body. In this instance, the smooth contraction (pumping) sequence of the heart is replaced by a useless quivering motion which prevents the heart from pumping out any significant amount of blood to the body. Ventricular fibrillation must be treated immediately or it can be fatal.

In addition to damage to the sinus node or the heart muscle, arrhythmia may be caused by the improper use of drugs, excessive smoking, or large quantities of foods and drinks containing caffeine. For example, drugs pre-

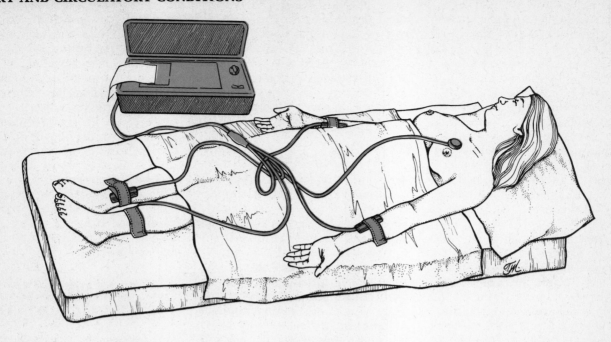

An electrocardiograph (EKG) is the primary tool used in diagnosing heartbeat irregularities because it measures the electrical impulses in the heart that control the rate of beating. Electrodes are placed on the skin and attached to the EKG which then produces a visual record of the impulses.

scribed to control arrhythmia may actually cause it if taken in too high a dosage. The nicotine in cigarettes may slow the heartbeat, while the caffeine in coffee, tea, cola, and chocolate (and some cold medications) may overstimulate the heart. Also, the heart may have congenital damage (present from birth) or may contain scar tissue from an earlier heart attack that is interfering with the transmission of the nerve impulses governing its beat.

Persons with high blood pressure or who have already suffered a heart attack are at a greater risk for arrhythmia. Poor function of the ventricles, the lower chambers of the heart responsible for pumping blood into the arteries, can also provide a tendency toward this condition.

SYMPTOMS

Many heartbeat irregularities are virtually symptom-free. However, light-headedness, fainting, a sensation of a pounding heart, dizziness, and chest pain can all be symptoms indicating that the heart is beating irregularly.

An electrocardiograph (EKG) is the primary tool used in diagnosing arrhythmia because it measures the electrical impulses generated by the heart to control the rate of beating. Electrodes (small metal disks) sensitive to these impulses are placed on the skin and attached to the electrocardiograph, which produces a visual record of the impulses. A normal heart will produce an EKG reading consisting of peaks and valleys occurring at regular intervals, while an arrhythmic heart, or one with some other disease, will produce an uneven, irregular pattern. Radioactive isotopes or X-ray opaque dye may be injected into the bloodstream as a means of tracing the flow of the blood through the heart. These substances can be scanned by special devices, and the path they take through the heart will reveal where any damage is located.

TREATMENT

Treatment for arrhythmia depends on the cause and the seriousness of the condition. An irregularity in the heartbeat may be so slight as to require no treatment at all, or so severe as to require drug therapy or implantation of a pacemaker. The treatment for the most severe form of arrhythmia, ventricular fibrillation, is application on the chest over the heart of a defibrillator, which jolts the heart back into a normal beating pattern by means of an electrical charge.

The drug digitalis may be prescribed to slow a speeding heart, while beta blocking drugs may be used to correct the problems of extra beats originating in the heart's lower chambers. Various other antiarrhythmics are also available, depending on the precise nature of the heartbeat irregularity.

For persons whose arrhythmia problem stems from a defect in the sinus node, a pacemaker may be implanted in the heart. The pacemaker is a tiny electrical device powered by a small generator sewn under the skin. It takes over the job of regulating the heartbeat by emitting the same type of im-

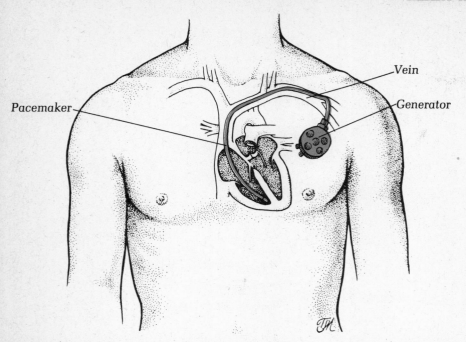

Pacemaker

Vein

Generator

Heartbeat irregularities may be corrected by a pacemaker, a tiny electrical device powered by a small generator. The pacemaker is inserted and threaded through a vein until it rests within the heart. This is called a transvenous (through the vein) placement. The generator is then sewn under the skin.

pulse as your own sinus node. The device is usually triggered only when your heart fails to beat after a specific time limit. Other types of pacemakers, however, are set so that the heart will always beat at a constant rate, usually 72 beats a minute. Implantation is a relatively simple procedure done under a local anesthetic: the pacemaker is inserted into and threaded through a vein until it comes to rest in the proper place in the heart. The generator is then sewn under the skin.

All arrhythmia patients will probably be advised to lose weight if necessary (to reduce the strain on the heart), to eliminate their consumption of caffeine, and to stop smoking. A well-supervised exercise plan may also be suggested.

HYPERTENSION

Blood pressure is the force with which blood pushes against the walls of the arteries, the blood vessels that carry blood from the heart through the body. Hypertension, or high blood pressure as it is commonly known, means that too much force is being exerted on the arteries. This may cause deterioration of the arteries and possible damage to body organs such as the heart, kidneys, and brain. (Hypertension does not mean a condition of excessive activity or tension, as many believe.)

Hypertension has been called the "silent disease," because it often has no obvious symptoms. Although an estimated 35 million people in this country have hypertension, only about one half of these people know they have the disease; of these 17 million, only about one half are treating their hypertension. These undetected and untreated victims run the risk of a shortened life, because hypertension contributes to strokes, heart attacks, and kidney failure.

Hypertension is not only "silent," it is also mysterious because in many cases there may be no known cause. When no underlying cause is discovered, the disease is called *essential* or *primary* hypertension. If another condition, for example, kidney disease, malfunctioning of the endocrine glands, or disorders of the circulatory system (such as narrowed blood vessels), is found to be causing the elevated blood pressure, it is termed *secondary* hypertension. In either case, detection and treatment are necessary to prevent complications.

Although there is no typical hypertensive person, there are some people who are at higher risk for developing hypertension. Persons with either one or two hypertensive parents are at greater risk, since heredity is believed to play a role in the development of hypertension. Blacks, both children and adults, have three to four times the incidence of hypertension as whites. Overweight, stress, smoking, drinking, and excessive sodium (salt) in the diet increase blood pressure, especially in those persons whose families have a history of hypertension. There is evidence, though inconclusive, that oral contraceptives contribute to the development of hypertension in some women; this is more likely to occur in women with a family history of hypertension or in those who are overweight.

Hypertension has been thought to be a part of aging, but there is increasing evidence that aging is not the primary factor; high blood pressure is found in men and women under the age of 35 and even in children (children of hypertensive parents, in fact, should have their blood pressure measured early in life).

SYMPTOMS

The first indication of elevated blood pressure is often the reading taken in your doctor's office. The real problem with hypertension is not the symptoms, but the lack of them. High blood pressure may be present in a person for years without causing noticeable symptoms.

Symptoms, if they occur, may include headache, fatigue, and dizziness. Sometimes flushing of

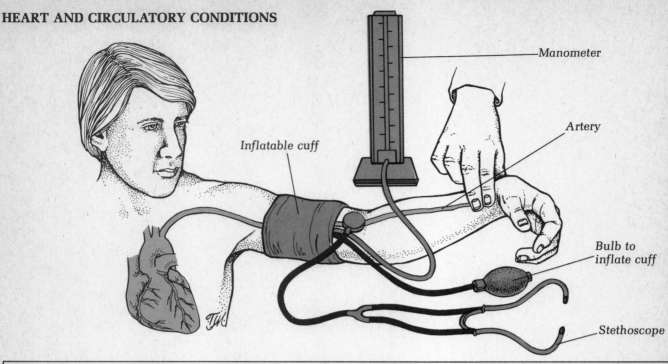

Manometer

Inflatable cuff

Artery

Bulb to inflate cuff

Stethoscope

Hypertension is diagnosed by a simple test using a stethoscope and a sphygmomanometer, an inflatable arm cuff attached to a graduated mercury manometer. The blood pressure is measured in the main artery of the arm by alternately closing and opening the flow of blood in the artery with the cuff and listening to the pulse of the artery with the stethoscope.

the face, ringing in the ears, thumping in the chest, and frequent nosebleeds may indicate high blood pressure. However, these symptoms may develop gradually, they may come and go, and they are frequently common to other conditions.

One form of primary hypertension that does exhibit symptoms is called *malignant* hypertension (this does not mean cancer but rather advanced, untreated hypertension). Its victim is often ill with headache, blurred vision, nausea, and dizziness. Some of these symptoms may be caused by uremia, a condition in which poisonous substances normally eliminated in the urine accumulate in the blood because of kidney damage resulting from untreated hypertension.

Hypertension is diagnosed by a simple and painless medical test. By using a stethoscope and a sphygmomanometer, a rubber or fabric arm cuff connected to a graduated mercury manometer (oversized thermometer), a doctor can take a reading of the blood pressure. The main artery in the arm is located by feeling for its

pulse just below the bend of the elbow. The head of the stethoscope is placed over the pulsating artery; the arm cuff is wrapped around the upper arm and is inflated by squeezing a rubber ball until the cuff is squeezing hard enough on the arm to shut off the flow of blood. This is indicated by the disappearance of pulse sound heard through the stethoscope.

At this point the doctor begins to release the pressure in the cuff until the pulse of the returning blood flow can be heard through the stethoscope. The doctor makes a note of the height of the mercury in the manometer and records it as the systolic pressure.

The systolic pressure measures the pressure of the heart during a contraction or heartbeat. To determine the diastolic pressure when the heart is at rest between contractions, the cuff is inflated and deflated again, but this time the doctor continues to let air out of the cuff after the blood flow returns. The mercury reading drops lower and a succession of murmuring sounds is heard. Eventually there is silence. The height of the mercury column at

this point is noted and recorded as the diastolic reading. While diastolic pressure is much lower than systolic, there is still pressure going through the body even though the heart is relaxed.

Both numbers count. A very high systolic reading means that the heart is pumping too hard, and a very high diastolic reading shows that the arteries are being subjected to constant wear and tear even when the heart is at rest.

A blood pressure reading of 120/80—120 is the systolic pressure and 80 is the diastolic pressure—is considered normal in an adult. At birth, blood pressure is typically about 80/46 and it goes up as age increases. Men generally have higher pressure than women until around age 50 to 55; at this age the trend reverses, and women have slightly higher pressure than men.

Since blood pressure can vary as much as 30 points, even within a few minutes, at least three separate readings under identical conditions on different occasions are recommended to make an accurate diagnosis of hypertension. If all the readings are higher than normal, a doctor may look for possible underlying causes by doing a thorough physical examination and a variety of laboratory tests.

TREATMENT

Fortunately, hypertension responds well to treatment. If the condition is mild and there is no indication of other disease, the doctor may prescribe lifestyle changes before prescribing medication. The initial changes may include weight loss if obese, a regular exercise program, and limitation of sodium (salt) intake. Limiting sodium does not mean simply cutting back on table salt; you should also read product labels carefully since many prepared and convenience foods, as well as over-the-counter drug items, have a high sodium content. All of these steps should be conducted under the close supervision of your doctor.

If medication is prescribed, your physician may try to find the right drug or drug combination. A "stepped care" program may be initiated, starting with a diuretic, a medication which increases sodium and water loss through increased urination. Step two might be a beta blocker, a drug which works by reducing the work of the heart. Step three could be a vasodilator, a drug which dilates or opens up narrowed blood vessels which could be contributing to high blood pressure. Step four, if none of the first three steps is effective, could be a combination of two or more of the earlier steps. Whatever program is prescribed, you should never change the dosage of or stop taking a drug without consulting your doctor. However, you can help the doctor monitor the treatment program by checking your own blood pressure on a regular basis. Home blood pressure kits are available, and you can easily learn to use the sphygmomanometer to keep a record of blood pressure.

A final word: while tension and stress do not directly cause hypertension, these factors do have an effect on the management of the disease. Persons with hypertension are urged to avoid high-pressure situations and learn to deal with stress. Studies have shown, too, that environmental factors as diverse as airplane noise and overcrowding can drive up blood pressure. Techniques such as biofeedback and self-hypnosis, in addition to meditation, are often thought to be useful in reducing stress and may therefore be helpful to a person with high blood pressure. It should be emphasized again, however, that even if stress is reduced, it is mandatory that instructions from the physician be followed carefully and that *medications are never stopped* except on the advice of the doctor.

THROMBO-PHLEBITIS

Thrombophlebitis is an inflammation of a vein accompanied by the formation of a blood clot (thrombus). Inflammation of a vein for any reason interferes with the blood's ability to flow smoothly through the vessel and provokes the formation of clots. The condition is most commonly seen in the deep veins of the leg, although it can occur in the veins of the pelvis and the arms.

Thrombophlebitis in itself is not life-threatening; however, a blood clot formed in a thrombophlebotic leg vein can break free and travel through the circulatory system to the lung where it can cause a pulmonary embolism (blood clot lodged in the lung). Since all blood in the veins ultimately returns to the lungs, this is the most likely place for a blood clot formed in inflamed veins to lodge. A pulmonary embolism can cause chest pain, coughing up of blood, and even death if a complete obstruction occurs.

Any condition that limits the free circulation of blood in the veins can cause thrombophlebitis. It is particularly prevalent among people who have undergone major surgery and have spent prolonged periods in bed or who are otherwise inactive. Congestive heart failure, which affects the heart's ability to pump blood efficiently through the body, can also contribute to thrombophlebitis. Additionally, any accident or infection which injures a vein can provoke the onset of this disease.

All these conditions allow blood to accumulate in pools in the elastic-walled veins. The resultant slowing of circulation causes clots to form, which, in turn, further reduce effective circulation.

Oral contraceptives, as well as pregnancy itself, are known to increase the risk of developing thrombophlebitis. Persons with occupations that require prolonged sitting or standing in one place are also more likely to be affected. Obesity, old age, and chronic infections can play a part in the development of this disease. On the other hand, the presence of thrombophlebitis may indicate a tumor in the pancreas or lung, since these malignancies seem to produce a substance that affects circulation.

SYMPTOMS

Swelling, aching pain, and a feeling of heaviness in the leg or other affected area are all signs of thrombophlebitis. The leg will appear white and will be painful to the touch, with the discomfort increasing when the foot is bent backward or forward. Walking may also increase the pain. Often, these symptoms do not occur until the disease is well advanced.

If thrombophlebitis is affecting a surface vein, your doctor can probably diagnose it through a physical examination alone. However, since the disease most commonly affects the deep veins, additional tests may be required. An X ray of the veins taken after the injection of contrast dye (called a venogram) will reveal the presence of a clot. Another test, called the Doppler test, can assess the blood mass flowing through the veins.

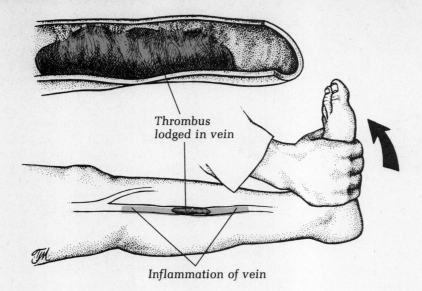

Thrombus
lodged in vein

Inflammation of vein

Thrombophlebitis is an inflammation of a vein accompanied by the formation of a blood clot. Inflammation of a vein interferes with blood flow through the vein and thus promotes the development of clots. Thrombophlebitis occurs most commonly in the deep veins of the leg and is often suspected if there is pain when the foot of the affected leg is bent backward or forward.

TREATMENT

Elevating the legs and wearing elastic hosiery, which help the muscles push the blood through the veins, are the standard treatments for thrombophlebitis of the legs. During the early stages of the condition, the patient should remain lying down with the legs elevated. Elastic stockings should be worn from the toes to just below the knees. After the symptoms subside, short periods of walking — but not sitting or standing — are permitted. These periods are increased each day.

Anticoagulant drugs, which thin the blood and help prevent the formation of clots, will be prescribed if the case is serious enough. Painkillers, as well as anti-inflammatory drugs to reduce swelling and inflammation, may also be recommended.

Sometimes, if a long period of bed rest is anticipated, such as before major surgery, your doctor may administer an anticoagulant to forestall the development of thrombophlebitis. Other preventive measures you can take include exercise, getting up to stretch after long periods of sitting, and elevating your legs.

VARICOSE VEINS

Varicose veins are dilated or swollen veins in the legs caused by pooling of blood. Veins are the blood vessels that carry blood back to the heart from the body. In all other parts of the body this is a relatively easy task. However, in the legs, blood must move uphill against the force of gravity. The veins are lined with one-way valves that prevent blood from flowing back down into the leg. When pressure on the veins causes them to stretch, the valves do not close properly and blood seeps back, forming pools that stretch the veins even further. The result is bulging, bluish lines down the legs which may cause pain, a feeling of heaviness, and cramps in the legs. Varicose veins, apart from being a cosmetic problem, may also result in leg ulcers (eroded patches on the skin), phlebitis (inflamed veins), and blood clots.

Anything that puts an undue strain on the veins of the legs, making the task of returning blood to the heart more difficult, can lead to varicose veins. Standing in one position for long periods of time, prolonged sitting in chairs especially with crossed legs, general lack of exercise, and confining clothes can all contribute to the development of varicose veins. The condition is also more common in countries, like the United States, where people maintain a diet low in fiber and high in refined foods. Experts believe that the hard stools that result from a low-fiber diet and the straining necessary to excrete them put severe pressure on the leg veins.

Experts differ on the role heredity plays in the development of varicose veins, but it seems that a tendency toward weakness in vein walls or valves can be inherited. Tall people may be at a greater risk since their blood must travel farther in its return trip to the heart, while obesity puts pressure on the veins and makes it more difficult for the muscles of the legs to help push blood upward.

Women are more likely to develop varicose veins than men. Female hormones, especially those released during pregnancy, may account for this, because the hormones tend to relax the smooth muscle walls of veins.

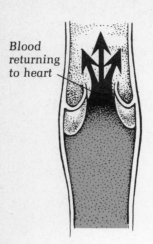
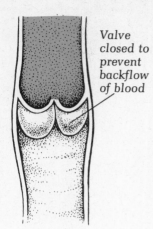

Blood returning to heart

Valve closed to prevent backflow of blood

Normal vein

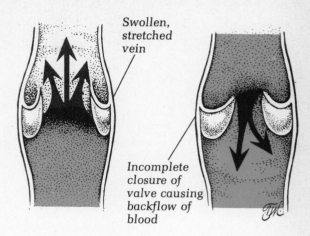

Swollen, stretched vein

Incomplete closure of valve causing backflow of blood

Varicose vein

Varicose veins are swollen, stretched veins that usually appear as bulging cords on the surface of the legs. Veins are equipped with one-way valves that prevent the blood returning to the heart from flowing back down into the legs. When pressure on the veins causes them to stretch, these valves do not completely close; and blood seeps back, further stretching the veins. The result is varicose veins.

Varicose veins often appear in the first few months of pregnancy because of the pressure of the enlarging uterus on the large veins leading into the leg veins. However, varicose veins may recede after the birth of the baby.

SYMPTOMS

Varicose veins only develop in the blood vessels close to the surface of the skin, so the bulging, bluish, cord-like appearance of the veins is always noticeable. The disorder generally causes a feeling of achiness, heaviness, and fatigue in the legs, especially at the end of the day. Itchy, scaly skin may also appear over the affected areas. As the disorder worsens, the ankles may swell, pain may extend down the leg, and night leg cramps may occur. Since varicose veins are highly visible, they are easily diagnosed by a simple physical examination.

TREATMENT

The primary treatment for this condition is wearing elastic hosiery, which acts like muscles to aid the flow of blood through the veins. If this produces no re-

lief, surgery to tie off and remove the affected veins may be recommended. This procedure is called "vein stripping" and is generally performed in a hospital under general anesthesia. After surgery elastic bandages will be kept on the legs for several days. After the varicose veins are removed, other healthy veins in the legs will take over the role of returning blood back to the heart. However, if none of the contributing factors such as obesity, lack of exercise, and poor diet has been altered, the disease may recur in the other veins.

Another treatment involves injecting a chemical into the vein which closes it off, forcing the blood flow into other channels. However, this approach has more complications and is therefore not used as often as surgery.

To prevent the likelihood of developing varicose veins, exercise regularly, improve your diet, and put your feet up whenever possible. If you must sit for extended periods in your job or while traveling, get up and stretch your legs occasionally. Do deep knee bends or rise up on tiptoe several times during the day to improve circulation in the legs.

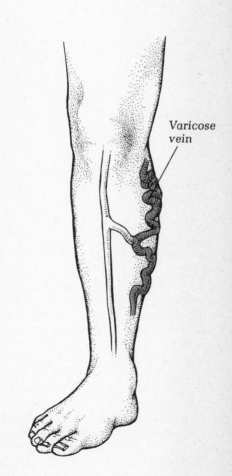

Varicose vein

PROBLEMS OF THE DIGESTIVE SYSTEM

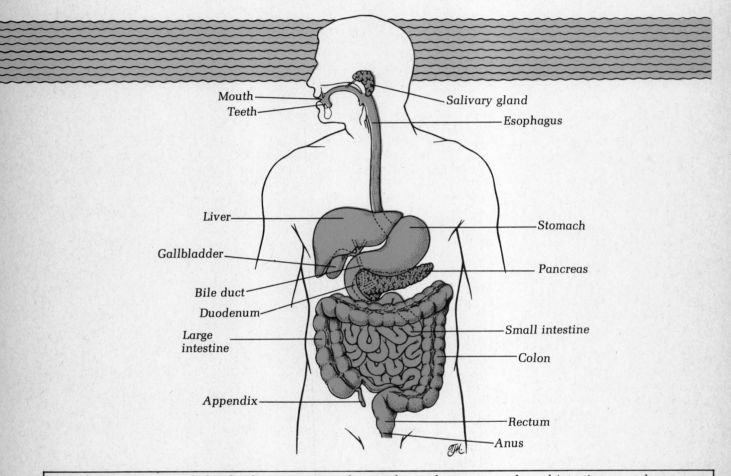

Mouth
Teeth
Salivary gland
Esophagus
Liver
Stomach
Gallbladder
Pancreas
Bile duct
Duodenum
Large intestine
Small intestine
Colon
Appendix
Rectum
Anus

The digestive system includes the digestive tract — the mouth, esophagus, stomach, and intestines — and accessory organs — the pancreas, liver, and gallbladder.

The digestive or gastrointestinal system processes food for use by the body and helps to regulate the amount of nutrients, water, and other substances that are absorbed into the bloodstream. It includes the digestive tube or tract — the mouth, esophagus, stomach, intestines — and several accessory organs — the pancreas, liver, and gallbladder. A mucous membrane lines the entire digestive system and aids in the absorption of nutrients. The mucus secreted by the membrane also lubricates the tract and protects it from irritating substances.

Mouth. The mouth is the beginning of the digestive tract, which is actually a tube over 30 feet long. More than simply an opening, the mouth is where the digestive process starts. In the mouth food is chewed into smaller pieces and mixed with saliva, secreted from the salivary glands in the mouth. The saliva moistens the food for easier swallowing and also contains an enzyme (a special kind of protein produced by the salivary glands) that helps to digest starches.

Esophagus. The esophagus transports food and liquid from the mouth to the stomach. It is a muscular tube about nine inches long.

Stomach. The stomach stores food entering the digestive system. It also churns food into smaller pieces and mixes it with acid digestive juices.

Small intestine. From the stomach, food passes into the small intestine. In the first 12 inches or so of the small intestine (duodenum), the food is mixed with more digestive juices. Through the remainder of the small intestine (more than 20 feet), nutrients are absorbed into the blood. Very little nutrient absorption occurs in either the stomach or large intestine.

Large intestine. The large intestine is approximately six feet long, and it is in the large intestine that the fecal mass (waste material) is formed and water is reabsorbed to help preserve the body's balance of fluids.

Colon. The colon, the lower portion of the large intestine, stores the feces before they are transferred to the rectum, the lower end of the colon. Finally, the feces pass out of the body through the anus, the opening at the end of the digestive tube.

Liver. An accessory organ of the digestive system, the liver controls many of the body's physiological functions. It purifies and removes waste products from the blood and manufactures many different chemicals used by the body. The liver also traps and processes old and worn-out red blood cells. Although not directly concerned with the process of digestion, the liver does manufacture bile which is required for the absorption of fat from the small intestine.

Gallbladder. The gallbladder is a hollow organ located beneath the liver. Bile produced by the liver is stored in the gallbladder. When the bile is needed, the gallbladder contracts and releases it into the small intestine.

Pancreas. The pancreas lies mostly behind the stomach. It has two primary functions. One function is the manufacturing and secretion of digestive enzymes that are delivered directly into the small intestine where they aid in digestion. The pancreas also contains the islets of Langerhans. These cells secrete insulin — the hormone required for carbohydrate digestion—into the blood.

APPENDICITIS

Appendicitis is an inflammation of the appendix resulting from a bacterial infection. Located at the juncture of the small and large intestines, the appendix is a small, worm-like piece of intestinal tissue with no known function in humans. It is called a vestigial organ because, although it may have previously served some function, it has no known function now.

Unfortunately, although the appendix is a useless organ, it can be the source of a serious or, at times, even fatal illness. When the appendix becomes swollen and filled with pus from bacteria, it may form an abscess or may break, allowing the infection to spread to the surrounding organs. Rupture may lead to peritonitis — one of the most serious of all diseases — an inflammation of the lining of the abdominal cavity. The infection can spread so quickly that gangrene (death of tissue) and rupture may occur within a matter of hours from the first symptoms.

Although appendicitis is not among the leading killers, it still claims some lives needlessly. It can affect anyone, but it is more prevalent among those in the age group between ten and 30.

The appendix is a hollow structure formed like a tube, so if it becomes plugged up by a hard bit of waste matter, intestinal worms, or other material, normal drainage cannot take place. Thus, many bacteria find this a fertile ground in which to multiply, causing infection and inflammation.

SYMPTOMS

Any fever with nausea and abdominal pain, especially in the lower right portion of the abdomen, may indicate appendicitis and should be checked immediately since the disease can worsen very rapidly.

At the beginning of an attack there will be either dull or severe pain in the naval area of the abdomen. The pain will sharpen during movement, coughing, or sneezing. The patient may suffer from a loss of appetite, and nausea may follow. Although constipation is usual, about 10 percent of patients may have diarrhea instead. Adults may have a mild fever (up to 102° F.), but children will generally have a higher fever. Occasionally, the pulse increases to about 100 beats per minute.

After a few hours the pain will become continuous and will shift to the lower right side of the abdomen over the appendix. The whole appendix region will feel extremely tender as the abdominal muscles tighten. (Because the tip of the appendix may be located in slightly different places in each individual, the pain may possibly be located in the back, the side, or in the pelvis. In the very unusual situation where a person is born with all internal organs reversed in position, the appendix may be located on the left side of the abdomen, and therefore the pain will be felt on the left side.)

If the fever rises and the pain becomes very severe, rupture is almost certain. At this point, the condition becomes a medical emergency.

Although there is no known way to prevent appendicitis, a prompt diagnosis can lead to the treatment or effective removal of the inflamed organ before serious complications set in.

The doctor will look for tenderness over the appendix when pressure is exerted there. A laboratory test to check for a high white blood cell count is also helpful in making a diagnosis. (During an infection or disease, the number of white blood cells increases to fight the condition.)

The doctor will also search for evidence of other diseases which are sometimes mistaken for appendicitis, including gallbladder attack, kidney stones, or kidney infection on the right side. In women, the symptoms of a ruptured ectopic (tubal) pregnancy or a twisted cyst on the ovary are similar to the symptoms of appendicitis.

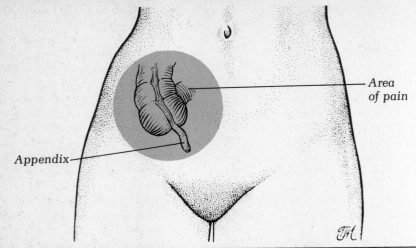

Area
of pain

Appendix

In appendicitis, the lower right side of the abdomen will be painful and tender to the touch.

TREATMENT

A mild case of appendicitis may subside by itself, and some people have actually had recurrent attacks. But the usual treatment for an acute case is surgical removal of the appendix. Removal is the preferred treatment to avoid the risk of infection and the possibility that the condition could worsen and the appendix rupture. Antibiotics will also be administered to prevent any further infection.

If you suspect that you're suffering an attack of appendicitis do not take any laxatives in an attempt to relieve your pains, since this could cause the appendix to rupture immediately by increasing activity in the intestine. In fact, all food, water, and drugs should be avoided until a doctor is consulted.

GALLSTONES

Gallstones are hardened, stone-like masses formed in the gallbladder or in the bile duct, the tube leading from the gallbladder into the intestine. The stones largely consist of cholesterol, a substance that is normally found in animal fats, bile, blood, the liver, and other tissues.

Although the gallstones themselves may not cause any symptoms, serious complications may develop. The gallbladder can become inflamed, a condition called cholecystitis, which causes severe pain 30 to 60 minutes after eating. The pain may be confused with a heart attack or severe ulcer complications.

If the stones block the flow of bile, severe liver damage, accompanied by jaundice (yellow skin and eyes discolored by excess bile pigment) may result. Occasionally, inflammation and damage of other nearby organs will also be caused by the stone's pressure.

A combination of factors is known to affect the formation of gallstones. These factors include concentration of bile and bile salts, eating too much fat, infection, liver disease, and certain forms of anemia such as sickle-cell disease.

Cholesterol-containing gallstones—the most common kind—form because the bile juice contains too much cholesterol as compared to its other major ingredients. The excess cholesterol cannot remain in the bile solution and it separates out as "stones." Unfortunately, it seems that you cannot prevent stones by cutting down the cholesterol in your diet. Cholesterol from the diet goes into the blood, and there is no direct relationship between the cholesterol content of the blood and that of bile.

Some factors that contribute to an increased risk of gallstones include diabetes, pregnancy, and obesity. The risk of developing stones increases, too, when an

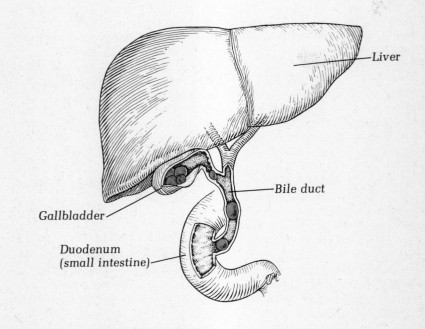

Liver

Bile duct

Gallbladder

Duodenum
(small intestine)

Gallstones can form in the gallbladder or bile duct. These stones may cause inflammation of the gallbladder or they may lead to liver damage if a stone blocks the flow of bile from the gallbladder to the duodenum.

overweight person starts losing weight. Therefore, obese people should avoid repeated weight losses and gains.

Women who have had more than one or two children are more likely to suffer from gallstones, and after the fortieth birthday, about twice as many women as men have gallstones. The reason for this is unclear.

SYMPTOMS

Gallstone symptoms are usually of a chronic (long-term) nature causing recurring discomfort and pain in the upper abdomen, indigestion, nausea, and an intolerance of fatty foods.

The indication of an acute gallbladder attack is pain in the upper abdomen, often more pronounced on the right side and sometimes traveling to the back and under the right shoulder blade. The pain develops suddenly, often after a meal, and can lead to fever, chills, vomiting, and often jaundice. Usually these symptoms will occur when a stone, previously floating freely in the gallbladder, becomes wedged in the bile duct. (Some stones can pass through the duct into the intestine and then be eliminated naturally.)

About half of those persons with gallstones have no symptoms at all. In these cases, the existence of gallstones may be discovered through a standard X ray of the abdomen. A doctor may also take a cholecystogram—an X ray taken after the patient swallows a tablet containing a dye which outlines the gallbladder as well as any stones that are present. Since this dye does not always work, another test that uses ultrasound is increasingly being used. In this test, sound waves bounce off internal body structures and form an image of them. This technique seems to be more reliable in detecting stones than both types of X rays.

TREATMENT

Persons with gallstones should avoid foods rich in fat or fried in grease as well as gas-forming vegetables such as cucumbers, radishes, and turnips.

Fortunately, we can live without our gallbladders, so many doctors recommend surgical removal for those who have an acute attack and experience severe and prolonged symptoms. The operation, called a cholecystectomy, is one of the most common forms of abdominal surgery performed on adults in this country. Many doctors even advise such a procedure in patients with "silent" stones to prevent complications that might develop in the future.

There may soon be an alternative to surgery for gallstone sufferers. Researchers are testing a drug that will be able to dissolve cholesterol gallstones.

HEMORRHOIDS

Hemorrhoids, often referred to as piles, are enlarged veins inside or just outside the anal canal, the opening at the end of the large intestine. The veins enlarge and swell, causing severe inflammation which promotes intense itching, discomfort, and pain that may be accompanied by bleeding.

Although the initial bleeding that is associated with hemorrhoids may appear slight and not seem serious, if it is continuous it may lead to anemia (a deficiency of red blood cells). In addition, a blood clot can form in the vein and can be extremely painful, requiring surgical removal. Furthermore, inflamed veins may become infected and even rupture, causing severe bleeding.

The initial development of a hemorrhoid is often due to an individual's toilet habits. Many times the cause can be traced to the hard, dry stools and the straining that accompany constipation. These irritate the veins and slow the flow of blood which leads to swollen, inflamed veins. Therefore, straining over a prolonged period of time encourages the development of hemorrhoids.

Personal habits, such as the tendency to postpone normal bowel functioning, can also contribute to the development of hemorrhoids. The bowels should be moved while the body's signal is still strong. Habitual postponing of bowel movements can lead to the loss of the rectal reflex, thus requiring undesirable straining to accomplish elimination. Also, the

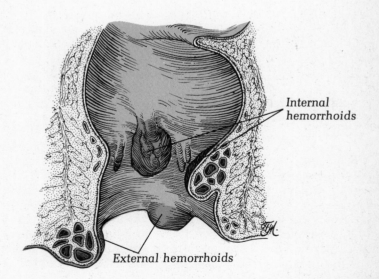

Internal hemorrhoids

External hemorrhoids

Hemorrhoids are enlarged veins inside (internal hemorrhoids) or just outside (external hemorrhoids) the anal canal, the opening at the end of the large intestine. The swollen veins cause itching, discomfort, and pain which may be accompanied by bleeding.

longer the feces remain within the bowels, the less moisture they retain. Therefore, postponing a bowel movement may contribute to hard, dry stools.

Dietary factors play an important role in the development of hemorrhoids. The proper diet to avoid constipation and the development of hemorrhoids includes a lot of roughage—natural grains, fresh fruits, and vegetables—instead of a diet which contains a high proportion of refined, fiber-depleted foods like white flour and sugar.

Hemorrhoids can also be caused by something potentially serious; for example, pressure on the veins from diseases of the liver or heart, or from a locally situated tumor or cancer, can inflame the veins.

Pregnancy seems to be a major contributing factor in the formation of hemorrhoids, because the enlarged uterus puts increased pressure on the veins. Although hemorrhoids may appear or become aggravated during pregnancy, recent research suggests that women who experience such a condition probably had hemorrhoids prior to becoming pregnant. The increased abdominal pressure is believed to cause their hemorrhoids to become more symptomatic.

There seems to be a tendency toward the development of hemorrhoids in some families, although this is usually due to similar dietary and personal habits rather than inherited physical characteristics.

SYMPTOMS

For most patients, hemorrhoids take many years to develop and it may be even longer before their appearance is obvious. Initial symptoms include itching and some discomfort during or after a bowel movement. The pressure of straining on the toilet will eventually result in a slight swelling of the lining of the anal canal. Although the swelling may not be noticed by the patient, the passage of hard stools may scrape this interior swelling and cause slight bleeding — an early clue that hemorrhoids are developing.

Following a period of continual straining, a portion of the anal canal may protrude at the anus during the course of a bowel movement. At this stage the elastic connective tissue is still strong enough to draw the hemorrhoid back into the anus unassisted, so the patient may still be unaware of the problem. In the next stage, however, the hemorrhoid's existence becomes obvious because the protruding tissue remains outside of the anus at the conclusion of the bowel movement and must be manually returned within the anus. While outside the anal canal, the hemorrhoid causes a dull, aching, uncomfortable sensation.

The situation may require emergency treatment when the hemorrhoid becomes difficult or impossible to return and a permanent bulge at the anal opening interferes with bowel movements. The patient may try to avoid additional discomfort by postponing bowel movements, thereby prolonging the constipation which is causing the problem.

To determine the presence and/or condition of the hemorrhoids, the doctor may examine the anal canal. Occasionally, instruments will be used, including an anoscope (a short, lighted tube) to inspect the lining of the rectum, and a sigmoidoscope, a longer instrument which gives a view of the entire inner area of the colon.

TREATMENT

In the early stages of hemorrhoid development, personal toilet habits should be adjusted to prevent the condition from worsening. Avoiding straining during bowel movements and improving the diet can also help to arrest further development.

Over-the-counter hemorrhoid preparations that can be purchased without prescription are generally helpful in reducing the itching and swelling associated with hemorrhoids. They do not, however, cure the hemorrhoids.

Occasionally, an individual may be sensitive to the chemicals in these preparations, and hemorrhoid symptoms may become worse. If this occurs, a physician should be consulted. The occasional use of non-irritating laxatives may also be helpful in maintaining soft bowel movements.

A case of extremely painful hemorrhoids may need some emergency home treatment. Apply very cold water on paper tissues or on a cloth directly to the anal area. Continue for five to 10 minutes till the pain is relieved. In addition, a hot bath may offer some relief. If severe pain persists after taking these measures, a physician should be consulted.

A severe case of hemorrhoids may require surgery. The dilated veins may be surgically removed and the remaining parts of the veins tied off. This is called a hemorrhoidectomy. However, the hemorrhoidectomy procedure is being replaced by newer medical techniques which are less painful and have fewer postoperative complications.

Cryosurgery is done by touching the hemorrhoid with an extremely cold probe that quickly freezes it. The frozen tissue will die, and the hemorrhoid will fall off within several days. This procedure can be done in the doctor's office and takes only a few minutes. There may be a slight watery discharge for a few days, but healing is rapid.

Rubber band ligation is another technique often used for internal hemorrhoids. This procedure can also be done in the doctor's office, although the patient may have to return for several treatments since only one hemorrhoid can be treated per session. With a special instrument, the doctor binds off the hemorrhoid's blood supply, causing it to die and drop off within three to nine days. When a hemorrhoid is eliminated in this way, there may be a brief spotting of blood and minor itching of the area.

Hemorrhoids are the most common cause of rectal bleeding

in an adult. It is important, however, that all cases of rectal bleeding are evaluated by a physician since a more serious problem such as a cancer may be present.

HEPATITIS

Hepatitis is an inflammation and infection of the liver, caused by a virus and characterized by jaundice, a yellowing of the skin and the whites of the eyes. Although there are several viruses associated with hepatitis, the two most common strains of the disease are hepatitis A, formerly called infectious hepatitis, and hepatitis B, known as serum hepatitis.

Hepatitis A, the less serious strain, is rarely fatal. However, without prompt care, permanent liver damage can occur. This form of the disease is also known to occur in epidemics when sanitation is poor and the virus is spread through water contaminated by sewage.

Hepatitis B, on the other hand, can produce lingering liver inflammation. Unlike the A virus which the body rids itself of by the time jaundice fades, the B virus can persist for years or even a lifetime. Persons who continue to harbor the virus are "carriers" and can transmit the disease to others even when they, the carriers, seem to be in good health. Type B can also produce chronic, or long-term, hepatitis — in up to five percent of its victims — which can lead to cirrhosis or irreversible liver failure. Cirrhosis is a condition in which fibrous scar tissue replaces most of the normal liver cells.

Hepatitis is caused by a virus that can be spread in many ways. It is generally thought that the two types of hepatitis are caused by different viruses.

Hepatitis A is passed through the human digestive tract and can be transmitted through the stool of an infected person or by contaminated food or water. Hepatitis B is traditionally thought of as being spread by blood transfer (such as through transfusions of

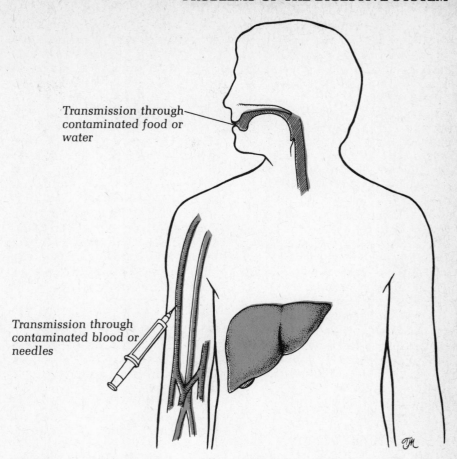

Transmission through contaminated food or water

Transmission through contaminated blood or needles

Hepatitis, an inflammation of the liver, can be transmitted through the digestive tract by contaminated food or water or by blood transfer involving contaminated blood or needles.

contaminated blood or through contaminated needles, particularly among drug users). However, it is now also known that hepatitis B can be communicated by intimate person-to-person contact. The virus is present in virtually all body fluids including tears, urine, saliva, and semen and may be spread even by such casual contact as shared razors or toothbrushes. In addition, hepatitis may be a complication of infectious mononucleosis (a viral infection).

SYMPTOMS

The symptoms of hepatitis A and B are similar except that the onset of symptoms in type B is often more gradual, appearing in stages. After contracting hepatitis B, 40 to 180 days may elapse before the first symptoms appear.

For hepatitis A, the incubation period is from 14 to 40 days. Infected persons are most contagious during the "prodromal state" — that is, before they even feel sick or before the appearance of symptoms. Some patients with hepatitis A have such a mild form, without the appearance of jaundice, that they never even know they have the disease.

Early symptoms include general fatigue, pain in the joints and muscles, and a loss of appetite. Nausea and vomiting follow, and diarrhea or constipation may occur along with a low grade fever (103° F. or less). The patient may suffer from chills, develop a distaste for smoking, and lose weight. Jaundice — caused by an accumulation of yellow bile pigment in the blood—appears as the other symptoms worsen. In hepatitis A, as the yellowing of the skin disappears, recovery follows.

Analysis of blood and urine specimens usually determines the existence and severity of hepatitis and will be the first tests administered to a person suspected of having the disease. A physicial exam will reveal the yellowish color of the skin if the disease has progressed that far, and a check for soreness in the upper right abdomen over the liver will help confirm liver involvement.

The diagnosis of the more severe chronic hepatitis may require a liver biopsy, a sample of liver tissue which is obtained by inserting a needle through the upper abdomen after a local anesthetic has been injected.

A new test has been developed to speed the diagnosis of hepatitis B and to identify carriers actively producing the virus. This test will be able to detect the presence in the blood of the virus that causes hepatitis B.

TREATMENT

There is no specific treatment for acute hepatitis. Once it occurs, recovery is up to the body's defense systems. Usually strict bed rest is suggested during the most acute phases, and hospitalization may be required in some serious cases. Exchange blood transfusion is credited with enabling some severely afflicted patients to recover.

During recovery, the patient is advised to avoid all strenuous physical activity. Most importantly, alcoholic beverages are to be avoided, because processing alcohol places a great strain on the liver.

Preventing or minimizing the effects of hepatitis is possible. For persons who have come into contact with the disease, an injection of gamma globulin — the disease-fighting portion of the blood — is recommended. This substance appears to offer potent protection against the A virus and gives modest protection against the B virus. But even if hepatitis develops after receiving a shot, the case is likely to be less severe.

There is also a new vaccine against hepatitis. (A vaccine is a preparation containing the virus that causes the disease. When the vaccine is introduced into the body, it stimulates the body to produce its own immunity — or protection — against the disease.) However, the vaccine is not yet available for general use because of its lengthy production time. It is recommended only for people at high risk such as health care workers or persons in daily contact with known hepatitis carriers. Nevertheless, scientists expect that the vaccine will eventually become available for widespread use in the near future.

IRRITABLE COLON

Irritable colon is the most common chronic, or long-term, abdominal disorder seen by physicians, and it has a variety of very descriptive names — mucous colitis, spastic colon, functional dyspepsia, colitis, nervous indigestion, and irritable bowel syndrome.

The irritable colon syndrome primarily refers to a disturbed state of the muscular contractions of the intestine which propel food and waste material through the digestive tract. It is a functional disorder, meaning that there is nothing wrong with the colon itself, but only with the way it acts. There are real symptoms, but no physical cause can be found and no deformities characteristic of more serious abdominal illnesses are apparent. Many people with chronic indigestion end up with the diagnosis of irritable colon. It very rarely develops into a more serious disease.

Irritable colon is usually caused by emotional upset, anxiety, or stress which stimulates the colon to overreact and cause the pain. Tension may aggravate a "nervous" bowel. However, many people have the symptoms despite their apparent ability to cope with their problems.

Other contributing factors to an irritated bowel may be poor di-

etary habits and the improper use of laxatives.

SYMPTOMS

The symptoms of irritable colon are extremely variable and their appearance often coincides with some emotional upset. Patients may have diarrhea or constipation and gassiness. Pain may spread across the abdomen and sometimes move into the chest or shoulders, perhaps creating the false impression of a heart attack. The abdomen is often bloated, and the patient may develop a headache, begin vomiting, or suffer from a loss of appetite and fatigue. Bowel movements are usually hard little pellets accompanied by a lot of gas, yet at other times they may be loose with mucus, but never blood, in the stool.

Diagnosing irritable colon is often a problem in that there is no apparent structural abnormality or disease that shows up on X rays and in other tests. All the patient has are symptoms, and a diagnostic search for cancer and other serious intestinal disorders will fail to turn up the physical signs characteristic of these problems.

Nevertheless, your doctor will probably attempt to rule out more serious diseases before concluding that your symptoms indicate irritable colon syndrome. This involves an examination of the stool and direct inspection of the interior of the colon with a sigmoidoscope — a long metal tube with a light on the end that permits a view of the rectum and colon. Such an exam is necessary because it can detect any silent, more serious problems that may exist.

TREATMENT

Anyone with an irritable bowel is immediately told to "relax." If the syndrome has been brought on by emotional anxiety, the symptoms may go away or lessen as the anxiety decreases. But for many people, the key to management of the condition is diet. The addition of high-fiber foods, such as bran and other cereals, fruits, and vegetables, will provide bulk to help relieve the chronic constipation that often accompanies irritable colon. Those with diarrhea, of course, should select foods that do not contribute to this symptom. However, the bland diet that was once believed to control the problem has proven itself to be ineffective.

People who suffer from irritable colon should avoid gas-forming foods such as cabbage, beans, and cauliflower, as well as tea and coffee which may cause diarrhea in some. Laxatives should not be taken for constipation because they will further aggravate an already irritated bowel, which needs rest, not stimulation.

Anti-spasmodic medications can be taken when necessary to reduce intestinal spasm, and the urge to move the bowels should never be ignored.

PEPTIC ULCERS

Peptic ulcer is an open sore or erosion in the wall of the stomach or of the duodenum, the first part of the small intestine extending from the stomach. The word "peptic" comes from the Greek word for digestion and simply means that the ulcer is located somewhere in the digestive tract.

Duodenal ulcers are much more common than those in the stomach, but the incidence of both types has been declining gradually over the past few decades. Still, ulcers are a fairly common disease, affecting about 10 million Americans of all ages. Furthermore, while ulcers are generally not considered to be life-threatening, if left untreated they can cause serious damage. If an ulcer erodes nearby blood vessels, there may be internal seepage of blood or even massive internal bleeding (hemorrhage). An untreated ulcer can also perforate the wall of the intestine or stomach and allow the contents to leak into the sterile abdominal cavity, thus contaminating it and possibly causing peritonitis, an inflamma-

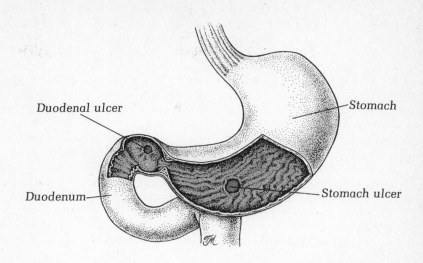

A peptic ulcer is an open sore or erosion in either the wall of the stomach or the beginning of the small intestine called the duodenum. Duodenal ulcers are more common than stomach ulcers, but both types are shown in this cutaway illustration of the stomach and duodenum.

tion of the membrane lining the abdomen. A perforated ulcer may also penetrate an adjoining organ. In addition, the scar tissue that can build up around an ulcer can sometimes lead to an intestinal obstruction. These complications are all the possible results of an advanced, untreated ulcer.

There are no firm medical conclusions about what causes ulcers, although heredity has been determined to play a large role in this disease. Ulcers are far more common among relatives of existing ulcer patients than among those whose family has no history of ulcers.

The duodenal ulcer has been linked to the secretion of an excessive amount of digestive juices by the stomach. Different factors, including coffee, alcohol, aspirin, cigarettes, some painkillers, and emotional stress, are known to increase the flow of stomach acid and are therefore thought to contribute to ulcers. However, the role emotional tension plays in causing ulcers is often overestimated. It is not the stress itself but the way a person copes with stress that will ultimately determine whether this factor will contribute to an ulcer.

The more uncommon stomach ulcers are not usually associated with the production of stomach acid. Instead, they may result from an inherent weakness in the stomach wall. However, the same environmental factors that aggravate duodenal ulcers may also affect the stomach variety.

A family history of ulcers is the most important element in determining a person's susceptiblity to ulcers. Additionally, for some unknown reason, persons with type O blood are more likely to be afflicted with ulcers. Those who suffer from certain diseases, such as cirrhosis of the liver, emphysema, and rheumatoid arthritis, may also be more vulnerable.

SYMPTOMS

Sometimes an ulcer may be present with no symptoms at all or the symptoms may be very mild, resembling heartburn or indigestion. On the other hand, the symptoms may be quite severe, with pain radiating throughout the entire upper part of the body and even mimicking angina, the chest pains that accompany heart disease.

The most common symptom of ulcer is a burning pain in the abdomen above the navel. The discomfort may sometimes be felt as a gnawing sensation not unlike hunger pangs. Usually the pain or discomfort occurs about one-half hour to two hours after eating or in the middle of the night when the stomach is empty and the acidic juices are irritating the exposed nerve endings in the open sore of the ulcer. The pain usually subsides upon eating something, drinking milk, or taking an antacid, all of which will neutralize stomach aid. Nausea and vomiting may sometimes occur, and constipation is common. In the case of an advanced ulcer, blood in the stool (indicated by a black, tarry appearance) or blood in the vomit are both signs of internal bleeding, as are weakness, faintness, and excessive thirst.

A barium X ray is the most frequent diagnostic procedure. After swallowing barium, a chalky substance which shows up as an opaque outline of the digestive tract on X ray films, the patient stands in front of a fluorescent screen, and, as the X ray tube moves down from shoulder level, the doctor can examine the digestive tract to determine if there are any abnormalities.

A gastroduodenoscope (a long, flexible, lighted tube inserted through the mouth and down the esophagus) may also be used to allow the doctor to directly view ulcers that may be missed by an X ray. If the ulcer is believed to be in the stomach, the scope should probably be used and a biopsy taken to eliminate the possibility of a cancer masquerading as a stomach ulcer. A biopsy involves removing a small tissue sample from the stomach for testing. It is a precautionary measure since some apparent stomach ulcers seen on an X ray may actually be a cancer.

TREATMENT

The aim of medical treatment is to relieve irritation of the ulcer so that it may heal naturally. This is accomplished by using various medications which either neutralize the excess stomach acid already produced or reduce the amount being secreted. Ulcer patients will also be advised to change living habits that are believed to aggravate their ulcers.

Antacids neutralize stomach acid, relieve symptoms, and thus promote healing. It is generally suggested that the antacids be taken hourly at the onset of treatment and less frequently thereafter. Although most antacids are over-the-counter items, you should not attempt self-treatment with massive doses of these products, since they can cause complications. For example, sodium bicarbonate, one of the main antacid ingredients, contains a significant amount of salt and should not be taken by persons with kidney disease or high blood pressure, since both conditions are aggravated by salt. Furthermore, the proper dosages and timing for antacids should be determined by your doctor who is familiar with your case.

Recent studies have shown that many popularly held assumptions about diet in treating ulcers are not really accurate. The famed "bland diet" consisting largely of milk products, hot cereals, and baby food, has proved to be unnecessary in the successful management of ulcers. Although a bland diet may be recommended for the first week of treatment until the more acute symptoms disappear, many doctors now suggest that only those foods which actually cause stomach distress should be avoided. Milk is also losing its status as the cure-all food for ulcer sufferers. Its neutralizing effects on stomach acid are mild and temporary; however, people who learn to substitute milk for beverages containing proven irritants, such as alcohol or caffeine, are less likely to be troubled by their ulcers. (Unfortunately, switching to decaffeinated beverages may not be helpful since these, too, have been shown to stimulate acid secretions.)

If, in spite of these measures, the ulcer persists, other drugs may be prescribed to relieve the symptoms and promote healing. These include anticholinergics which act by delaying the emptying of the stomach. This is particularly helpful at bedtime, since the presence of food in the stomach cushions the stomach against excess acidity. Anti-spasmodics are prescribed to relax the muscles of the digestive tract, and sedatives may also be given to relieve tension and stress if these are considered to be significant contributing factors.

An important new drug for ulcer patients is called cimetidine (Tagamet). This product works by actually suppressing the production of excess stomach acid. Cimetidine is not in itself a cure for ulcers, but it produces rapid and sustained relief of ulcer pain and promotes healing.

There is also a new drug called sucralfate (Carafate). Unlike cimetidine, sucralfate is not absorbed into the bloodstream in any significant amount and thus poses less of a risk of side effects. The ingredients of sucralfate work by forming a chemical barrier over the raw exposed ulcer. In short, the drug acts as a "bandage" which protects the ulcer from the surrounding stomach acid. This seems to promote the healing of the ulcer.

Despite the best drug therapy, however, surgery may be necessary if an ulcer recurs repeatedly or if a life-threatening complication (such as perforation) develops. A portion of the stomach may be removed and parts of the vagus nerve (which controls secretion of digestive juices) may be cut in order to reduce the production of stomach acid. After surgery most ulcers do not reappear. Despite this success rate, surgery should not be a hasty decision, since the operation itself is a risk and may cause chronic complications.

The recovery rate for ulcer patients is extremely favorable, if assistance is sought at the onset of symptoms and if the recommended treatment is followed carefully. Most ulcers will heal in two to six weeks after treatment begins. However, even after an ulcer has healed, cigarettes, caffeine, alcohol, and other substances that are known to stimulate the production of stomach acid or to irritate the lining of the digestive tract should be avoided.

PERIODONTAL DISEASE

Periodontal disease is a progressive inflammation of tissue around the teeth. Left unchecked and untreated, the inflammation advances as food particles and bacteria lodge on the sides, between, and at the base of the teeth, causing the gums to recede, or pull back, from the tooth surface. Pockets formed in the tissue around the teeth harbor bacteria and pus and allow for more debris to accumulate.

As the gum disease progresses, the fibers holding the teeth in their sockets weaken, and gradually the bone supporting the teeth is destroyed. The teeth become loose and fall out or move out of alignment with one another, causing difficulty in eating.

Like tooth decay (dental caries), periodontal disease is caused by the accumulation of bacteria (although of a different type from that which causes tooth decay) on and around the teeth. These bacteria give off toxins (poisons) that cause gum tissue to swell, bleed, and recede. The bacteria also produce a plaque or film that covers them—in a sense, that seals them in against the teeth — which allows them to continue to cause damage. Sealed in, these bacteria create pockets in the gum tissue which finally lead to the destruction of the bone that supports the teeth.

SYMPTOMS

Although in the early stages the symptoms of periodontal disease may not seem very important, they are really the beginning of gum deterioration and require prompt treatment.

The first stage is gingivitis, in-

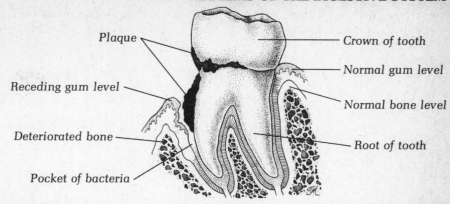

Plaque

Receding gum level

Deteriorated bone

Pocket of bacteria

Crown of tooth

Normal gum level

Normal bone level

Root of tooth

Periodontal disease is a progressive deterioration of the gums and bone around the teeth. It is caused by an accumulation of bacteria on the teeth, and if untreated this disease can lead to pockets of bacteria and pus around the teeth, receding gums, and eventual destruction of the bone supporting the teeth.

flammation of the gums. The gums become tender, slightly swollen, and red. They may bleed when the teeth are brushed or flossed. If pus develops in the gums around the teeth, the condition has entered a second stage called pyorrhea (pus flowing). If the pus is harbored in the gum tissue and does not drain off, there will be acute pain and swelling.

A visit to the dentist for a cleaning or checkup will confirm the beginning of periodontal disease from the initial gum swelling and deposits of bacteria and plaque around the teeth. If the condition is diagnosed early, continual home care may be able to reverse the deterioration process.

TREATMENT

Just as in tooth decay, it has been proven that proper mouth care can prevent periodontal disease and reduce gum problems. The patient should learn correct methods in toothbrushing. Use a soft-bristled brush gently in the crevices between the gum and teeth to dislodge material in this area and firmly on the tooth surface to remove plaque. Flossing is equally important to clean away plaque from the sides and from between teeth. Vigorous rinsing, after brushing and flossing, with a mouthwash containing antimicrobials (substances that kill bacteria) can also aid in eliminating

other bacteria-forming materials. (However, mouthwashes do not in themselves prevent plaque or tooth decay.)

A dental mirror can be used for self-checking, especially the teeth and gums in the back of the mouth. Disclosing wafers, which, when chewed, stick to and color plaque deposits, can be used to detect this invisible film.

Ideally, the mouth should be cleaned immediately after every meal or snack. But since that is not practical for everyone, even a single thorough cleansing at night before bed can help minimize gum disease.

For the far advanced cases of gum disease, a periodontist—gum specialist — is necessary and surgery may be the only way to eliminate deep gum pockets. Once this procedure is done, a patient may be able to keep the disease under control with the usual home care methods.

Before a dentist will take that step, however, alternatives to surgery may be tried, such as deep scaling of the affected areas at frequent intervals. The dentist may use this nonsurgical treatment to scrape the tissue pockets every few months and then to clean them with antiseptics (germ-killers). Although surgery is more likely to provide a long-term solution, scaling, along with a vigorous home care program, may control the infection process and arrest the disease.

HORMONAL DISORDERS

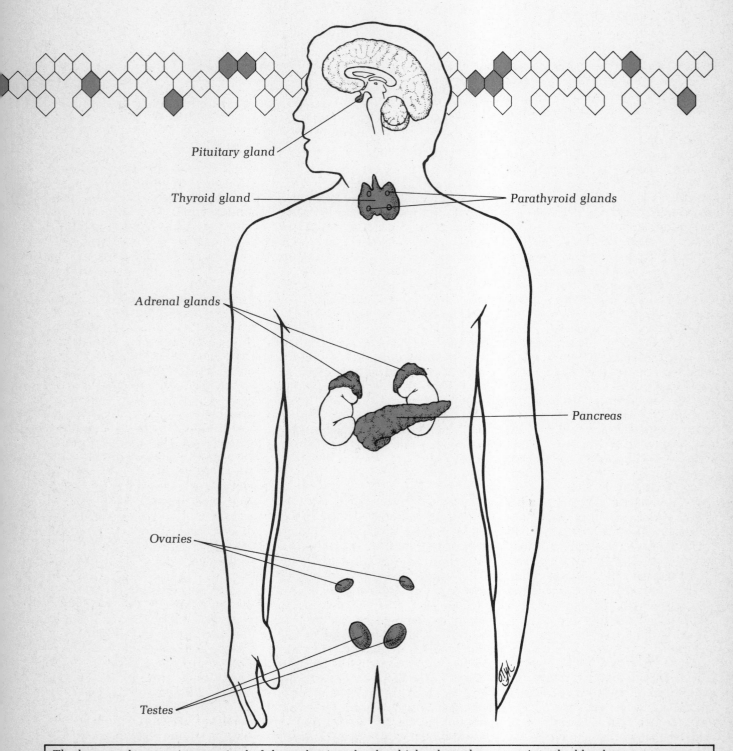

Pituitary gland

Thyroid gland

Parathyroid glands

Adrenal glands

Pancreas

Ovaries

Testes

The hormonal system is comprised of the endocrine glands which release hormones into the bloodstream.

Hormones are chemical messengers secreted by the endocrine glands into the bloodstream. The blood carries the hormones to various parts of the body where they direct cell activity. Generally, hormones have three major functions. They regulate the activities of differing groups of cells so that the groups act together in a coordinated way. For example, some hormones help certain cell groups process food so that other cell groups can be nourished. Hormones also control the type and rate of growth throughout the body. And they help the body maintain its internal environment.

The endocrine glands send their hormones directly into the bloodstream. In contrast, other glands called exocrine glands — for example, sweat glands — deposit their secretions into tubes or ducts rather than directly into the bloodstream. Thus, the endocrine glands are called ductless glands.

The endocrine glands include the pituitary, the thyroid, the parathyroids, the pancreatic islet cells, the adrenals, and the sex glands—the testes in the male and the ovaries in the female.

Pituitary gland. The pituitary gland lies at the base of the brain. It is often called the master gland because it oversees the activity of the other endocrine glands. Some of the hormones the pituitary sends out directly regulate the other endocrine glands. It secretes these hormones in response to a signal from the brain or from another gland. For example, if another endocrine gland is not secreting sufficient hormone, the pituitary automatically stimulates the other gland to produce more of its own hormone.

The pituitary gland also sends out other kinds of hormones. For instance, it secretes growth hormone which helps to control the growth and development of all parts of the body. It also releases hormones that govern the transition of a child into a sexually mature adult and that control other functions of the reproductive system.

Thyroid gland. The thyroid gland is located in front of the throat just above the breastbone. The thyroid consists of two main sections, one on each side of the trachea (windpipe). The two sections are connected at the midline by a thin piece of tissue that extends over the trachea. This gland produces thyroid hormone which regulates the body's temperature, its energy production, growth, and fertility.

Parathyroid glands. The four small parathyroid glands are located just behind the thyroid gland. They secrete parathyroid hormone that controls calcium levels in the blood.

Pancreatic islet cells. The islet cells in the pancreas — called islets of Langerhans — produce the hormones insulin and glucagon. Insulin's function is to reduce the amount of sugar in the blood by helping the body cells absorb the sugar. Glucagon, on the other hand, stimulates the liver to release its stored sugar into the blood, thus raising the blood sugar level. With insulin and glucagon working together properly, an individual's blood sugar level can remain normal and stable throughout life.

Part of the pancreas also functions as an exocrine gland. A second type of cell in this gland produces a secretion that flows through the pancreatic duct into the small intestine to aid digestion.

Adrenal glands. There are two adrenal glands, one lying atop each kidney. The adrenal glands secrete steroid hormones that help produce energy from food and regulate the body's loss of water. In addition, the adrenal glands secrete the hormone adrenaline during stressful situations. Adrenaline increases the heart rate and the blood pressure, thus preparing the body to cope with stress. (This is often called the "fight or flight" reaction.) A small amount of the male hormone, androgen, is also produced by the adrenal glands in both men and women.

Testes. The testes, or male sex glands, are oval-shaped glands in the scrotum, the external pouch of skin lying behind the penis. The testes produce sperm and male sex hormones. The sex hormones are responsible for the secondary male sex characteristics such as development of the penis, body hair, beard growth, voice changes, and increased muscle mass.

Ovaries. The ovaries are two small glands located in the abdomen of the female. Two hormones, estrogen and progesterone, are secreted by the ovaries. These hormones are important in the reproductive process. Estrogen also controls secondary female sex characteristics including breast development, body hair growth, ovulation (monthly release of egg from the ovary), and menstruation. In addition to its function during reproduction, progesterone is responsible for enlargement of the breasts during pregnancy and for development of the breast's milk-producing cells after childbirth. Both estrogen and progesterone work together to control the menstrual cycle, and changes in the level of either hormone may lead to irregularities in menstruation.

The endocrine system affects every action and reaction of our bodies. It governs our physical health, as well as many aspects of our behavior. In turn, our behavior and health influence the functioning of the endocrine glands. The result is an intricate relationship vital to our well-being.

DIABETES

Diabetes mellitus, or sugar diabetes, is a disease in which the body does not properly use carbohydrates (sugars and starches), the body's chief sources of energy. During digestion, carbohydrates release a form of sugar called glucose into the blood. Normally, the increased glucose in the blood stimulates the pancreas to secrete the hormone insulin. Insulin helps transport the glucose from the blood to the body cells for fuel

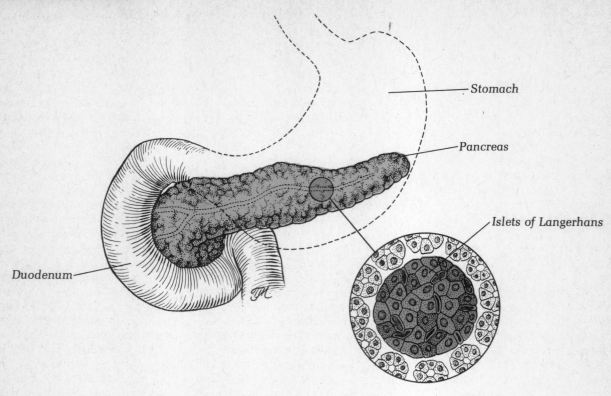

Stomach

Pancreas

Islets of Langerhans

Duodenum

The islets of Langerhans in the pancreas produce the hormone insulin which helps reduce the amount of sugar in the blood by helping the body cells absorb sugar. One type of diabetes may be the result of a defect in the islets of Langerhans, causing decreased insulin production.

or to the liver for storage until it is needed for fuel.

In a diabetic, however, either the pancreas does not manufacture sufficient insulin or the body is unable to use what insulin is produced. As a result, a high sugar concentration builds up in the blood because glucose continues to circulate without being used. Eventually, the excess blood sugar is filtered from the blood by the kidneys and eliminated in the urine.

Diabetes and the diseases that it may contribute to are the third highest cause of death in the United States. Untreated diabetes can lead to such high levels of blood sugar that unconsciousness and even death may result. However, the most common risk of uncontrolled diabetes is the strain it puts on other organs. Diabetes contributes to atherosclerosis, the hardening and consequent narrowing of the arteries that supply blood to the body. Atherosclerosis, in turn, can lead to an in-

creased chance of heart attack, stroke, kidney disease, impotence, eye disorders, and blindness. Diabetics may also be subject to gangrene — the death of tissue caused by insufficient blood circulation. This is why diabetics are urged to take special care of their feet, one of the most common sites for impaired circulation.

There are two major types of diabetes. Type I, or insulin-dependent, diabetes requires treatment with injections of insulin. It is often the result of a defect in that part of the pancreas that produces insulin. This form of the disease may develop as early as childhood, and scientists still are not sure what causes insulin-dependent diabetes. Therefore, they do not know why certain people develop the disease.

Type II, insulin-independent, diabetes normally strikes adults, primarily after the age of 40. This type of diabetes does not usually require insulin injections, because Type II diabetics may produce

sufficient insulin. However, their bodies are unable to use the insulin efficiently. This may stem from a shortage of insulin-receptor cells — the sites throughout the body where the interaction of sugar and insulin takes place. Thus, the insulin is floating in the bloodstream, unable to do its work. Obesity is often a contributing factor because as the fat cells become larger, the number of insulin receptor cells decreases.

Another possible reason for Type II diabetes is a slow-down in the production of insulin by the pancreas. In addition, other disorders in the endocrine system, especially in the adrenal or thyroid glands, may cause a hormonal imbalance that interferes with the insulin-sugar reaction.

Type II diabetes is closely linked to heredity — there is a definite tendency for members of the same family to be afflicted with the disease. Obesity is also a great risk factor, since excess fat causes a decrease in insulin-receptor cells. Type II diabetes is more likely to affect women than men, and the chances of developing it double with every decade you live past 40.

Pregnancy is often considered a risk factor in diabetes. In fact, some women develop diabetes during pregnancy and return to normal after childbirth. However, women who show symptoms of diabetes during pregnancy and who have babies weighing over ten pounds may run a greater risk of developing diabetes in the future.

SYMPTOMS

The classic symptoms of Type I, insulin-dependent, diabetes are excessive thirst and urination, irritability, fatigue, slow-healing cuts and bruises, a change in vision, and occasionally fainting. There may be weight loss despite intense hunger and overeating.

Type II, insulin-independent, diabetes may display the same symptoms as Type I. However, Type II diabetics often show no symptoms at all. Many of these people are unaware that they have the disease or only learn that their blood sugar is high after a routine physical or an exam for another medical problem.

A diagnosis of diabetes is made after testing the blood and urine for high sugar content. The blood may also be tested for insulin levels, and the urine tested for ketones. Ketones are the end products of breaking down fat for energy. Because the diabetic's body cannot use sugar, it burns fat for fuel and the end products of this energy production are eliminated in the urine.

TREATMENT

Treatment of both forms of diabetes centers on maintaining normal, steady blood glucose levels. This is usually accomplished by insulin injections and/or diet, and is monitored by blood and urine testing.

Insulin treatment for Type I diabetics aims to improve sugar utilization during the course of the entire day without causing blood sugar levels to dip or soar widely. If the blood sugar level rises, the standard symptoms of diabetes (increased thirst and urination, weakness, fatigue) will result. The treatment prescribed for this is to increase the insulin dosage. On the other hand, if the blood sugar level drops too low, insulin reaction sets in with symptoms of dizziness, fatigue, faintness, hunger, headache, sweating, and trembling. An insulin reaction can be countered rapidly by eating simple sugar, such as a candy bar. To prevent these fluctuations in blood sugar levels, the type of insulin and the timing of injections are coordinated with the timing and content of meals. Unusual or extra exercise on a given day can also affect insulin requirements. Most Type I diabetics can control their blood sugar level with a single daily injection of the appropriate insulin before breakfast.

Insulin injections are not the usual treatment for Type II, insulin-independent, diabetics — although some may need to take insulin at times. Type II diabetes often can be managed by proper diet. Certain Type II patients may also be treated with oral anti-diabetic drugs which act to stimulate the pancreas' production of insulin. However, research studies have indicated that prolonged use of these drugs may contribute to the development of heart problems. Furthermore, there is evidence that these drugs are not any more effective in diabetes control than diet alone.

Both Type I and Type II diabetics monitor their blood sugar levels by periodically testing their blood and urine. For the Type I diabetic, these tests help to determine the proper insulin dosage. For the Type II diabetic, the tests are useful in planning the proper diet. There are commercial blood glucose and urine tests available which are simple to use at home.

Proper diet is crucial in the treatment of diabetes. Persons with Type II, insulin-independent, diabetes can frequently control their diabetes with diet alone. Overweight individuals will probably be required to lose weight. After weight loss is achieved, balanced meals that maintain the proper weight will be stressed. It is recommended that the diet be low in fats (to reduce the chances of developing atherosclerosis) and limited in simple sugars. Fibrous roughage is also recommended because it is not only filling and low-calorie, but also reduces or slows the absorption of sugar in the digestive tract.

Type I, insulin-dependent, diabetics are not usually overweight and should not decrease their calorie intake. Young diabetics need sufficient calories to maintain their weight and to allow for normal growth and development. Type I diabetics must also plan their meals so that their daily food intake balances their daily insulin injections.

Diabetic diets, whether tailored to Type I or to Type II diabetes, need not be complicated or rigid. In most cases, a diabetic can adapt the regular family meals to meet the proper dietary needs. There are various medically approved diet plans and food exchange lists which can help in planning the appropriate diet.

By carefully controlling the blood sugar level, either by diet or with medication, a person with diabetes can lead a normal life.

HYPOGLYCEMIA

Hypoglycemia is an abnormally low level of sugar (glucose) in the blood. Anyone who has not eaten for quite a while may experience the symptoms of low blood sugar. True chronic hypoglycemia, however, is not especially common.

There are two types of hypoglycemia. The most common form is reactive hypoglycemia. In this condition, the blood sugar level drops sharply several hours after a large portion of sugar or starches has been consumed. When sugar is eaten, the pancreas is normally stimulated to produce the hormone insulin which enables the body to use the sugar. However, in reactive hypoglycemia the pancreas continues to produce insulin long after the need has passed. The result is abnormally low blood sugar levels.

Reactive hypoglycemia may result from an insulin overdose or a faulty insulin response in diabetics. Sometimes reactive hypoglycemia occurs after surgical removal of part of the stomach. This surgery may cause a more rapid than normal absorption of sugar with a corresponding outpouring of insulin. Most often, however, the cause is unknown; therefore, those persons likely to be afflicted cannot be determined.

The other type of hypoglycemia, fasting hypoglycemia, may have several causes. Fasting hypoglycemia can occur during pregnancy, strenuous exercise, and infections accompanied by fever. All of these situations increase the body's need for sugar; if sugar intake is not increased, temporary hypoglycemia may result. Fasting hypoglycemia may also result if an insulin-secreting tumor is present on the pancreas. And disorders of the liver, which stores and releases sugar as needed, may lead to fasting hypoglycemia. This is especially common in heavy drinkers, since alcohol upsets the sugar-release response in the liver. Consequently, alcoholics are at a greater risk of developing fasting hypoglycemia.

SYMPTOMS

The symptoms of hypoglycemia are sweating, hunger pangs, faintness, fatigue, headache, nervousness, vision impairment, and rapid heartbeat. Anxiety, difficulty in concentrating, confusion, and blackout spells may also result. In its most severe form hypoglycemia can produce convulsions and eventually deep coma as the nervous system is deprived of the sugar it needs to function normally.

To determine a diagnosis of

hypoglycemia, your doctor will perform a blood sugar analysis, preferably during an attack of the disease when symptoms are at their peak. A glucose tolerance test may also be administered in which blood samples are taken every hour for four or five hours after a measured amount of sugar has been eaten. If during this period your blood sugar falls below a certain level or shows a rapid drop in a short time, a diagnosis of hypoglycemia is reasonable.

TREATMENT

Treatment of hypoglycemia depends on the underlying reason for the disease. For instance, diabetics with reactive hypoglycemia will need to adjust their insulin dosages until the proper balance of sugar and insulin is achieved. Or a pancreatic tumor causing fasting hypoglycemia may require surgical removal.

However, reactive hypoglycemia without a discernible cause is the most common form of the disease, and there is no known way to correct the pancreas' tendency to go on producing insulin long after it is needed. Therefore, the treatment for this form of reactive hypoglycemia involves avoiding the foods that bring on the attacks. The best diet for this type of hypoglycemia is one low in sugar and starches — to eliminate the body's overreaction to sugar intake — and high in protein which causes only a gradual elevation in blood sugar. Foods with a high fiber content such as whole-grain breads and fruits and vegetables are also helpful because they have been shown to slow the absorption of sugar as it passes through the digestive tract. Smaller meals eaten more frequently are also helpful in keeping blood sugar levels stable.

THYROID DISORDERS

The thyroid gland is a small, butterfly-shaped gland located in

the front of the throat just above the breastbone. The thyroid gland affects every organ and tissue in the body because it secretes hormones that help to maintain proper body temperature, convert food to energy, regulate growth, and influence fertility. The amount of thyroid hormone produced is regulated by the pituitary gland. In addition, the mineral iodine is necessary for the production of thyroid hormone.

The thyroid gland is subject to various disorders. An overactive thyroid, which produces too much hormone, leads to *hyperthyroidism* ("hyper" meaning higher than normal). An underactive thyroid, producing too little hormone, leads to *hypothyroidism* ("hypo" meaning lower than normal).

Although thyroid imbalances are not usually life-threatening, untreated thyroid disorders can develop serious complications. Untreated *hypothyroidism* in infants may lead to *cretinism* in which both physical and mental growth are severely retarded. *Hyper*thyroidism in adults may cause an overactive heart and protruding eyes which, if serious enough, can impair vision.

Heredity may play a role in the development of thyroid imbalances. In addition, women are more likely to develop thyroid disorders than men. However, in many instances, it is not known why certain people develop thyroid disorders.

Proper diagnosis of thyroid disorders is very important. One reason is that symptoms of the milder forms of thyroid diseases may be attributed to sources other than the thyroid. On the other hand, weight changes and vague feelings of tiredness or nervousness are often ascribed to a thyroid condition when they may actually be due to an entirely unrelated emotional or physical problem. Also, an incorrect diagnosis of thyroid imbalance may actually cause a thyroid imbalance. If a thyroid supplement is prescribed when there is, in fact, no thyroid problem, the supplement may lead to excessive levels of hormone in the blood or may cause the normal thyroid gland to underproduce hormone in an effort to compensate.

Therefore, in order to make an accurate diagnosis, your doctor may run a number of tests. The amount of thyroid hormone circulating in the blood can be measured accurately with blood tests. If blood tests indicate that the thyroid is not functioning properly, the doctor may recommend a radioactive iodine tracer test. Since any iodine — the mineral necessary for the production of thyroid hormone — introduced into the body eventually goes to the thyroid, the doctor will be able to "trace" the action of the iodine in the thyroid gland. An overactive gland will take up more of the substance, while an underactive one will absorb less.

Modern diagnostic procedures can accurately pinpoint thyroid abnormalities, and treatment is usually quite effective. However, persons diagnosed as having a thyroid disorder should remember that continual, lifelong follow-up may be required.

Hyperthyroidism

Hyperthyroidism results from an overactive thyroid gland which produces too much hormone. The disorder may be due to a breakdown in the control mechanisms of the thyroid, especially faulty pituitary regulation of the thyroid. The onset of hyperthyroidism may be linked to extreme stress or emotional upheaval.

SYMPTOMS

The classic symptoms of hyperthyroidism are nervousness, weight loss despite a ravenous appetite, extreme sensitivity to heat, bulging eyes, rapid heartbeat, insomnia, sweating palms, and occasionally decreased fertility and high blood pressure. The hyperactive thyroid is often enlarged and may have lumps, or nodules, growing on it. These nodules act independently of the gland itself and may produce excessive amounts of hormone.

TREATMENT

Hyperthyroidism is treated by stopping the excessive secretion of thyroid hormone. This is accomplished either through drugs, radioactive iodine, or surgery. Anti-thyroid drugs block the manufacture of the hormone within the thyroid. These drugs are usually taken for one to two years. However, if the gland again becomes overactive, drug therapy is reinstated or treatment by one of the other methods will probably be necessary.

Radioactive material combined with iodine will travel to the thyroid and work directly on the gland by suppressing its activity — sometimes permanently. Although there is no conclusive evidence of increased risk from the radioactive iodine, this treatment is not recommended for persons under the age of 40 or for pregnant women.

Surgery to remove part of the thyroid is performed when other methods of treatment are ineffective or inappropriate. Although the surgery itself is not extremely risky, a specialist is often consulted because the thyroid's location is near important nerves and other glands.

Hypothyroidism

Hypothyroidism results when the thyroid gland is underactive and does not produce enough hormone. The disease may stem from a chronic thyroid infection, from a deficiency of pituitary hormone, or from an unknown cause. Hypothyroidism can also be the end result of the suppression or partial removal of the thyroid gland as treatment for hyperthyroidism.

Hypothyroidism is sometimes overlooked and untreated because its symptoms are nonspecific, that is, the same symptoms can be caused by other health problems.

SYMPTOMS

A person with hypothyroidism may be overweight, easily tired, and subject to repeated infections. Menstrual disorders, extreme sensitivity to cold, dry hair and skin, puffiness of hands and face, and memory disturbances are also common.

A long-standing case of hypothyroidism may be revealed in a general slow-down of the other functions of the body. Anemia, a deficiency of red blood cells, may be present because the bone marrow produces red blood cells more slowly than normal; the heart rate will perhaps be decreased; brain waves, as recorded on a special measuring device, may be irregular; and reflexes will be slow.

TREATMENT

Hypothyroidism is treated with thyroid hormone supplements. In other words, the thyroid hormone not manufactured by the body is replaced by either synthetic hormone or natural hormone extracted from the glands of animals. Both are highly effective, although the natural form is usually less expensive. Treatment often continues throughout life.

URINARY TRACT CONDITIONS

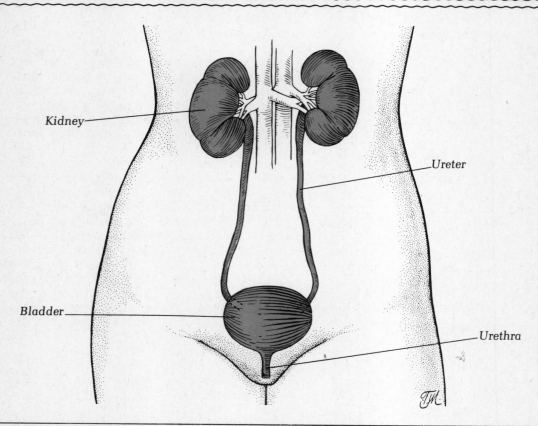

The urinary system includes the kidneys, the ureters, the bladder, and the urethra.

The urinary system consists of the kidneys, the ureters, the bladder, and the urethra. The function of the urinary system is to produce and eliminate urine — a combination of water and waste products that passes out of the body as a fluid. In performing this job, the urinary system also helps to maintain the proper water balance in the body as well as the proper concentration of salts and other nutrients necessary for health.

Kidneys. The kidneys are two bean-shaped organs that lie in the back of the upper abdomen, just above the waist. All the blood in the body goes through the kidneys to have the wastes filtered out. In addition, while the kidneys are combining waste products with water to form urine, they are also reabsorbing and returning important nutrients to the blood. This reabsorption process insures that the body does not become depleted of necessary substances.

Ureters. The ureters are tubes that carry urine from the kidneys to the bladder. There is one ureter leading from each kidney.

Bladder. The bladder serves as a storage depot for urine before it is eliminated from the body. A muscle around the outlet of the bladder prevents the urine from escaping. When the bladder is about half full of urine, there is an urge to empty it. At this point the muscle can be relaxed to release the urine from the body.

Urethra. The urethra is the tube that transports urine from the bladder to the outside of the body. The male urethra is approximately nine inches long; the female urethra is about one and one-half inches in length. The male urethra passes through the penis and has the dual function of transporting urine and semen (the fluid, including sperm, from the male reproductive organs).

ACUTE KIDNEY FAILURE

The kidneys have three main functions: they remove waste materials from the blood and concentrate them into urine; they reabsorb and return to the body valuable nutrients; and they help maintain the body's water balance. Acute kidney (renal) failure is dangerous because the kidneys suddenly quit regulating the chemical balance of various substances in the body and allow poisons and excess fluid to collect instead.

If not treated immediately, a person with acute kidney failure may die within two weeks. Death results from the accumulation in the blood of toxic substances normally filtered out by the kidneys. This rapid buildup of poisons in the body can initially lead to confusion, disorientation, delirium, and eventually result in coma and death.

Kidney failure may be due to a variety of causes: kidney stones or any blockage of the urinary tract; the ingestion of various chemicals or drugs; injury or burns; infectious diseases; shock following surgery; heart attacks; transfusion with incompatible blood; severe water depletion; pregnancy complications; or congenital (existing at birth) defects in the kidneys.

Although anyone may experience these causes that lead to kidney failure, persons with high blood pressure have an increased risk of renal failure. In addition, kidney failure may be a complication of cirrhosis of the liver, a disease often caused by drinking too much alcohol.

SYMPTOMS

A major symptom of acute kidney failure is a sudden reduction in urine output. Urine flow may be decreased to as little as two tablespoons a day. Any changes in the color of urine — if it appears bloody, wine-colored, cloudy, or full of pus — may be a sign of kidney disease and should be reported immediately to a doctor.

Loss of kidney function may also lead to fatigue, drowsiness, loss of appetite, diarrhea, nausea, breathing disturbances, and dry skin. Disease in the kidneys may also cause pain in the lower back and puffiness around the eyes or a swelling of the hands and feet. This swelling — or edema — results from fluid accumulation in the tissues because of decreased urine production.

Blood and urine tests can reveal a problem developing in the kidneys. If these organs are damaged, they may allow needed substances to slip through the otherwise efficient filtering system and be lost to the body. This will be apparent if such substances as red or white blood cells, sugar, or proteins are found in the urine. Also, the kidney may not be filtering from the blood the waste materials it should be disposing of, and a blood analysis will indicate that these waste products remain in the blood.

X rays or an ultrasound scan of the kidneys can also determine if there is a structural problem or a blockage. Ultrasound is a diagnostic technique using high-frequency sound waves to create an image of the internal structures.

Additional tests will be given to a patient with high blood pressure to determine the individual's heart and kidney status. If high blood pressure is a factor, effective treatment is available to reduce the risk of kidney failure, heart disease, and strokes.

TREATMENT

Immediate identification and treatment of acute kidney failure will often restore the function of the kidneys to normal. Proper therapy for kidney stones, for example, may eliminate the conditions contributing to kidney failure.

While the kidneys are returning to normal, bed rest is essential. Also, fluids should be restricted unless there is an unusual fluid loss from vomiting or diarrhea. A low protein diet is often recommended, since processing protein can place a strain on the recovering kidneys.

If these measures are ineffective, many patients can be helped by dialysis — a process in which the blood is filtered and cleansed daily by an artificial kidney machine to remove toxic materials. This machine was developed in the Netherlands in the early 1940s and has helped many people who suffer from either temporary or chronic kidney failure. Most dialysis patients must go to the hospital several times a week to receive treatment. Recently, however, a new, portable technique has been developed as an alternative to hospital dialysis. This portable system keeps pace with the body's functions and requires no machinery, thus allowing dialysis patients to lead relatively normal lives.

Even at its best, however, dialysis is a stopgap measure that can prolong life but cannot overcome the underlying kidney disease. Only kidney transplant can "cure" end-stage kidney disease by replacing the diseased kidney with a healthy one. More than 10,000 Americans live with the aid of someone else's kidney, and thousands more are waiting for a suitable organ to be available. Recently, there have been many improvements in the methods for matching donor to recipient as well as in techniques for preventing transplant rejection. For these reasons, kidney transplantation is now regarded as a highly successful procedure in the fight against kidney disease.

KIDNEY STONES

Kidney stones are deposits of mineral or organic substances formed in the kidney. They may vary in size from tiny pebbles to walnut-like formations. Usually several stones form at the same time.

Although they are a fairly common problem, kidney stones may cause complications. Even if they are too small to be noticed, kidney stones may move about in the kidney and their mobility can damage delicate tissues. If they pass out of the kidney into the ureter—the tube that carries urine from the kidney to the bladder—they may cause internal scars as they move toward the bladder. Small stones will usually pass through and be eliminated in the urine; however, larger ones may become lodged in the ureter. If a kidney stone blocks a ureter, urine may back up, distending and injuring the urinary tract (including the kidneys) above the blockage. This is a medical emergency requiring immediate treatment.

Kidney stones usually develop when certain substances in the urine — for example, the mineral calcium — condense into hardened masses in the kidney. This may happen if there is an abnormally high level of these minerals in the urine. Drinking large quantities of milk may cause high calcium levels in the urine. Excessive amounts of Vitamin D, which helps the body absorb calcium, can also be a contributing factor. And a fractured bone may give off extra calcium which can condense into stones in the kidney.

Other disorders may also help to start this process. Overactive parathyroids, the endocrine glands that regulate calcium absorption, allow excessive amounts of that mineral to be absorbed by the body. Gout, a disease affecting the joints, can also lead to kidney stones. Gout is caused by high blood levels of uric acid—a waste product from the breakdown of protein — which can crystallize into stones in the urine. A urinary infection that prevents the blad-

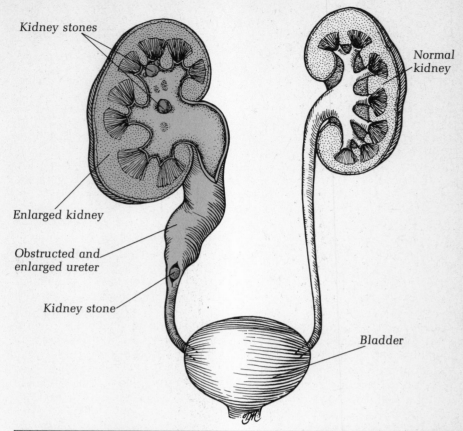

Kidney stones may remain in the kidney or may obstruct an ureter, causing swelling and injury above the blockage.

der from being completely emptied leaves urine with a higher concentration of minerals and substances which can solidify into stones.

Kidney stones occur more frequently in middle-aged men and in those persons with gout or chronic urinary tract infections. However, in many cases, no one knows why some individuals form kidney stones while others do not.

SYMPTOMS

Kidney stones may remain silent for years and in fact may never cause symptoms or lead to any trouble. Some stones, however, display symptoms when they start to pass out of the kidneys, causing severe pain and tenderness above the kidney area, frequent and painful urination, nausea, blood in the urine, fever, chills, and complete exhaustion. A serious situation develops

when a stone enters and blocks a ureter producing excruciating pain across the back, abdomen, and genitalia — the external reproductive organs. If a stone blocks the urethra, urine output will decrease. The patient must be treated at once to prevent loss of consciousness, shock, and possible kidney damage.

Because of the many ways kidney stones may form and their potential for trouble, a physician will perform special blood and urine studies to determine the nature of the stones. In addition, X rays or an ultrasound scan and a physical examination will reveal the condition of the kidneys and urinary tract.

TREATMENT

People with a tendency to form kidney stones require a large daily intake of water — about three or four quarts—to dilute their urine, since stones develop more readily when urine is highly concentrated. Sometimes it is even necessary to drink an additional glass of water during the night to make sure the urine does not become too concentrated. Extra water may also flush any small stones out of the system.

Diet may be helpful in managing less severe cases of kidney stones. Reducing consumption of foods high in the minerals that form stones can keep the condition from worsening. Such a diet can also prevent additional stones from forming. Since calcium compounds are the basis of most kidney stones, a diet low in milk products and Vitamin D foods is recommended. Those persons with gout should lower their protein intake, since uric acid is a by-product of protein digestion.

There are no drugs available that will dissolve kidney stones. However, a new method using tiny shock waves to disintegrate the stones, thus allowing them to be painlessly passed out, is currently being tested. There are also medications that inhibit the absorption of calcium from the blood. Painkillers may be prescribed if the discomfort caused by the passage of stones is too great.

Kidney stones too large to be passed may require surgical removal.

LOWER URINARY TRACT INFECTIONS

The lower urinary tract is subject to a number of problems — ranging from annoying to potentially dangerous. Sometimes the condition is a simple irritation, while at other times the ailment is a true bacteria-caused infection.

Cystitis is probably the most common urinary tract infection (UTI) which affects the lower part of the urinary tract. The other common lower UTI is urethritis. Cystitis is an infection of the bladder, while urethritis is an infection of the urethra, the passageway through which urine is carried away from the bladder to the outside of the body.

It often happens that a person develops cystitis after first having urethritis, since the bacteria usually enter the bladder by way of the urethra. On the other hand, a non-bacteria irritation of the urethra does not necessarily affect the bladder.

If untreated or if partially treated, cystitis may cause inflammation of the lining of the bladder and eventually scarring and impaired functioning of the muscular walls of the bladder. Long-standing chronic, or recurring, cystitis can also lead to a more serious infection, *cystitis cystica*, which is characterized by small, bacteria-filled cysts in the bladder lining. Symptoms of this condition are identical to those for simple cystitis, but the symptoms can disappear and recur periodically over months or years.

The greatest danger of untreated lower urinary tract infection, however, is the potential risk to the kidneys. Proper treatment is essential in order to prevent the infection from spreading to the kidneys and affecting their functioning.

Urinary tract infections occur when bacteria invade the urinary tract and the urine. Under ordinary circumstances, the urine is free from bacteria — or sterile — while it is in the body. This is because any bacteria at the outside opening of the urethra are prevented from entering the urinary tract by the constant outpouring of urine. However, if the flow of urine is obstructed, the bladder may not be completely emptied. The urine remaining in the bladder then becomes a breeding ground for bacteria which enter the urinary tract unimpeded by the downward flow of urine. The obstruction may be caused by a tumor, stones, or, in men, by an enlarged prostate — the reproductive gland which lies at the base of the bladder and surrounds the urethra.

Other factors can also lead to a bacterial invasion of the urinary tract. A defect in the protective lining of the urethra may make it easier for the bacteria to enter the tract. Injury to the tissues of the lower urinary tract—for example, after frequent sexual intercouse— and distortion or compression of the bladder by an enlarged neighboring organ (such as the uterus during pregnancy) may lead to a UTI. In men, urethritis may be a result of a sexually transmitted disease, such as gonorrhea, or an infection of the prostate gland, since the male urethra is shared by both the urinary and reproductive systems.

The bacteria responsible for UTIs most often comes from the large intestine or bowel. The intestine contains bacteria which are normally helpful or at least harmless while in the intestine. But if these bacteria travel from the anus—the outside opening of the intestine — to the urethra opening, they may cause an uncomfortable and possibly serious urinary infection.

Another source of infection can be bacteria from the vagina, the passageway in the female from the uterus to the outside of the body. Again, if bacteria travel from the vaginal opening to the urethra opening a UTI may develop. In the female the external openings of the urethra, the vagina, and the large intestine are close to each other which makes it easy for the bacteria to migrate from one to the other. This is one reason why lower urinary tract infections are nearly ten times more common in women than in men. Another reason is that the urethra is much shorter in women than in men (an inch and a half versus about nine inches respectively); thus the distance the infecting bacteria must travel in the female is less.

SYMPTOMS

Sometimes a urinary tract infection can be entirely without symptoms, but most often it is characterized by increased frequency of urination, increased urge to urinate, burning pain upon urination, cloudy, foul-

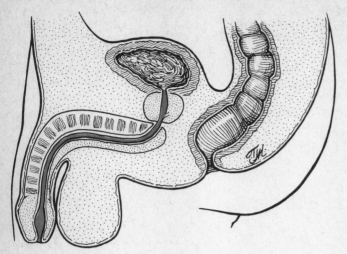

The male urethra is about nine inches long.

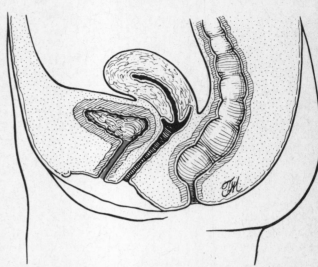

The female urethra is about an inch and a half long.

Lower urinary tract infections are nearly ten times more common in women than in men because the urethra is much shorter in women than in men. Therefore, the infecting bacteria have less distance to travel in women.

smelling or blood-tinged urine, lower back pain and/or pain in the lower abdomen, and a generally worn-out feeling. Examination of a urine sample under a microscope will usually reveal pus cells and bacteria. A culture of the urine will aid the physician in identifying the offending bacteria and in prescribing the appropriate medication.

TREATMENT

Anti-infectives, such as antibiotics or sulfa drugs, are used to treat urinary tract infections. In most cases, the physician will prescribe these drugs in a capsule or tablet form to be taken by mouth. In cases of severe kidney infection, hospitalization may be necessary and antibiotics will be administered intravenously (directly into the vein).

Medications that are used to treat urinary tract infection are excreted in the urine in high concentration. These drugs will destroy the offending bacteria in the urine and in all parts of the urinary system. The drugs should be taken according to instructions for the recommended period of time to eliminate the infection completely and to prevent reinfection. It is important to follow these instructions because individuals with a urinary tract infection are more likely to be reinfected by the same or another strain of bacteria if the course of drug therapy is not completed.

Thorough follow-up is a crucial part of the treatment. Urine samples should be analyzed after the course of drug therapy to check for bacteria. In the case of chronic infections, drug therapy may have to be continued intermittently for months or even years. If an obstruction such as a tumor or a stone is found to be the underlying cause of the infection, surgery may be suggested.

In addition, there are measures that help treat or even prevent a urinary tract infection. Drinking eight to ten glasses of water a day will promote urine flow through the kidneys and flush out bacteria in the urinary tract. Urinating frequently — completely emptying the bladder each time—will aid in preventing the bacteria from invading the urine left in the bladder. Showering rather than bathing is advisable since bacteria from bathwater can enter the urethra. Washing thoroughly after each bowel movement can prevent the spread of bacteria. Urinating immediately after intercourse is also advisable since this will flush out any bacteria introduced to the urethral opening at this time. (Some doctors will recommend abstaining from sexual intercourse during short-term treatment for a UTI, while others believe that sexual intercourse is permissible after the symptoms subside.)

In general, persons who are susceptible to UTIs are wise to avoid excessive coffee, tea, alcohol, and spicy foods, since these tend to irritate the urinary tract. Comfortable, absorbent underclothes that are not too tight are also recommended. And it cannot be repeated too often that careful hygiene is essential in preventing the spread of bacteria.

REPRODUCTIVE SYSTEM

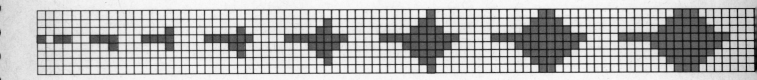

The reproductive system includes those organs whose function is the creation of new individuals. These organs include the sex glands (testes in males, ovaries in females) as well as other structures which assist the reproductive process and protect and nourish the new life.

Both the male and female produce a reproductive or sex cell that is different from any other cell in the body. In the male this cell is called the sperm cell; in the female it is called the ovum or egg cell. Each of these sex cells differs from other cells because it contains only half the components of a typical human cell. When the male sperm cell combines with the female egg cell, their two halves combine, and a new individual is created. This is called conception, and the result is an embryo — a new developing human being.

Although the individual's sex is determined at the time of conception, the male or female characteristics do not develop until after the embryo stage, about the end of the second month of pregnancy. During this stage the embryo has all the parts for either a male or female reproductive system. Thus, in the very beginning, the reproductive system for either sex is the same. Later each reproductive organ of one sex has a counterpart in the opposite sex. For example, in the embryo the sex glands are called gonads. As the embryo develops into a fetus (the name for an unborn child after the second month of pregnancy), the gonads differentiate into either testes in the male or ovaries in the female. In the mature adult, the testes and ovaries release, respectively, sperm cells and egg cells. And the process can begin again.

Despite their common beginning, the adult male and female reproductive systems are different in both appearance and in the way each functions. The male reproductive system has external parts, the penis and the scrotum (the pouch of skin which holds the testes). The female system is enclosed within the body. In the male, the reproductive and urinary systems are closely related— the urethra, for example, is used by both systems as an exit for sperm or urine (although not at the same time). In the female the reproductive and urinary systems are separate. The female reproductive system operates on a cycle, based on ovulation, the monthly release of an egg by the ovary. This monthly cycle also includes menstruation. The male system does not function in a cyclical fashion. Perhaps the greatest difference between male and female is the fact that the female's ability to reproduce ends with menopause when the ovaries stop producing an egg each month and menstruation ceases. The male's reproductive capacity does not end, though it may diminish. (It is important to remember that reproductive capacity is not the same as sexuality. Both men and women can maintain their sexuality — sexual ability and pleasure — with little or no reproductive ability.)

The reproductive system also has other functions besides reproduction. The ovaries and testes secrete hormones, chemical messengers that travel in the bloodstream to all parts of the body. These sex hormones affect physical development and behavior. Thus, the sex glands are important parts of both the reproductive system and the hormonal system.

Male Reproductive System

The male reproductive organs include the testes, a system of ducts, a set of glands, and the penis.

The testes. Besides secreting male sex hormones, the testes produce the sperm cells. The testes lie outside the body in the scrotum, a pouch of skin hanging behind the penis. There is a reason why the testes are not enclosed within the body; sperm production is slowed by the higher temperature within the body. From the testes the sperm cells move to the epididymis, the first structure in the duct system of the male reproductive system.

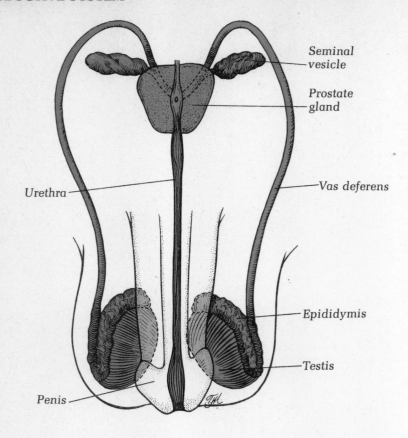

A front view of the male reproductive system.

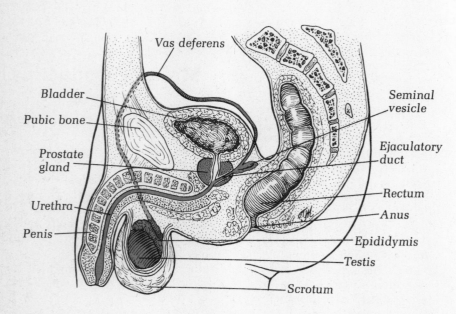

A side view of the male reproductive system.

The duct system. The duct system includes the epididymis, the vas deferens, the ejaculatory duct, and the urethra.

The epididymis lies along the top and side of each of the testes. It contains several ducts which conduct the sperm from the testes into the vas deferens, which is actually a continuation of the epididymis. The vas deferens loops up into the body and then descends to combine with a duct from the seminal vesicle gland to become the ejaculatory duct. The ejaculatory duct travels through the prostate gland and enters the upper segment of the urethra. The urethra is the duct from the bladder to the outside.

This duct system conveys the sperm from the testes to the outside of the body. Along the way, the sperm cells are joined by various fluids from the male glands.

The glands. The primary male glands are the seminal vesicles and the prostate gland. The seminal vesicles lie near the underside of the bladder, and they secrete a thick sticky fluid which is added to the sperm cells traveling from the testes. The prostate gland rests just below the bladder and surrounds the urethra as it emerges from the bladder. The prostate secretes a thin fluid which is also added to the sperm cells and seminal vesicle fluid as they travel through the ejaculatory duct to the urethra. The prostate fluid is thought to have a beneficial effect on the sperm, causing them to be more active.

The sperm cells have now combined with fluids from the glands to form semen. Semen is the substance that moves through the urethra and out of the penis during sexual excitement. This is called ejaculation.

The penis. The penis is the external organ by which sperm are transferred to the female. The penis contains large, internal spaces—called corpora cavernosa — which fill with blood during sexual excitement. When this occurs, the penis becomes rigid or erect and is therefore able to enter the female vagina.

Female Reproductive System

The female reproductive system includes the ovaries, fallopian tubes, uterus, cervix, and vagina. In addition, the breasts are often considered part of the reproductive system. Strictly speaking, the breasts — called mammary glands — are a kind of sweat gland. However, their development and functions are both related to and controlled by the reproductive system. For example, hormones secreted by the ovaries regulate the growth of the breasts at puberty (the time of life when the sex organs begin to mature) as well as the production of milk after childbirth.

Ovaries. The ovaries are small, firm, and roughly egg-shaped. Once a month, an ovary produces an egg (two or more eggs on rare occasions). Ovulation occurs when the egg matures and passes from the ovary into a fallopian tube. The ovaries also produce reproductive hormones.

Fallopian tubes. Above the ovaries are the openings of the fallopian tubes which extend to the uterus. Conception occurs in the fallopian tube, which helps direct the sperm to the egg and then propel the fertilized egg to the uterus.

Uterus. The uterus is a muscular, pear-shaped hollow organ, normally about the size of a lemon. The uterine walls stretch considerably as an unborn child develops within the uterus. In late pregnancy the uterus may be as large as a medium-sized watermelon.

The rich, soft lining of the uterus (the endometrium) is renewed each month; it sloughs off and leaves the body as menstrual discharge if conception does not occur. If a pregnancy does occur, the endometrium serves as a nourishing lining to receive the fertilized egg.

Cervix. The cervix is the narrow opening at the lower end of the uterus. It projects into the

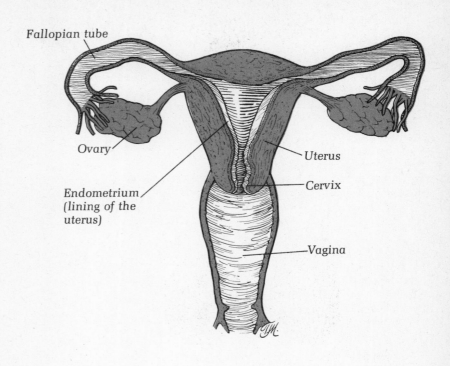

A front view of the female reproductive system.

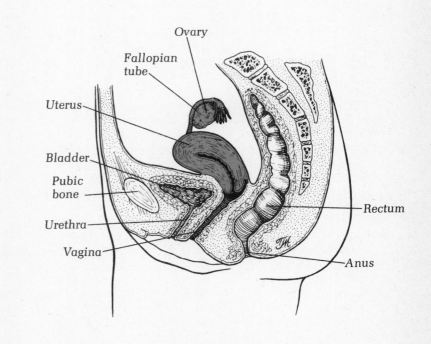

A side view of the female reproductive system.

upper end of the vagina. A tiny opening in the cervix leads to an inch-long canal connecting the vagina and uterus. This canal is the passageway for sperm on their way to fertilize an egg, and for menstrual discharge and babies leaving the uterus.

Vagina. The vagina or birth canal is the muscular passage leading from the uterus to the outside of the body. It measures four to five inches in length. Normally the vaginal walls lie close together; however, during sexual intercourse they separate to accommodate the erect male penis. During childbirth they stretch greatly to allow the baby to emerge.

The vagina has few nerve endings, and most of these nerve endings are located near the opening to the outside of the body. Within the vagina, little can be felt but pressure.

The vagina is naturally moist although the quantity and quality of the vaginal secretions vary with the menstrual cycle and emotional state. This natural, continuous lubrication is a self-cleansing process that makes vaginal douching normally unnecessary.

ENDOMETRIOSIS

Endometriosis is a condition in which fragments of tissue from the lining of the uterus grow outside the uterus. Endometrial tissue, also called the endometrium, normally lines the uterus, growing and thickening in the course of each monthly menstrual cycle to prepare the uterus for possible pregnancy. If no pregnancy occurs, the endometrium then breaks down and flows out of the body during menstruation. These changes are governed by the female hormones secreted by the ovaries.

In a woman with endometriosis, the displaced endometrium may grow on the ovaries, the outside of the uterus, the bowel, or anyplace else in the abdomen. This tissue behaves in much the same way as

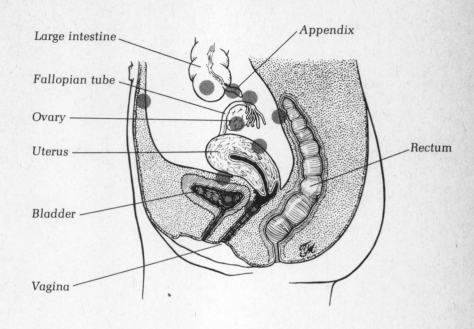

Endometriosis patches—displaced tissue from the lining of the uterus—may grow anywhere in the abdominal cavity. This illustration shows some of the common sites of endometriosis in the abdominal cavity.

the tissue lining the uterus; it swells and bleeds every month in response to the hormones from the ovaries. However, when it breaks down at the end of the menstrual cycle, it has no place to go. Therefore, the body responds by surrounding this abnormally-located menstrual blood with scar tissue which builds up month after month. This often leads to the formation of blood-filled pockets or cysts (called ''chocolate cysts'') on the affected organs.

Endometriosis can cause pain during menstruation and during sexual intercourse. It is also considered a cause of infertility—the inability to conceive a child. Scar tissue around the fallopian tubes and ovaries can prevent an egg from entering the tube to be fertilized.

No one is certain exactly what causes endometriosis. One theory holds that in some women

menstrual blood may flow back through the fallopian tubes into the abdominal cavity. In most cases, the reason for this backflow is not known. Occasionally, it may be caused by a blockage of the cervix or vagina. Other possibilities include the migration of endometrial tissue through the veins, or the transfer of some of this tissue outside the uterus following surgery for another condition.

Endometriosis only occurs in women during their childbearing years. After menopause the endometrium is no longer active (unless you are receiving hormone therapy) and it withers naturally in time. Pregnancy and breast feeding usually have a beneficial effect on endometriosis because they interrupt the menstrual cycle, thus preventing the buildup and breakdown of endometrial tissue outside the

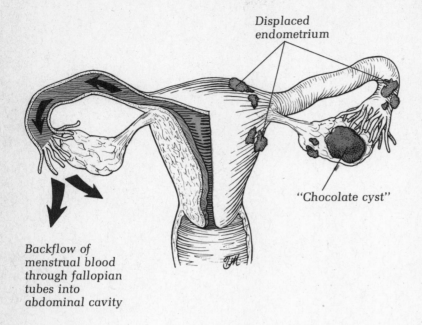

Displaced
endometrium

"Chocolate cyst"

Backflow of
menstrual blood
through fallopian
tubes into
abdominal cavity

Endometriosis is a condition in which fragments of endometrium—the tissue lining the uterus—become displaced and begin growing on the ovaries, the fallopian tubes, the outside of the uterus, or anywhere in the abdominal cavity. Sometimes these growth patches are surrounded by scar tissue, leading to the formation of blood-filled sacs called "chocolate cysts."

---

uterus. Childbirth enlarges the cervix, which also may be helpful in preventing the disease. However, endometriosis may prevent pregnancy.

The disease seems to occur more frequently in women who have delayed childbearing to their late 20s and 30s. Although it can strike as early as the teenage years, it is more prevalent among women from 30 to 40 years of age.

SYMPTOMS

The most common sign of endometriosis is pain during menstruation, or immediately before or after. The disease may also be associated with irregular or heavy menstrual flow, pain during intercourse, and discomfort in the lower urinary tract or the bowel. If the disease affects these organs seriously there may even be bleeding from the rectum or blood in the urine. Infertility is often a symptom. In fact, many women discover they have the disease in the course of seeking treatment for infertility.

To determine the presence of endometriosis, your doctor will take a complete medical and menstrual history and will do a pelvic exam. Often one pelvic exam is performed during your period and one between periods to distinguish the changes in your pelvic area at different points in your cycle.

To make a completely accurate diagnosis, a laparoscopy may be necessary. In this procedure, a small lighted tube is inserted into the lower abdomen through a tiny incision made under general or local anesthetic. The tube allows your doctor to actually see any endometrial tissue that may be present in the abdomen outside the uterus.

TREATMENT

The goals of treatment for endometriosis are to halt the disease, to eliminate pain, and to restore normal menstrual function and fertility.

In some cases, birth control pills may be prescribed because they contain hormones that in high enough doses halt ovulation and menstruation. This gives the endometriosis patches an opportunity to shrink and disappear. There are also various other methods of female hormone therapy that modify the normal hormonal secretion and thus slow the progression of endometriosis.

There are disadvantages to hormone therapy. Since these drugs, including birth control pills, temporarily stop ovulation, this course of treatment will not allow the patient to become pregnant. Furthermore, some women cannot tolerate the high doses of hormone necessary for treatment. The side effects, for example, nausea and fluid retention, may be too severe. Also, high doses of these hormones may carry a potential risk of blood-clotting problems.

Recently, a new synthetic hormone has been developed which does not have the same side effects or the blood-clotting risk of conventional hormone therapy. This new drug, called Danazol, causes ovulation and menstruation to cease, and the areas of endometriosis begin to shrink almost immediately. In essence, the drug creates a menopause-like condition. This new medication seems effective, although it may not work in all cases and it can be expensive.

If this therapy does not work, surgery may be suggested. There are two approaches to surgical treatment. One is to remove scar tissue and as many spots of endometrial tissue as possible without damaging the reproductive organs. The other surgical procedure recommended in severe cases is to remove the uterus and ovaries to eliminate the source of the abnormal endometrial growth.

FIBROCYSTIC DISEASE OF THE BREAST

Fibrocystic disease, also known as benign breast disease and cystic mastitis, is a condition in which noncancerous lumps form in the breasts. The condition may be temporary and may disappear without treatment in a few months; however, in many women it lasts throughout the reproductive years.

Although fibrocystic disease is not dangerous in itself, it can be painful. Furthermore, the constant presence of some lumpiness in the breast makes it difficult to detect new lumps that may be cancerous. Most important of all, there is reported evidence that women with fibrocystic disease may be two to four times more likely to develop breast cancer.

The cause of fibrocystic breast disease is unknown. In some women with fibrocystic disease solid masses may appear in the breasts. In other women fluid-filled cysts (sacs) may occur. During the course of the menstrual cycle under the influence of hormones secreted by the ovaries, these lumps may increase slightly in size. In many cases, these areas become painful. There is a slight reduction in the size of these lumps after the menstrual period once the body's hormones naturally fall.

There is some indication that fibrocystic disease may run in families. Furthermore, the condition appears to be more common in women who have never breast-fed their children.

SYMPTOMS

The breasts of women with fibrocystic disease are irregularly thickened and tender. The symptoms are an exaggeration of the soreness and heaviness of the breasts that most women experience prior to their menstrual periods. However, in the case of fibrocystic disease, the symptoms may persist between menstrual

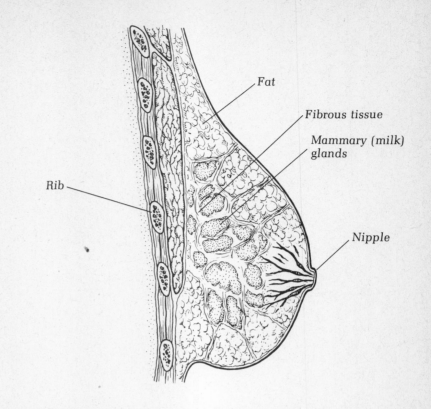

A normal breast has some fibrous tissue to support the milk glands.

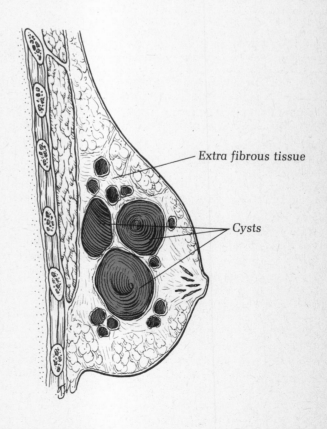

A fibrocystic breast may contain extra fibrous tissue and fluid-filled cysts.

periods. A slight discharge from the breast may also be present.

Diagnosis is made by physical examination, in conjunction with the patient's description of her symptoms. Mammography, a special breast X ray, or diaphanography, in which a light is shined through the translucent tissue of the breast to illuminate its interior, may be used to see if the lumps are fluid-filled cysts or solid masses. If the masses are solid, a biopsy—the removal of a small piece of tissue for analysis —will be necessary to exclude the possibility of cancer.

TREATMENT

Treatment of fibrocystic disease is rarely necessary. However, a large or particularly bothersome cyst can be removed by aspiration, a technique performed under local anesthesia in which your doctor inserts a thin hollow needle into the cyst and drains the fluid. Since this is impractical if you have many small lumps or develop the lumps repeatedly, treatment to prevent the formation of cysts may be necessary. In some women, birth control pills, which equalize the amount of hormones circulating in the blood throughout the month, may relieve the condition. In other women, however, birth control pills may stimulate the growth of cysts. Large doses of Vitamin E, given under a doctor's supervision, have also been shown to help some cases of fibrocystic disease. Recent research also suggests that nicotine and chemicals called methylxanthines — found in coffee, tea, cola, chocolate, and some cold preparations — may promote the growth of fibrocystic disease. Thus, eliminating these substances from your diet and giving up smoking may relieve the condition.

Whether treatment is recommended or not, women with fibrocystic disease should have a checkup at least twice a year. This periodic monitoring is necessary because of the increased risk of breast cancer in women with fibrocystic disease. Between visits to the doctor, a monthly breast self-examination is advisable. (For instructions on how to do a breast self-examination, see the section on breast cancer.) It is important that a patient report any new growths or any significant enlargement of existing lumps.

FIBROID TUMORS

Fibroid tumors are common benign—noncancerous—growths of various sizes and shapes that appear in and on the uterus. They are usually solid and unyielding, composed of interlacing smooth muscle fibers within a connective tissue framework.

Fibroid tumors can grow in the muscular walls of the uterus or may grow out from the uterus, extending into the abdominal cavity. In rare instances, fibroid tumors can occur on the cervix, the narrow opening at the lower end of the uterus. Occasionally, fibroids can fill the entire uterus, push through the cervix, and appear in the vagina.

Although most fibroid tumors grow slowly and cause few problems, in some cases they may create difficulties. Exceptionally large fibroids can press on neighboring organs, such as the bladder or intestine, thus contributing to annoying urination frequency or constipation. During pregnancy fibroids tend to enlarge and may cause complications as the baby grows. If the tumors bulge into the interior of the uterus, heavy and long menstrual periods may occur.

In addition, fibroid tumors are sometimes found with other disorders such as endometriosis (the migration of tissue from the uterus' lining to other parts of the abdomen) or a generalized infection of the abdomen (called pelvic inflammatory disease or PID). Cancer, however, rarely develops in a fibroid tumor.

The cause of fibroid tumors is unknown; however, their growth appears to be linked to stimulation by estrogen, a female hormone. This connection between fibroids and estrogen seems to be confirmed by the fact that fibroid

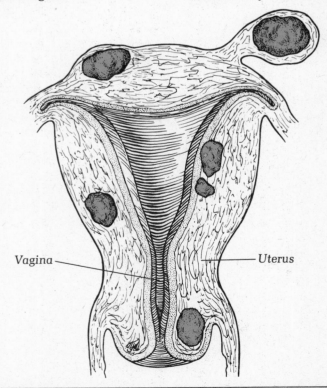

Vagina — Uterus

Fibroid tumors are noncancerous growths that can grow in the muscular walls of the uterus or may grow out from the uterus on a stalk.

tumors rarely appear before puberty (sexual maturity) and tend to stop growing after menopause (the end of reproductive ability). They most often appear in the middle to later reproductive years when the body's estrogen production is at its peak.

Fibroid tumors are considered the most common abdominal tumor — occurring in about one fourth of the women over 30. They are also more prevalent in black women.

SYMPTOMS

Fibroid tumors may produce no symptoms at all and may only be discovered during the course of a routine physical examination. However, in many cases they cause dysmenorrhea (pain during menstruation), gushing or flooding of menstrual flow, and a vaginal discharge that is either thick and slippery or thin, brown, and watery. Abdominal pain and pressure may also be present, although pain is not usually a symptom unless a complication involving the tumor develops. For example, a fibroid may twist on its base and cut off its blood supply, causing severe pain. If the tumor or tumors are well advanced, the abdomen may become enlarged and the patient will be aware of a noticeable mass.

Fibroid tumors are diagnosed largely through physical examination. Curettage (scraping the walls of the uterus) or endometrial biopsy (removing a tissue sample from the lining of the uterus) may also be recommended to test for the possibility of cancer. X rays and ultrasound may be used to view the location and nature of the tumors. Ultrasound is a technique using sound waves to outline internal structures.

TREATMENT

Fibroid tumors that produce no uncomfortable symptoms may require no treatment at all. Your doctor will keep you under observation to make certain that no adverse changes occur. If the tumors are causing serious complications, however, surgery may be necessary. For women who are in the early years of their reproductive life and whose symptoms are not too severe, surgery may involve removal of only the tumor. This operation is called a myomectomy. However, some cases are serious enough to warrant removal of the uterus, rendering the patient sterile. This operation is called a hysterectomy and is usually considered for older women or for women who are not interested in becoming pregnant.

IMPOTENCE

Impotence is the inability to achieve and maintain an erection of the penis. The penis contains internal spaces, called corpora cavernosa, which normally fill with blood during sexual excitement. When this occurs, the penis becomes rigid or erect and is therefore able to enter the female vagina during sexual intercourse. Doctors distinguish between primary impotence — never being able to have an erection adequate for sexual intercourse — and secondary impotence — described as a chronic or recurring failure to complete intercourse to the satisfaction of both partners. Secondary impotence is the more common form. Both types are more likely to affect men over the age of 40.

Many men will experience episodes of temporary impotence at some point in their lives, usually brought on by psychological stress or too much alcohol or drugs. However, chronic impotence can undermine a man's self-esteem and strain his marriage or social relationships.

Until quite recently doctors believed that almost all cases of impotence were a result of psychological problems. Now they are beginning to realize that many physical disorders may also account for impotence, although emotional factors are still one of the leading causes of impotence.

Several physical conditions may lead to impotence. An imbalance in the hormonal system may cause a decrease in the production of testosterone, the male hormone needed for a man to have an erection. Malfunctioning of the circulatory system can affect the responses necessary for erection. For example, if atherosclerosis, the hardening and consequent narrowing of the arteries, strikes the artery that supplies the penis, blood flow will be insufficient to produce an erection. (Atherosclerosis may be a complication of diabetes.) Also, certain drugs used to treat high blood pressure may cause impotence, but the reasons are not clearly understood. And diseases of the nervous system such as multiple sclerosis can affect the ability to have an erection, as can structural abnormalities or injuries of the penis.

Overuse of drugs and alcohol also leads to impaired sexual ability. Psychological problems that can bring on impotence include: job-related stress; a concern that sex will be dangerous after major surgery or a heart attack; a fear of causing pregnancy, and unresolved conflicts about sexuality. Sometimes a man may be impotent with one sexual partner but not with another.

SYMPTOMS

Impotence is indicated when the penis is repeatedly too flaccid (limp) to penetrate the vagina or to complete sexual intercourse. This condition may be accompanied by a lack of interest in sex. However, impotent men are not necessarily infertile. Discovering the cause may be difficult since the symptoms are the same whether impotence is a result of physical or psychological factors. However, there are some tests which may be able to pinpoint the reason for the condition.

A blood test will reveal whether there are adequate levels of sex hormone, testosterone. Another test uses both a special blood pressure cuff, designed to be placed around the penis, and ultrasound, which uses sound waves to create an image of internal structures. This test can reveal blood pressure and blood vessel problems in the penis.

There is also a test that registers the size of erections that occur spontaneously during sleep. If the penis is able to enlarge by 20 percent under these circumstances, doctors theorize that there is probably nothing physically wrong with the body and that psychological problems may be causing the impotence.

TREATMENT

Injections of testosterone may relieve impotence caused by hormonal problems. Surgery to repair the veins and arteries serving the penis can improve blood flow; however, these procedures are not suitable for everyone and are not always successful.

A penile implant is a successful new treatment for impotence. One variety is a silicone rod implanted in the corpora cavernosa, the hollow spaces in the penis that normally fill with blood during an erection. The rod results in a penis that is semi-erect all the time. Another version, made of silicone surrounding a flexible silver wire, allows the penis to be manually adjusted to the angle required for intercourse. Yet another model involves placing balloon-like cylinders in the corpora cavernosa; these cylinders are attached to a reservoir full of fluid that, when activated by a hand pump, swells the penis in much the same way as the flow of blood would.

Men whose impotence is caused by psychological factors may require counseling by trained psychologists or sex therapists. Most sex therapy programs also request that the man's wife or regular sexual partner accompany him in the treatment process. Often, too, those whose impotence is the result of physical disorders, will benefit from counseling.

INFERTILITY

Infertility is defined as a couple's failure to conceive a child after one year of regular sexual intercourse without birth control, or the woman's repeated failure to carry a child to term. Roughly one in six couples has some trouble in conceiving. In approximately 40 percent of the cases the problem lies entirely with the male; in 60 percent of the cases the problem lies with the woman or with both partners. Sterility is defined as the complete inability to conceive a child.

The term "infertility" is often used interchangeably with "sterility." This is incorrect since, from a medical standpoint, "infertility" implies that the condition can be reversed and fertility restored. The term "sterility," however, means that the condition is permanent and cannot be reversed.

It is important to remember that recent reports have shown that a woman's fertility normally drops significantly between 31 to 35 years of age, and declines gradually but steadily until menopause — the end of ovulation and menstruation — renders her unable to conceive. Although men are capable of fathering a child despite old age, their fertility also begins to decline after age 40.

Male Infertility

Male fertility is measured by the number of active sperm present in a milliliter (less than one-half teaspoon) of semen — the fluid ejected through the penis during intercourse. A fresh sample of semen is examined under a microscope to determine the quantity and quality of the sperm it contains. The average man has approximately 90 million sperm per milliliter. A count between 40 and 60 million is considered necessary for conception; when the level drops below 20 million the man's ability to father a child becomes extremely unlikely. However, since only one sperm is necessary to fertilize the ovum

(egg from the female), there is always a remote possibility that a man with an extremely low sperm count could father a child.

Even a man with a normal sperm count may be infertile if his sperm has poor mobility (ability to propel themselves through the woman's reproductive tract to reach the egg) or if his sperm are irregularly shaped. Only oval-shaped sperm are able to fertilize the egg.

Low levels of testosterone, the male sex hormone, can cause a low sperm count, as can exposure to certain chemicals, pesticides, and radiation. A low sperm count can also be accounted for simply by having sex too often, thus reducing the number of active sperm in each ejaculation — in other words, the supply of sperm is depleted faster than it is replaced. Heat is also a factor in low sperm count since sperm production is slowed by high temperatures. Men who wear tight underwear or pants, sit all day in hot cars or trucks, or work near ovens or kilns can experience a reduction in their sperm production. Removing the source of excess heat usually restores the sperm count to normal.

There are other causes of male infertility. A man may be infertile because of varicose veins in the scrotum, the pouch containing the testes. Varicose veins are veins that are abnormally swollen and twisted. It is thought that the increased blood flow in swollen veins may bring extra warmth to the area, thus slowing down sperm production. Furthermore, an obstruction anywhere in the tubes that transport sperm from the testes to the penis can prevent healthy sperm from being ejected. Retrograde ejaculation, in which the semen is passed back into the bladder during intercourse rather than out through the penis, is a problem sometimes encountered by men who have had surgery to remove part of the prostate gland or who are taking certain drugs for hypertension. Local infection or injury to the testes may cause infertility, but sperm production is

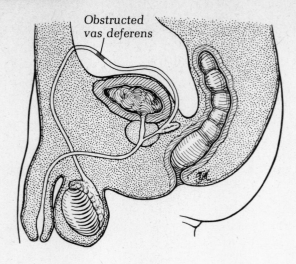

Male infertility may be caused by an obstruction anywhere in the tubes that transport sperm from the testes to the penis.

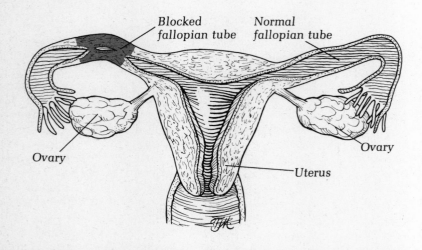

One of the causes of female infertility is an obstruction in the fallopian tube which conducts the egg from the ovary to the uterus. Such an obstruction prevents the egg from uniting with the male's sperm.

usually restored when the infection clears or the injury heals.

TREATMENT

Men whose infertility is caused by varicose veins in the scrotum can be helped by an operation to eliminate the problem. Those with an obstruction somewhere in the tubes that transport the sperm may be candidates for microsurgery to bypass the obstruction. The procedure is very delicate, but the success rate is improving all the time.

If a man's low sperm count is caused by insufficient production of testosterone, hormone therapy may bring his sperm levels up to normal. Avoiding exposure to offending chemicals, radiation, or high temperatures may be the answer for those whose low sperm count is a result of one of these factors. However, if sperm count is low for some unknown reason, often there is nothing that can be done. Nevertheless, researchers continue to search for new methods of restoring or increasing a man's fertility.

Female Infertility

The causes of female infertility and sterility are far more various and require more complicated tests to be diagnosed. First, a physical examination will be performed and a complete medical, menstrual, and sexual history will be taken.

The next question to be answered is whether or not the woman is ovulating (releasing an egg every month). This is done by measuring the basal body temperature (the body temperature upon awakening and before eating or drinking) every morning for a month. If the temperature rises by 6/10 to one degree for several days in the middle of the menstrual cycle, ovulation is probably taking place. An endometrial biopsy, a test which determines the condition of the lining of the uterus, will also confirm whether or not the patient is ovulating.

If failure to ovulate is not the problem, one of two tests will be performed to check for an obstruction in the fallopian tubes which conduct the egg from the ovary to the uterus. One test involves taking an X ray after injecting a dye into the reproductive tract. The other test requires an injection of carbon dioxide into the fallopian tubes; if there is pain felt in the upper part of the body this indicates that the gas has passed through the fallopian tubes and there there is no obstruction.

Obstructions in the fallopian tubes can be caused by pelvic inflammatory disease (PID), a generalized infection of the pelvic organs that causes the fallopian tubes to become inflamed and then to form scar tissue, which renders them incapable of transporting eggs. PID can result from a reaction to an IUD (intrauterine device used for birth control), a sexually transmitted disease that has not been treated promptly, a ruptured appendix, or any other infection of the lower reproductive tracts.

Other problems in the female reproductive system that may

cause infertility are related to a weakness in the cervix that prevents the woman from being able to hold the pregnancy in the uterus. This weakness may be the result of a previous abortion or previous surgery on the cervix. This problem can be diagnosed through physical examination and X ray.

Some women have what is referred to as a "hostile cervix," that is, the environment in their cervix makes it impossible for sperm to survive. To diagnose this problem, there is a test that involves examining the woman's cervix shortly after she and her partner have had intercourse to determine the rate of sperm survival.

Endometriosis, the abnormal location outside the uterus of the tissue that lines the uterus, may interfere with conception. This happens when the endometriosis patches cause scar tissue to form around the opening of the fallopian tube; thus, the egg is prevented from entering the tube to be fertilized. This condition is diagnosed by looking at the uterus, tubes, and ovaries through a laparoscope. The procedure involves inserting a small, lighted instrument into the abdominal cavity through a small incision made under a general or local anesthetic.

Hormone imbalances can also account for infertility. An imbalance of the female hormones, estrogen and progesterone, or of other hormones from the pituitary or thyroid glands can reduce fertility by interfering with the reproductive cycle. Hormone levels are measured by blood tests. For more about the effect of hormones on reproduction, see the section on hormonal disorders.

Psychological factors can also contribute to both male and female infertility. Sometimes a deep-seated fear of having a child prevents a couple from being able to conceive.

TREATMENT

Failure to ovulate accounts for about 25 percent of female in-

fertility problems and it is commonly treated by administering the fertility drug clomiphene (Clomid), which stimulates the production of the hormones that regulate ovulation. About 60 percent of these patients become pregnant. The chances of multiple births are relatively low. For those for whom Clomid is not effective, a stronger drug, Pergonal, may be tried. However, it does carry an increased risk of multiple births.

Women who have obstructions in their fallopian tubes can sometimes be helped by microsurgery that allows the damaged area to be bypassed. Another new procedure involves removing an egg and replacing it in the fallopian tube beyond the point of obstruction where it can then be fertilized normally through intercourse.

A hostile cervix can sometimes be treated by administering the female hormone, estrogen, which stimulates the woman to produce more of the mucus necessary to transport the sperm through the reproductive tract. In other instances, the cervix is simply bypassed by having the sperm introduced directly into the uterus.

Infertility problems caused by endometriosis can often be helped by surgery to remove both the endometrial tissue located outside the uterus and any scar tissue formed around the displaced tissue.

Hormone therapy may be prescribed to correct any hormonal imbalances that interfere with the normal reproductive process.

Despite great strides in treating female infertility, about 15 percent of all women's problems remain undiagnosed, and therefore untreatable.

MENSTRUAL DISORDERS

Menstruation is the monthly breakdown and discharge of the endometrial tissue that lines the uterus. The endometrial tissue thickens during each menstrual

cycle to prepare the uterus for possible pregnancy. If no pregnancy occurs, the lining of the uterus breaks down and flows out of the body. This monthly cycle is controlled by the female hormones, estrogen and progesterone, secreted by the ovaries.

Menstruation may be accompanied by complications of varying degrees of seriousness in many women at some point in their reproductive lives. The most common problems are *dysmenorrhea*, painful menstruation; *amenorrhea*, the absence entirely of a menstrual period or the missing of several periods; and *premenstrual tension* (PMT), distinct feelings of irritability and discomfort in the days before the period begins.

For many years the symptoms of these disorders have been attributed to hysteria and emotional instability. Recent research, however, has shown that most are caused by very real physical changes, and many new methods of treatment have been developed.

Although the disorders themselves are generally not dangerous, they can be physically and emotionally incapacitating. Furthermore, they may be symptoms of a disease in the reproductive organs. Therefore, medical treatment for annoying symptoms accompanying menstruation should always be sought.

Dysmenorrhea

There are two classifications of dysmenorrhea, or painful menstruation.

Primary dysmenorrhea may begin shortly after the onset of menstruation in a young girl. It is thought to be caused by the release of prostaglandins from the menstrual uterus. Prostaglandins are substances that stimulate contractions of the uterus. This temporarily deprives the uterus of its blood supply, causing pain in the same way that a decrease in blood supply to the heart causes chest pain. Researchers are not certain why some women produce

Stages of the Menstrual Cycle

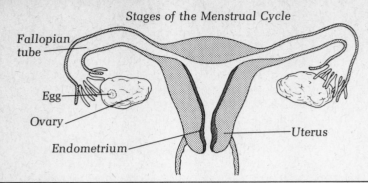

Fallopian tube

Egg

Ovary

Endometrium

Uterus

In the first stage, the female egg is within the ovary and the endometrium (lining of the uterus) is relatively thin.

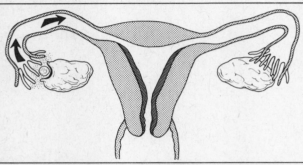

As the egg is released from the ovary and prepares to move into the fallopian tube, the endometrium begins to grow and thicken in preparation for a possible pregnancy. These changes are controlled by female hormones.

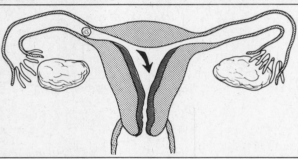

The egg continues its journey through the fallopian tube to the uterus. During this time the endometrium continues to thicken and secrete substances to nourish a possible embryo (fertilized egg). This is the stage in which conception may occur. The sperm from the male unites with the egg in the fallopian tube, and the fertilized egg then continues to the uterus.

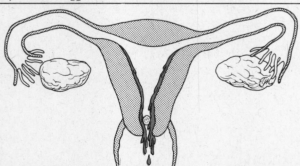

If conception does not occur, the female hormone levels drop, and the endometrium no longer grows and thickens. At this point, the lining of the uterus is shed, along with the unfertilized egg. This is menstruation. (The egg shown here has been enlarged for the purpose of illustration. It is normally not visible without the aid of a microscope.)

more prostaglandins than others.

Secondary dysmenorrhea starts later in life after a woman has been menstruating for some time. These painful periods are usually secondary to—a result of—other problems in the reproductive system. Examples of these problems include endometriosis (the abnormal location outside the uterus of the tissue that lines the uterus), fibroid tumors, or a narrow cervix.

Women who are overweight are a greater risk for dysmenorrhea. In addition, painful periods are most common among teenagers and among those women who have never had children. Childbirth seems to relieve the problem, perhaps by enlarging the cervix, perhaps by damaging some nerve fibers in the uterus which never regenerate.

SYMPTOMS

The symptoms of both forms of dysmenorrhea are cramp-like pain in the lower abdomen which may radiate to the lower back. Nausea, vomiting, diarrhea, headache, fatigue, and nervousness are symptoms commonly associated with the pain. The symptoms usually begin at the onset of the monthly period or slightly before and continue for several hours to several days.

In diagnosing dysmenorrhea your doctor will perform a complete physical examination, along with taking a medical and menstrual history. It is important to differentiate between cases of primary and secondary dysmenorrhea so that appropriate treatment may be given. Typical symptoms present in young women, or in older women who have suffered them since the onset of menstruation, usually means a diagnosis of primary dysmenorrhea. However, the sudden development of the typical symptoms in an older woman indicates secondary dysmenorrhea, and X rays and/or tissue samples of the reproductive organs may be necessary to determine the underlying cause.

TREATMENT

Primary dysmenorrhea is now being treated very successfully with certain anti-inflammatory drugs also used in the treatment of arthritis. These drugs—ibuprofen (Motrin), naproxen sodium, and mefenamic acid — suppress the production of prostaglandins and thus reduce the uterine contractions which cause pain. Because these drugs prevent release of prostaglandins, they are more effective if taken before a period begins.

Secondary dysmenorrhea can be handled by treating its cause; for example, endometriosis may be treated with hormone therapy or surgery. When the endometriosis is eliminated, pain during menstruation will probably cease.

Many women have discovered their own methods to ease painful periods. A hot water bottle or heating pad placed on the abdomen or even a hot bath can provide comfort. Some women find that lying on their backs with knees bent relieves pressure and pain.

Amenorrhea

Amenorrhea, the absence of menstruation, is also divided into two categories.

Primary amenorrhea, the failure to begin menstruating by the age of 16, may be caused by endocrine gland disorders (such as hyper- or hypothyroidism) or by genetic abnormalities. It may also stem from damaged or missing ovaries, uterus, or vagina. Sometimes the hymen — the membrane that covers the opening of the vagina in young girls — may be so thick that the menstrual flow cannot be released.

Secondary amenorrhea, the skipping of more than three periods in a row by a woman who has previously menstruated, is much more common. The most common cause is pregnancy. However, it may also result from strenuous sports training, jet lag, drastic weight gain, medications (including birth control pills),

serious surgery or disease, emotional shock, or poor nutrition. In addition, women whose percentage of body fat falls below a certain point (different for each individual) may temporarily stop menstruating. In these cases, amenorrhea is usually temporary and menstruation will resume when the underlying problem is resolved.

SYMPTOMS

Apart from the absence of the period for three or more months, secondary amenorrhea is without symptoms. Primary amenorrhea, on the other hand, may be accompanied by abnormal physical development. A young woman who has failed to develop breasts and body hair may be suffering from some genetic disorder that prevents her from attaining sexual maturity.

By asking detailed questions and taking a pregnancy test, your doctor will attempt to rule out all the most obvious causes of secondary amenorrhea. If none of these causes seems to be responsible, tests will be run to determine the possibility of genetic or hormonal disorders. X rays may be necessary to determine the status of the reproductive organs. These same tests may be recommended for women with primary amenorrhea.

TREATMENT

Primary amenorrhea may require extensive hormonal therapy. If it is caused by a thick hymen, surgical correction is possible. However, it is essential to remember that some forms are untreatable.

Secondary amenorrhea will, in many cases, correct itself, especially if the cause is a disruption of the patient's normal routine, an emotional upset, or, obviously, a pregnancy. In more persistent cases, a hormone may be administered to trigger ovulation, which in turn will reestablish a regular menstrual cycle.

Premenstrual Tension

Premenstrual tension is believed to be caused by fluctuations in the production of female hormones during the menstrual cycle. These hormonal fluctuations seem to increase the amounts of salt and fluids retained by the body's tissues in the week before menstruation begins. However, the exact way this works is not known. For this reason, there is no way to determine who will be affected by premenstrual tension.

SYMPTOMS

Premenstrual tension is marked by feelings of nervousness and irritability in the week preceding menstruation. Because of the generalized fluid retention (edema), there is usually a feeling of being bloated and puffy. Many women also experience depression, headaches, fatigue, tenderness in the breasts, and acne. These symptoms tend to disappear as soon as the menstrual flow starts.

TREATMENT

Premenstrual tension can be helped by cutting down on salt intake and by taking diuretics (medications which help eliminate excessive fluid from the tissues) during the week before the period is due. A balanced diet, adequate rest, and moderate exercise may also be beneficial. In cases where emotional problems are considered to be a contributing factor, tranquilizers and counseling may be recommended.

PROSTATITIS

Prostatitis is an infection or inflammation of the prostate, the male gland that lies just below the urinary bladder and surrounds the urethra — the tube that carries urine from the bladder to outside the body. Most men in their lifetime will have at least one bout

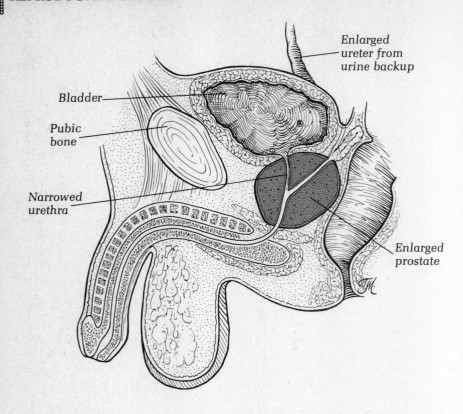

Enlarged ureter from urine backup

Bladder

Pubic bone

Narrowed urethra

Enlarged prostate

Prostatitis, an inflammation of the prostate gland, can lead to an enlarged prostate. The enlarged prostate may constrict the urethra passing through it and interfere with urination. There may even be a backup of urine into the ureters and kidneys.

SYMPTOMS

A man should suspect a developing prostate problem when the force of his urinary stream is reduced, when he has trouble starting to urinate, and when the flow dribbles at the finish. Prostatitis creates a feeling of urgency and frequency even during sleep.

When the prostate is infected, a man will also experience discomfort in the lower back and genital area and a burning sensation while urinating. In addition, there may be fever and chills.

Urine analysis usually shows evidence of infection and sometimes a trace of blood. A doctor will feel the prostate through the rectum to determine the size, shape, and firmness of the gland. An infected prostate gland is a little tender to the touch and when massaged, pus cells are forced out which then appear in the urine. The doctor makes a culture of the urine specimen to see what organisms grow — although very often no bacteria are identified in chronic prostatitis. If there is blood in the specimen, a portion of the urine will be tested for the possibility of a malignancy.

To diagnose an enlarged prostate, your doctor may use an intravenous pyelogram (IVP). In this procedure, dye is injected into a vein in the arm; the dye travels through the bloodstream to the kidneys, then to the urinary bladder, and out through the penis. This dye appears in both kidneys and shows any enlargement as well as an obstruction in the ureters. The patient then urinates, after which the IVP reveals whether there is any urine left behind. A large quantity of urine remaining in the bladder usually indicates a partial obstruction generally caused by an enlarged prostate.

TREATMENT

Most prostate infections can be easily treated with an appropriate antibiotic. Chronic nonbacterial prostatitis, on the other hand, is not usually treated with antibiotic

of prostatitis, and some become the victims of a chronic case—recurring low-grade infections which, while not life-threatening, cause considerable discomfort.

Prostatitis can occur at any time during adult life, but it is more common in older men. As men grow older, they may develop an enlarged prostate which obstructs the outflow of urine. This, in turn, causes a set of symptoms known as prostatism — the urine may be slow to start, have decreased force, and end with dribbling. Urination may require prolonged effort and several attempts, and there will always be some urine left in the bladder. The leftover urine becomes a fertile breeding ground for bacteria, leading to the infection common in prostatitis. In advanced stages, prostatism may produce a sudden and complete blockage of the flow of urine. This requires emergency treatment since the backup of urine may result in bladder and kidney damage.

Prostatitis can also be an aftereffect of a sexually transmitted disease or a urinary tract infection. The urinary tract is comprised of the kidneys, ducts from the kidneys to the bladder, the bladder, and the urethra. In these cases the bacteria responsible may also infect the prostate gland.

However, chronic prostatitis, the more common form of the disease, is not usually the result of a bacterial infection. In fact, the cause of chronic prostatitis is unknown. It is thought that, occasionally, the prostate may become congested from too much or not enough sexual activity (the prostate secretes a substance used to transport sperm cells during ejaculation). And some doctors believe that emotions can play a role in a chronic case, but no real scientific evidence supports this theory.

drugs. Instead, drinking large quantities of nonalcoholic fluids and taking hot baths may offer some relief. If the problem keeps recurring, however, a physician will have to determine the cause and prescribe further treatment.

The usual treatment for an enlarged prostate that causes symptoms is surgical removal of the excess tissue. One approach is transurethral surgery (performed through the urethra) in which a special instrument is inserted into the penis and the central portion of the prostate gland is scraped out in small sections.

A more complicated surgical technique is a prostatectomy. This requires an incision in the lower abdomen or between the legs.

Most surgical procedures for prostate enlargement do not result in any degree of impotence; however, they may cause retrograde ejaculation where the semen is passed back into the bladder during intercourse instead of out through the penis. The semen will eventually be expelled from the bladder along with the urine. This is in no way harmful and will not change the emotional sensations of sexual intercourse.

SEXUALLY TRANSMITTED DISEASES

Sexually transmitted diseases (STDs), also known as venereal diseases, comprise a number of highly contagious illnesses spread primarily through direct sexual contact. (The term "venereal" comes from Venus, the ancient Roman goddess of love.) STDs are extremely common—in fact, the incidence of some of these diseases has reached epidemic proportions, particularly in the 15- to 35-year-old age group.

If left untreated, many STDs can cause serious, systemic infections (infections that affect the entire body). Pregnant women can pass the disease along to their children, either directly to the unborn baby or during birth. STDs can cause a wide range of complications in infants, from blindness and brain damage to death.

All forms of STDs require that every sexual partner of the patient be examined and, if necessary, treated for the disease to which they have been exposed. The chances of contracting a sexually transmitted disease increase with the number of different sex partners you have.

Some of the more common sexually transmitted diseases include gonorrhea, syphilis, herpes, nongonococcal urethritis, and genital warts. For more information about other infections that may be sexually transmitted, see the section on vaginitis.

Gonorrhea

Gonorrhea is the most commonly reported sexually transmitted disease. It is caused by a bacterial infection, and if left untreated can lead to a generalized blood infection, sterility, arthritis, and heart trouble. The disease can be passed to an infant by an infected mother during birth as the baby moves through the birth canal. The gonorrhea bacteria may infect the baby's eyes and cause blindness. However, most states require that a few drops of silver nitrate, an antiseptic, be placed in the eyes of all newborns to prevent this. Adults, too, can develop eye infections if the eyes come into contact with secretions from the genital area—for example, if a person rubs the eyes after handling the genital organs.

Gonorrhea is spread by direct sexual contact with an infected person. Besides affecting the penis in men and the vagina in women, it can also affect the throat and anus (the external opening to the intestines) in both sexes.

SYMPTOMS

In women, the disease is often entirely without symptoms; however, it may cause a discharge from the vagina and urethra, frequent and painful urination, cloudy urine, vomiting, and diarrhea. Often, gonorrhea develops into pelvic inflammatory disease (PID) before it is detected in women. PID, one of the leading causes of female sterility, results when an infection in the lower reproductive or urinary tract spreads upward and invades the

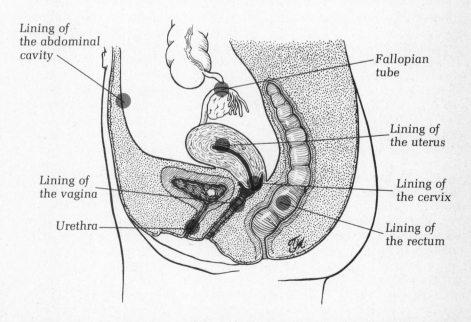

Lining of the abdominal cavity

Fallopian tube

Lining of the uterus

Lining of the vagina

Lining of the cervix

Urethra

Lining of the rectum

In females, gonorrhea may spread to various sites in the pelvic area causing pelvic inflammatory disease and possibly sterility.

abdomen. This produces an inflammation in the fallopian tubes and adjacent structures. The inflammation, in turn, leads to scarring, which may permanently block the fallopian tubes and prevent conception. (Symptoms of PID include lower abdominal pain, fever, chills, and vaginal discharge.)

In men, a yellowish discharge from the penis appears within two to ten days of exposure to gonorrhea. It is accompanied by pain and burning upon urination. If unchecked, the disease may spread to involve the prostate gland and parts of the duct system, causing a painful inflammation and possible sterility. Anal gonorrhea causes a discharge from the anus, often with blood and mucus, and pain during bowel movements. Gonorrhea in the throat may be without symptoms or may cause a sore, scratchy throat.

Gonorrhea is diagnosed by taking smears — or samples — of the discharge. These are then examined under a microscope to identify gonorrhea bacteria. The diagnosis of gonorrhea is confirmed by culturing a sample of the discharge in a test tube or in a specially prepared culture plate.

TREATMENT

Gonorrhea is generally treated by either an injection or an oral dose of penicillin. Recently, new forms of penicillin-resistant gonorrhea have developed. They can be treated with spectinomycin, a synthetically-produced antibiotic. (This drug is also used to treat people who are allergic to penicillin.) While being treated, the patient should refrain from sexual activity until it is confirmed that gonorrhea is no longer present. This is done by again testing smears from commonly infected sites — such as the urethra or cervix—after one week of treatment. Many doctors also recommend additional testing two weeks later. If the patient still shows signs of gonorrhea, drug therapy can be reinstated, often

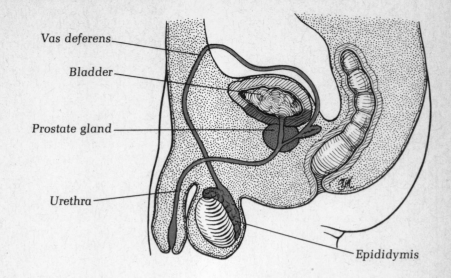

In males, gonorrhea can spread throughout the reproductive and urinary systems. Untreated gonorrhea may involve the male duct system, the prostate gland, the bladder, and the urethra.

with the same or a different antibiotic at higher dosages.

Additionally, men being treated for gonorrhea may be advised to avoid alcoholic beverages during treatment. Studies have suggested that drinking may increase the chance of developing an inflammation of the urethra.

Syphilis

Syphilis is more serious but less common than gonorrhea. It is also contracted by direct sexual contact with an infected person.

Syphilis is caused by a type of spiral-shaped bacteria called spirochetes. It can eventually affect any part of the body and can be passed from a woman to her unborn child — often with devastating results including mental retardation and blindness.

SYMPTOMS

The disease has four stages — called primary, secondary, latent, and late. Primary syphilis is characterized by an open but painless sore on the genitals which appears ten to 90 days after exposure to the infection. Although there can be several sores, as a rule the disease begins with just one sore.

This is called a chancre and usually begins as a red bump which soon erodes into a painless ulcer. A red ring may surround the chancre and a clear fluid may seep out. Most chancres appear on the external sexual organs, although they may occur in the rectum in men and on the cervix in women. Occasionally, chancres may appear on the lips, tongue, or fingers. The chancre disappears within several weeks without treatment, but the body still harbors the disease.

In three to six weeks the symptoms of secondary syphilis appear — general flu-like symptoms such as fever, sore throat, headache, fatigue, aching joints, enlarged lymph nodes, rash, and sometimes loss of hair. (Lymph nodes are small bean-shaped structures that contain the clear fluid from around the body's cells. This fluid carries away bacteria and waste products.) The rash during this stage of syphilis consists of round pin spots occurring in patches and often on the palms of the hands and the soles of the feet. The rash does not itch and eventually heals. During this stage there may also be grayish-white erosions in the lining of the mouth, on the penis, on the female external sexual organs, and in the anus. These eroded areas are extremely contagious. In addition, wart-like growths may appear in the genital area. (These growths, however, should not be confused with the more common genital warts.) If untreated, these rashes, sores, and growths usually heal within three to six weeks, and the disease enters the latent stage — latent means present but not visible or active.

During the latent stage of syphilis, all symptoms disappear and the individual seems normal. Latent syphilis may exist for an indefinite time and is probably not contagious (except in a pregnant woman who can infect her unborn child). Approximately one third of the individuals with latent syphilis eventually enter the stage of late syphilis.

By the time the disease reaches the late stage, it is no longer contagious; however, the entire body is under attack. The brain, bones, spinal cord, and heart may all be affected. This stage of syphilis can lead to blindness, brain damage, heart disease, and death.

Diagnosis of syphilis is made through physical examination, blood tests, and microscopic examinations of smears taken from the chancres or rash sites. The bacteria may not show up in the blood test in the first three weeks after the initial contact with an infected person, so several tests may be necessary.

TREATMENT

Syphilis is treated with penicillin or other antibiotics. In addition, as with any diagnosed STD, sexual activity should be curtailed until all tests show that the individual is no longer contagious. Furthermore, anyone else who may have had sexual relations with the patient should be contacted, examined, and, if necessary, treated.

In some cases of late stage syphilis, treatment is of little value.

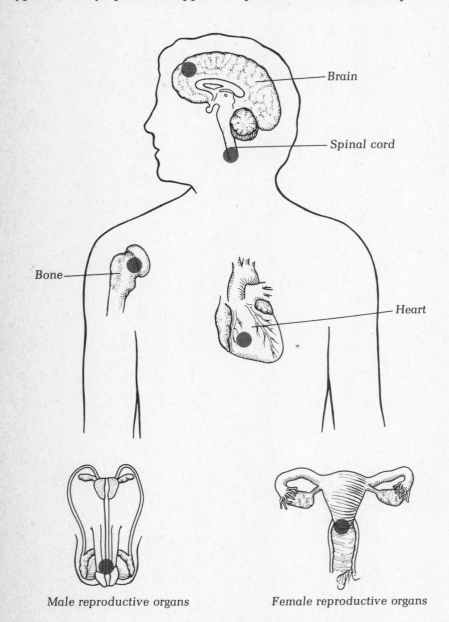

Male reproductive organs   *Female reproductive organs*

Brain

Spinal cord

Bone

Heart

Syphilis is a sexually transmitted disease that, if untreated, may attack all parts of the body. In its late stage, untreated syphilis may affect the brain, the spinal cord, the bones, and the heart as well as the reproductive organs.

Herpes

Herpes appears to be even more prevalent than gonorrhea. The disease is caused by infection with the herpes simplex type 2 virus, similar to the virus that causes cold sores and fever blisters on the lips.

Persons taking drugs that suppress the body's natural immune response — such as cancer or organ transplant patients — are at higher risk for developing herpes. The disease has also been linked to a higher rate of cancer of the cervix in women.

Herpes can be transmitted to an infant during childbirth, so if a woman has active signs of the disease when she goes into labor, the child will be delivered by cesarean section (delivery through a surgical incision in the walls of the abdomen and uterus). If the disease is transmitted to the child, it can cause brain damage and death.

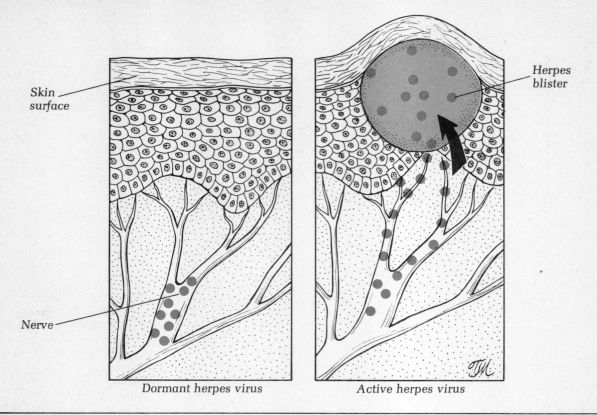

Skin surface

Herpes blister

Nerve

Dormant herpes virus

Active herpes virus

Herpes simplex type 2 virus causes painful, fluid-filled blisters which are highly contagious. The blisters eventually disappear, but the herpes virus lies dormant within nerve cells in the body until stress or illness reactivates the virus. This triggers a new outbreak of active herpes blisters. Herpes can be treated but not cured.

SYMPTOMS

Genital herpes is marked by outbreaks of fluid-filled blisters on and around the external sex organs. These blisters cause varying degrees of pain and itching and may be accompanied by vague, flu-like symptoms including fever, loss of appetite, and fatigue. Women may have a discharge from the vagina.

The blisters clear up by themselves in approximately two weeks; however, the virus is still present in the body. It lies dormant, hidden in clusters of nerve cells until another outbreak of symptoms is triggered by stress, a cold, fever, or, in women, menstruation. The disease is only contagious during outbreaks of symptoms, when sexual activity should be avoided. Many persons can anticipate an outbreak by a tingling sensation called a "prodrome," or premonition of disease.

Herpes is diagnosed by a micro-scopic examination of the fluid from the blisters.

TREATMENT

There is no cure for herpes. It is thought that the virus is untouchable when dormant in nerve cells since it is difficult to find a drug that will attack the virus without harming the nerve cells. However, some headway has been made recently in treatments for the disease. Acyclovir, an anti-viral drug, has been found to reduce the reproduction of the virus in initial outbreaks, thus lessening the number of recurring outbreaks. Acyclovir also speeds the healing of the blisters. Laser therapy has also proved to reduce pain and eliminate herpes blisters. By killing large numbers of the virus, it reduces the number of subsequent outbreaks; however, the laser treatment must begin immediately after the sores appear.

Nongonococcal Urethritis

Nongonococcal urethritis (or NGU), also known as nonspecific urethritis, is an inflammation of the urethra. This sexually transmitted disease produces gonorrhea-like symptoms in the absence of the gonorrhea bacterium. Instead, various other bacteria, among them one called *chlamydia*, cause the inflammation.

Left untreated NGU can lead to arthritis, prostatitis (inflammation of the prostate), and epididymitis (inflammation of the ducts leading from the testes) in men, and to pelvic inflammatory disease (generalized abdominal infection) in women. When transmitted to an infant during birth, NGU can lead to ear infections and pneumonia in the child. It has also been linked to a higher incidence of still-births and to sudden infant death.

SYMPTOMS

NGU causes a discharge from the penis or vagina, accompanied by pain and burning upon urination. At times the disease may have no symptoms. NGU can occur in conjunction with gonorrhea, so if gonorrhea-like symptoms persist after treatment for that disease, it is possible that NGU is also present.

NGU is often hard to diagnose since there is not one simple test for the bacteria that cause it. Often a tissue sample will be taken to test for the presence of *chlamydia*, the organism thought to cause NGU. However, many labs do not perform this procedure and it is expensive, so your doctor may diagnose NGU by ruling out the other possible causes of your symptoms, such as gonorrhea or cystitis (bladder infection).

TREATMENT

NGU is not affected by penicillin and must be treated with other antibiotics such as tetracycline. Therefore, treatment for gonorrhea—that is, penicillin—will not clear up NGU.

Genital Warts

Genital warts (condylomata acuminata) appear on the external genital areas and are caused by a virus similar to the virus that causes other warts on the skin. Approximately 60 percent of the people exposed to them through direct sexual contact develop the disease. There is a six-week to eight-month incubation period before the symptoms appear.

If left untreated, genital warts can sometimes grow quite large, making sexual intercourse, urination, and/or bowel movements difficult. They may even block the birth canal, making a cesarean delivery necessary.

Genital warts are more common in uncircumsized men — men who have not had the foreskin of the penis removed. Pregnancy may cause the warts to grow more rapidly than usual, although they commonly shrink spontaneously after birth. Although the wart virus may be transmitted directly to an unborn baby, the warts are not known to cause any serious complications in infants.

SYMPTOMS

Genital warts can appear on the penis, vagina, and anus. They are also seen less commonly in the mouth or on the cervix. The warts are soft, moist, and pink. They may occur in clusters or alone. In clusters, they often have a cauliflower-like appearance. Although they generally cause no pain, they may be irritated by sexual intercourse. In fact, genital warts appear most frequently on the areas of the sex organs which receive the most friction during sex.

Genital warts are diagnosed by physical examination. Generally, their appearance is distinctive enough to make a definitive diagnosis of warts. In some instances, your doctor may test a sample of the wart to rule out the possibility of some other kind of growth, such as cancer or the wart-like swelling that is a symptom of syphilis.

TREATMENT

Genital warts are treated with a drug called podophyllin applied directly to the warts, then washed off several hours later. The treatment may have to be repeated several times. Since this chemical can be toxic in large quantities, big or stubborn warts may be removed with cryotherapy (the application of liquid nitrogen, which freezes the growths off) or with other methods that destroy the warts through the application of heat which allows them to be scraped off.

TOXIC SHOCK SYNDROME

Toxic shock syndrome is a rare and sometimes fatal disease that occurs when a toxin (poison) produced by the bacterium *Staphylococcus aureus* enters the bloodstream, causing leaks in cell walls that allow blood to seep into tissues. This, in turn, can lead to a dangerous drop in blood pressure, shock, and possibly death.

The disease develops very suddenly and progresses rapidly. Although most victims recover, a severe case may lead to liver and heart damage because of low blood pressure and the weakening of cell walls that allows foreign substances to invade these organs. Furthermore, the disease has been known to recur in cases where the body has not produced sufficient antibodies to fight off the infection. An antibody is a chemical formed by the body to protect the body against invasion by a specific bacterium or foreign substance.

Toxic shock syndrome was first officially defined in 1975 and is considered by many to be a new disease. Since its first reported appearances, scientists have been trying to determine exactly which toxin produced by *Staphylococcus aureus* causes the syndrome and the precise link between the prevalence of the disease and the use of tampons. Since the bacterium can be present in the body without producing the toxin that causes the disease, why toxic shock syndrome occurs is still unclear.

Toxic shock syndrome has been linked to the use of menstrual tampons. However, the tampons themselves do not cause the disease although they may promote in some unknown way the growth of the staph bacteria. Researchers theorize that wearing tampons may contribute to the development of the disease in three ways: (1) the new "superabsorbent" tampons containing synthetic fibers may swell so much in the vagina that they block the elimination of blood entirely and create an ideal breeding ground for bacteria; (2) because these tampons are so absorbent, women tend to leave them in longer, increasing the likelihood of infection; and (3) the tampon applicators may scratch the walls of the vagina allowing bacteria to enter the bloodstream.

It is estimated that only three of every 100,000 women in their menstruating years have contracted the disease. Five to 15 percent of these cases are fatal. However, the disease does not strike only menstruating women. Of the total number of toxic shock cases reported, 10 percent have been in men or nonmenstruating women.

Without regard for age or sex, toxic shock syndrome also affects patients recovering from surgery, burn victims, and persons suffering from boils or abscesses. Thus it is apparent that the bacteria can enter the body in ways other than through the vagina.

Nevertheless, since almost 90 percent of the reported cases of toxic shock syndrome have occurred in menstruating women under the age of 30 using tampons, tampon use is clearly a risk factor for the disease. Although tampon manufacturers have been required to warn purchasers of this, the disease is still so rare that there is not enough evidence that tampons should be taken off the market. Tampons can be safely worn, although as a precaution, they should be changed every three to four hours and should be alternated with the use of sanitary napkins whenever possible. It is also advised that tampons not be worn at night while sleeping, since they may then be left in for prolonged periods of time.

Women who have just given birth are also at a greater risk for toxic shock syndrome, because the vagina or birth canal is more susceptible to bacterial invasion.

SYMPTOMS

Toxic shock symptoms include high fever, vomiting, diarrhea, sunburnlike rash, peeling of skin on soles and palms, blurred vision, and disorientation. The symptoms come on very suddenly and rapidly progress to a drop in blood pressure and shock.

The disease frequently occurs during or just after menstruation, so anyone with the symptoms of the disease at these times should immediately seek medical assistance.

There is no quick and definite test for toxic shock syndrome. Diagnosis depends largely on the ability to recognize the symptoms. A test for the presence of *Staphylococcus aureus* can be performed, but the presence of the bacteria alone does not indicate that a patient has the disease.

TREATMENT

Most cases of toxic shock respond well to treatment. The patient is usually hospitalized where treatment of the disease consists of supportive medical assistance similar to that provided for cases of poisoning. Fluids and even whole blood transfusions may be administered into the vein to raise blood pressure. In addition, an ice blanket may be used to bring down fever and antibiotics prescribed to combat infection.

VAGINITIS

Vaginitis is an inflammation of the vagina, the passageway in the female from the uterus to the outside of the body. If left untreated, vaginitis can become chronic, or recurring. An untreated infection may also spread to the urinary tract opening, causing a urinary tract infection.

Vaginitis often arises from imbalances of the microorganisms in the vagina. Normally, several different types of microscopic organisms exist in the vagina, keeping each other in check. But various factors can cause one or another of the strains to reproduce rapidly, leading to the itching and burning typical of vaginitis. The exception to this is nonspecific, noninfectious vaginitis. This is not due to the overproduction of any microorganisms, but rather to general irritation from an external source.

Several factors can throw off the balance of microorganism growth in the vagina. These include birth control pills and certain antibiotic drugs. Birth control pills contain high levels of estrogen, a female hormone, which changes the vaginal lining so it is more likely to nourish microorganisms that cause infections. Some antibiotics seem to cause vaginitis because they may destroy bacteria that normally help maintain the balance of microorganisms in the vagina. This unbalance may allow the microorganisms that cause vaginitis to flourish.

Excessive douching (washing out the vagina with water or antiseptic solutions) and the use of so-called feminine hygiene sprays may also disrupt the healthy environment in the vagina. Bubble baths, talcum powder, and scented and colored toilet paper can all irritate the vagina, leading to vaginitis.

Since bacteria are stimulated to reproduce excessively in warm, moist environments, vaginal infections are more prevalent in the summer. Similarly, wearing tight pants or panty hose, nylon underwear, and wet swimming suits promotes dampness in the vaginal area, creating a breeding ground for bacteria.

Although any woman may develop vaginitis under these conditions, those who have diabetes or are pregnant are at a higher risk for these infections. Women with gonorrhea, a sexually transmitted disease, also have a lower resistance to vaginitis.

Before proper treatment can be prescribed, your doctor must determine the precise cause of your infection. A smear of vaginal secretions will be taken in order to analyze under a microscope types of microorganisms present. The microscopic analysis will usually reveal that a vaginal infection is caused by one of three microorganisms—a fungus, a bacterium, or a protozoan (a one-cell organism).

SYMPTOMS

The fungus *Candida albicans*, or *monilia*, produces a thick, white vaginal discharge that re-

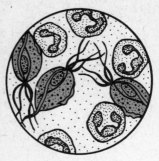

Protozoa

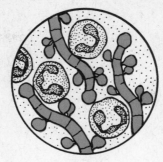

Fungi

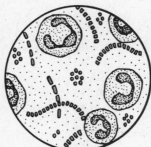

Bacteria

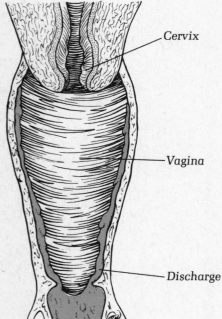

Cervix

Vagina

Discharge

Vaginitis is an inflammation or infection of the vagina and is characterized by a discharge from the vagina. A vaginal infection may be caused by a protozoan, a fungus, or a bacterium, each of which is shown above as it would appear under a microscope.

of vaginitis in diabetic and pregnant women.

Haemophilus vaginalis is a bacterium that causes a creamy white or grayish, foul-smelling discharge. Burning and itching are also typical of this type of infection. Men too can be infected, although the condition may cause no symptoms in the male.

Trichomonas vaginalis, a protozoan, also causes itching and burning but it is distinguished from other infections by its characteristic greenish-white discharge and foul odor. It is more likely to appear during or immediately after menstruation. *Trichomonas* can also be passed between sexual partners.

Noninfectious, nonspecific vaginitis produces irritation and dryness, usually without any discharge.

TREATMENT

Most types of vaginitis are treated with appropriate medications. The fungus *Candida albicans* requires an anti-fungal cream which is applied to the vagina. Bacterial infections can be managed by sulfa drugs or antibiotics. These drugs may be taken orally (by mouth) or as suppositories — solid cones of medication that are inserted into the vagina where they melt and are absorbed into the body. Because the bacterial infections can be passed back and forth between two sexual partners, both partners are usually treated with oral antibiotics.

Trichomonas is also treated with an oral antibiotic — metronidazole — and again both sexual partners are treated to prevent constant reinfection. This drug is quite effective, but because some studies have linked it to cancer and to genetic damage in the offspring of laboratory animals given the drug, it should not be taken during the first half of pregnancy.

Nonspecific, noninfectious vaginitis can usually be helped by eliminating irritants such as tight clothing or perfumed soaps, sprays, or tissues.

sembles cottage cheese in texture. Because the discharge has a "yeasty" odor, this condition is commonly known as a yeast infection. It causes severe itching of the external genital organs and pain during intercourse. A yeast infection is the most frequent kind

131

DISORDERS OF THE NERVOUS SYSTEM

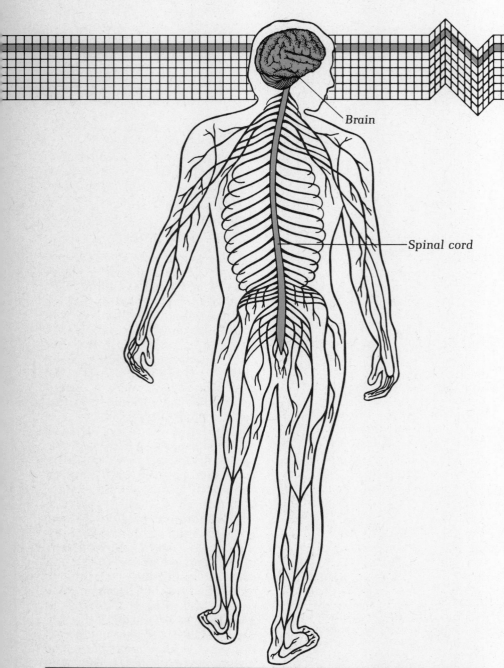

Brain

Spinal cord

The nervous system has three major divisions: the central nervous system, the peripheral nervous system, and the autonomic nervous system. Shown here are the central nervous system — the brain and spinal cord — and the peripheral nervous system — the nerves that branch out from the brain and spinal cord.

Our nervous system is an intricate network of specialized tissue that is responsible for our thoughts, emotions, sensations, and actions as well as for control of all the functions of living.

The basic element of the nervous system is the neuron, or nerve cell. Individual neurons are among the largest cells in the body; and they combine together to form nerve fibers which convey impulses throughout the body. As with every part of the nervous system, the neurons and nerve fibers are protected and cushioned so that they can do their jobs. Myelin, a fatty substance, forms an insulated coating around the nerve fibers.

The nerve fibers are specialized depending on their location within the nervous system. The nervous system has three major divisions:

The *central nervous system* consists of the brain and spinal cord. They are protected and cushioned by bone, layers of tissues (called the meninges), and spinal fluid.

The *peripheral nervous system* includes the cranial nerves (those that branch directly from the brain) and the spinal nerves (those that branch out from the spinal cord). The peripheral nerves convey sensory messages to the central nervous system from receptor cells in the body. And they carry motor impulses from the central system back to the body so that the muscles and glands can act on those impulses.

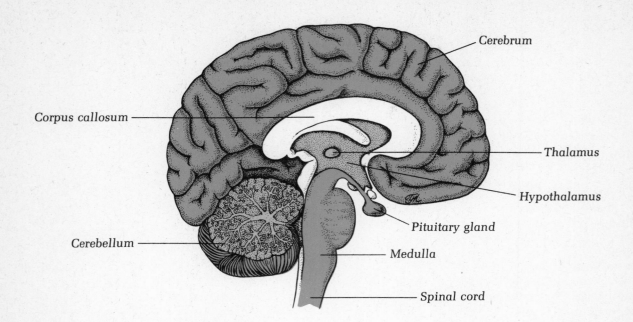

Cerebrum

Corpus callosum

Thalamus

Hypothalamus

Pituitary gland

Cerebellum

Medulla

Spinal cord

The brain is the control center of the body. Each of the areas of the brain shown here has its own function.

The *autonomic nervous system* is a subsidiary system that governs all functions, such as gland secretion, not subject to willful control. It also controls the heart, lungs, and digestive tract.

The control center of the nervous system — indeed, of the entire body—is the brain. The brain is often compared to a computer, but it is thousands of times more complex than the most sophisticated electronic computer. Composed of more than ten billion interconnected nerve cells, the brain controls more body functions than have yet been catalogued. All of our actions, sensations, and thoughts—whether we are asleep or awake—are influenced by the brain.

There are distinct areas within the brain, each with its own function. At the back of the skull is the cerebellum which controls posture, balance, and muscular activity. Deep within the center of the brain is the thalamus, the center for pain, touch, temperature, and consciousness. The thalamus is the main relay station for impulses coming in from the body; it relays these impulses to other parts of the brain. Underneath the thalamus is the

hypothalamus which governs the body's automatic functions, such as heartbeat, blood pressure, and blood circulation. The pituitary gland, or master gland of the endocrine system, is part of the hypothalamus, and this gland controls most of the hormones in the body. This causes the hypothalamus to be the seat of basic drives influenced by hormones—drives like hunger, thirst, and sexual desire.

Above the thalamus and hypothalamus is the cerebrum, consisting of the cerebral hemispheres. The cerebral hemispheres contain the nerve centers that control conscious thought and action. There is a left and right cerebral hemisphere, connected by a band of fibers called the corpus callosum. Each hemisphere controls the opposite side of the body. For example, the left hemisphere controls the right side of the body. This occurs because the nerve fibers from the hemispheres cross over each other in the brain stem (medulla) before they progress down the spinal cord.

Although a great deal is known about the brain, many of its functions and activities remain a

mystery. The brain's capacity for reasoning, memory, and complex intellectual processes, for example, are not understood. The brain remains the most important, most complex, and least understood organ in the body.

ANOREXIA NERVOSA

Anorexia nervosa means literally "nervous loss of appetite." Actually, however, persons with this condition — almost always female — do not lose their appetite, but rather willfully suppress the urge to eat in an unhealthy desire to lose more and more weight. In short, they starve themselves because they mistakenly believe that they are fat and need to diet.

Anorexia nervosa leads to the cessation of menstruation and to the destruction of healthy muscle and organ tissue which the body must use as an energy source in the absence of food. Ultimately, anorexic patients may starve themselves to death.

Anorexia nervosa is considered to be principally caused by serious psychological problems. Anorexic youngsters are usually obedient, successful children who try to do everything expected of them by parents, teachers, and friends. As a result, the strenuous dieting and exercising by an anorectic may represent the patient's desire to gain absolute control over at least one part of her life.

Anorectics may also try to deny the onset of adulthood by dieting away all the signs of mature femininity: breasts, curved hips, and rounded thighs. The lack of menstrual periods, too, is a reminder of childhood. In addition, the current preoccupation with thinness as the ideal of attractiveness contributes to the anorectic's desire to starve herself to the "perfect" weight. Frequently, the disease is precipitated by a casual remark that the girl is slightly overweight.

Ninety-five percent of all anorectics are female. Most are teenagers from upper and upper middle-class homes. Roughly one in 200 women of this age and class is estimated to have anorexia nervosa. Anorexia is also more common among people whose professions or hobbies demand careful weight control, such as ballerinas, athletes, or fashion models. The legitimate need to maintain a certain weight often slips into an unhealthy obsession with dieting. The rare cases of anorexia among males usually occur in those trying to qualify for some athletic team.

SYMPTOMS

The anorectic develops an aversion to eating which cannot be overcome by threats or appeals to reason. The dieting is accompanied by overly vigorous exercise to burn off the few calories that she does consume. Although she refuses to eat more than tiny amounts of certain foods, she is often obsessed with the subject of food and will prepare elaborate meals for others.

Often the anorectic may go on an eating binge after which she

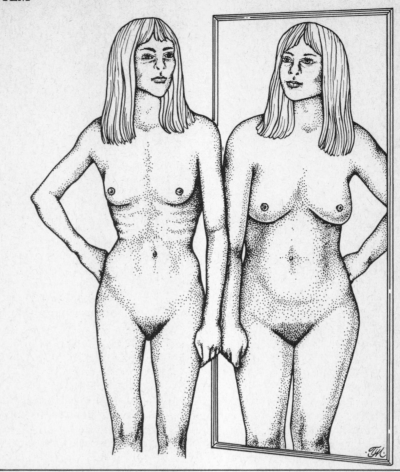

A person with anorexia nervosa often has a distorted sense of body image. When she looks into the mirror, she perceives herself as fat when in reality she is unusually thin.

forces herself to vomit. Excessive use of laxatives is also common.

The patient's fear of becoming fat is accompanied by a distorted body image that makes it impossible for her to realize how unattractively thin she has become. Often when an anorectic looks in the mirror, she perceives herself as fat when in reality she is exceedingly thin.

After a certain percentage of body fat is lost, menstruation will automatically cease. Fine, downy hair may begin to grow all over the patient's body.

The doctor will first attempt to rule out any physical causes for extreme weight loss, such as cancer, infectious disease, disorders in the digestive organs, or problems in absorbing the nutrients from food. If the patient has lost more than 25 percent of her original body weight, if she

displays the classic behavior, and if the onset of symptoms occurs before the age of 25, a diagnosis of anorexia is usually warranted.

TREATMENT

Anorectics may require hospitalization and forced feeding if their disease has led to severe malnutrition. However, most anorectics can be treated on an outpatient basis by a family physician, psychiatrist, or a specialist in eating disorders.

The underlying psychological problems should be exposed and resolved. In the meantime, however, the patient must be convinced to gain weight, but that her doctor and parents will not allow her to become obese. Healthy attitudes toward body weight and normal eating patterns must be restored.

EPILEPSY

Epilepsy is a brain disorder accompanied by periodic seizures and perhaps loss of consciousness. A sudden surge of disorganized electrical activity released by a cluster of nerve cells in the brain leads to the seizures which vary in severity. This pattern of disrupted brain activity can occur in association with a variety of conditions.

Left untreated, severe seizures can be fatal. Recurrent seizures present a high risk of injury to the brain, especially in young children. However, most persons experiencing seizures are in no physical danger unless there is the possibility of their falling or hitting their heads. Furthermore, the epileptic seizures of up to 70 to 80 percent of patients can be controlled by drugs.

Some of the underlying conditions which can cause the surges of electrical activity in the brain characteristic of epilepsy include head injury, cerebral palsy, brain tumor, central nervous system infection, and drug withdrawal. All of these may affect the brain in such a way that the brain's electrical activity is disturbed.

However, many cases of epilepsy appear to be entirely without cause. No one knows why these people have epilepsy, and, therefore, no one can predict who will develop the condition. Nevertheless, it is known that epilepsy is more common among men and usually begins before age 30. Furthermore, the tendency to have seizures may be inherited.

SYMPTOMS

Epilepsy is defined by the type of seizures experienced, not all of which are convulsive. A convulsion involves the nerves that control movement and produces jerking, spastic muscle movements. "Seizures," denoting simply an attack of epilepsy, is a more definitive term.

In the past, seizures were classified as *grand mal* (for big sickness), *petit mal* (little sickness), psychomotor, and focal. A newer classification method lists seizures as partial or generalized, depending on the extent of involvement of the brain. The currently accepted classifications of seizures are:

Simple partial seizures which are confined to small areas of the brain. The patient does not lose consciousness and may simply experience a tingling sensation in the arm, finger, or foot, or may perceive bad odors, see flashing lights, or speak unintelligibly.

Complex partial seizures marked by episodes of automatic behavior. The patient again remains conscious, but may sit motionless or move in a strange, repetitive, or inappropriate way.

Generalized convulsive seizure, the seizure most often associated with epilepsy, involving a total loss of consciousness. The patient may cry out, stiffen, and fall to the ground. Muscle spasms may cause the limbs to assume unusual positions, and urinary and bowel control may be lost. Then, wild thrashing movements, followed by a lapse into deep sleep occur. Headache and dazedness may be felt upon awakening. Sometimes, there are warning signals when this type of seizure is approaching. These may include a headache, sleepiness, yawning, and tingling sensations in the arms and legs.

Generalized non-convulsive or *absence* seizures are attacks which usually occur only in children. They are marked by periods of staring into space, rapid blinking, and "daydreaming." Although remaining conscious, the patient may be utterly unaware of the seizure. These seizures may be responsible for poor performance in school and may be mistaken for short attention span or a learning disability.

Epilepsy is diagnosed by observing the symptoms and by using the electroencephalograph (EEG) which measures the electrical activity of the brain. Electrodes (small, metal disks) sensitive to this brain activity are placed on the head and attached to the electroencephalograph which then produces a visual record of these brain impulses. Spurts of disorganized electrical activity will show up as steep, jagged lines on the EEG. Sometimes the patient is monitored over a 24-hour period to note the occurrence and location of abnormal electrical discharges.

TREATMENT

Managing a seizure, particularly a generalized convulsion, should be limited to preventing injury. Clothing can be loosened around the neck and a pillow placed under the head. Most importantly, patients should not be left face downward or in a position where they can swallow or inhale their own vomit. Epileptic patients who fall into a deep sleep at the end of a seizure should not be awakened.

The epileptic seizures of 70 to 80 percent of patients can be controlled by a variety of drugs, primarily anticonvulsants. But a number of other factors also affect control of the disorder. Many patients have more seizures during periods of emotional stress, and patients who are particularly susceptible to stress-precipitated seizures often receive tranquilizers. Physical stresses, such as lack of sleep, poor diet, and overexertion may also initiate seizures.

Epileptics usually need anticonvulsant drug therapy throughout life. However, if seizures are controlled for three to five years, the doctor may slowly reduce the dose over a period of one to two years to see if the patient will remain seizure-free. Sometimes, all medication will be withdrawn.

Many epileptics can lead normal lives with their seizures controlled by medication. Driving, for example, may be permitted if the patient has gone several years without a seizure. Epileptics can hold jobs and raise families. It is essential to remember that with proper treatment an epileptic is as normal as those who control their high blood pressure or their diabetes.

HEADACHES

Headache is a symptom, not a disease. There are three basic types of headache: vascular, muscle contraction, and traction or inflammatory. *Vascular headaches* occur when the blood vessels in the head dilate, or enlarge, thus pressing on nerves and causing pain. Migraine headaches are an example of this type. *Muscle contraction headaches* occur when the muscles of the face, neck, and/or scalp contract or have spasms. Tension headaches are an example of this type headache. *Traction or inflammatory headaches* arise from pressure within the head. Conditions as common as sinusitis (inflammation of the air-filled cavities in the facial bones) or as serious as a brain tumor may cause this type of headache.

Everyone has an occasional headache, but a doctor should be consulted if pain is persistent or recurring. Headache is rarely the symptom of a serious illness, but frequent migraine or sinus headaches can be exhausting and can affect work and personal lives. Since they can usually be treated fairly successfully, headaches should not be ignored.

Vascular Headaches (Migraine)

Vascular headaches can be caused by many different physical factors and triggered or worsened by many emotional ones.

Researchers do not know why some persons suffer from migraine headaches. They theorize that these persons' blood vessels may simply overreact to normal stimuli, causing some of them at first to constrict, shutting off the blood flow to parts of the brain and causing the visual impairment and numbness that sometimes accompany these headaches. The vessels then become engorged with blood, exerting pressure on nerves. Stress, as well as allergies or reactions to certain foods and food additives, can

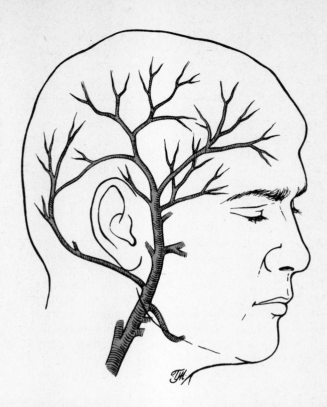

These are the blood vessels typically involved in a vascular headache.

trigger migraines. Chocolate, fatty foods, alcohol, citrus fruits, monosodium glutamate (a flavor enhancer in many Chinese foods), and nitrates (found in many preserved meats) are often cited as foods that trigger migraines. Suddenly consuming much less caffeine than usual may also set off a migraine. Many persons experience migraine after a stressful episode, while others seem to get them only on weekends or holidays, possibly because of changed eating and sleeping patterns.

The tendency toward migraine headaches can be hereditary, and they are seen most frequently in women. Furthermore, there seems to be a migraine personality: a compulsive, excessively neat, success-oriented, perfectionist person seems more prone to migraines.

SYMPTOMS

Migraine headaches can produce pain on one or both sides of the head. The pain is likely to be sharp and pulsating and often is incapacitating. The patient's skin may be pale and sweaty. Nausea and sensitivity to light are also present, and the migraine sufferer may wish to lie down in a dark, quiet room until the attack passes.

Frequently, migraine patients can anticipate the onslaught of a headache from sensations preceding the actual pain. These warning sensations are referred to as an aura. The approach of a headache may be indicated by seeing flashes or shooting "stars" in the field of vision, hearing noises, smelling fragrances, or feeling a tingling sensation in the limbs.

The headaches may also occur in cycles in response to certain cyclical environmental or emotional factors, for example, as a part of the menstrual cycle.

Cluster headaches, a form of migraine seen most often in men, occur in groups or clusters of one to six a day. They cause intense pain on one side of the head, accompanied by tearing of the eyes and runny nose. The bouts of headaches last for weeks or months at a time and may be provoked by drinking or smoking.

Your doctor will probably question you extensively about the circumstances surrounding your headaches in an effort to determine exactly what factors may trigger them. Additionally, a thorough physical will be performed to see if any diseases may be causing the headaches.

TREATMENT

Migraines are most often treated with a combination of painkillers, sedatives, and drugs designed specifically for migraine. The foremost among these is ergotamine, a drug which constricts the blood vessels, thus preventing the swollen vessels that cause migraine pain. It is usually taken to stop a migraine that is about to begin, and thus has no effect on the pre-headache aura experienced by some.

Antidepressant drugs taken in small doses every day may help prevent migraines in those who experience them regularly, while sedatives and tranquilizers may be prescribed to help the occasional migraine sufferer weather an attack.

For those whose headaches appear to be triggered by a certain change in routine or ingestion of a specific food, tests may be run to determine the culprit. All the suspect substances will be eliminated, then reintroduced one by one until the offending substance is found.

Muscle Contraction Headaches

Muscle contraction headaches are most often caused by tension, which seems automatically to make people clench their jaws and generally contract the muscles of the head and neck. Any abnormalities of the eyes, neck, teeth, or jaw can also cause a muscle spasm headache. Poor posture, especially holding the head at an odd angle while reading, driving, or watching television, can also lead to this type of headache.

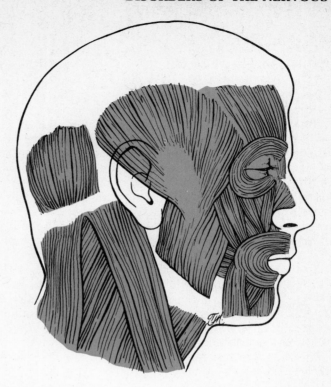

These muscles are the ones most likely to cause a muscle contraction headache.

SYMPTOMS

Muscle spasm headaches produce a tight squeezing pain around the back of the head or neck, or in the forehead. The jaws may also ache. The pain is constant and dull, most often occurring on both sides of the head. The headaches vary in frequency and severity, but usually are preceded by some specific stressful episode that causes the muscles to tense.

The doctor will probably try to discover what events or tensions precede your headache. In addition, a physical exam may be performed to determine if there is a reason that the pain radiates from a given area in the head or neck. (For example, poor alignment of teeth may cause pain in the jaw.) A psychological exam may also be suggested since so many of this type of headache are either triggered or caused by psychological factors.

TREATMENT

A combination of painkillers, muscle relaxants, tranquilizers, and antidepressants is often used in treating muscle spasm headaches. However, neither the painkillers nor muscle relaxants should be used on a constant, everyday basis. For persons who have frequent muscle spasm headaches, regular treatment with antidepressants to prevent the headaches may be the safest, most effective route.

Naturally, too, eliminating the tension that may cause the headaches is recommended. Also, correcting any underlying physical reasons (such as misalignment of teeth) will be helpful.

Traction or Inflammatory Headaches

Traction or inflammatory headaches may be caused by sinus problems, aneurysm (a bulge in a blood vessel), infections, high blood pressure, or a brain tumor. Of these, sinus headaches are probably the most common. The sinuses are cavities lined with mucous membrane within the facial bones. When the mucus produced in the sinuses cannot drain out through the nose, it collects in the sinus cavities causing pressure that leads to headache. Similarly, tumors and aneurysms press directly on the brain, while high blood pressure causes blood to circulate through vessels with too great a force, producing pressure. General infections cause headaches because of the inflammation of sensitive tissues, as well as the enlargement of blood vessels which may occur during a fever.

SYMPTOMS

Inflammatory headaches produce a dull, aching pain accompanied by a sensation of pressure. The headaches frequently occur early in the day. The pain is heightened by sneezing and coughing, shaking the head, bending over, or doing anything else that increases the amount of blood in the head.

The doctor will probably attempt to determine if your headaches are caused by sinus pressure or something less common. If sinus problems are ruled out, the doctor may prescribe X rays; a CAT (computerized axial tomography) scan, which provides a three-dimensional picture of the brain; or an EEG (electroencephalogram), which monitors electrical activity in the brain. These tests are used to determine the presence of an abnormality in the brain, a tumor, or an aneurysm.

TREATMENT

Inflammatory or traction headaches are treated according to their cause. Mild inflammatory headaches brought on by a sinus infection can usually be treated with painkillers, antihistamines (which dry the sinus tissues), or decongestants which promote sinus drainage. Headaches resulting from tumor or aneurysm will almost always require surgery.

HYPERKINESIS

Hyperkinesis — also called hyperactivity, minimal brain dysfunction, and attention deficit disorder—is a childhood disorder thought to be the result of some deficiency or malfunctioning of certain neurotransmitters in the brain. Neurotransmitters are chemicals whose job it is to transmit impulses across the junctions between nerves. The disorder results in increased levels of physical activity and an inability to concentrate for extended periods of time.

Hyperkinesis can be diagnosed as early as age one and usually lasts into adolescence. After the teenage years, the patient begins to outgrow the disorder, although some symptoms may linger into adulthood. The disorder is four to five times more common in boys than in girls.

While hyperkinesis does not damage the body physically, it can have lasting effects on a child's social, emotional, and educational development. Because hyperkinetic children cannot sit still and concentrate, they may have problems learning to read, write, and do arithmetic. They are often loud and boisterous, earning the disapproval of their parents and teachers and the scorn of their peers, which in turn leads to low self-esteem. Although most of the obvious symptoms of the disease disappear by adulthood, many adults who were hyperkinetic as children still show signs of impulsiveness and have trouble forming close relationships.

The precise cause of hyperkinesis is unknown, although theories are abundant. The theory that has received the most attention is that some cases of hyperkinesis are caused by additives, preservatives, and colorings found in processed foods. Proponents of this idea say that these substances have a toxic (poisonous), allergic effect on some children.

Another theory holds that some genetic defect or damage done to the unborn child during preg-nancy may account for hyperactivity. Still another theory is based on research showing that the brain has two systems: one that inspires immediate action and one that causes the person to hesitate while contemplating the outcome of proposed activity. Researchers deduce that the neurotransmitters necessary to control the latter behavior are not properly functioning in hyperkinetic children.

Apart from the fact that this disorder is more prevalent among boys, there seem to be no definite risk factors associated with hyperkinesis. Also, there are no studies to show whether adults who were hyperkinetic are more likely to have similarly affected children.

SYMPTOMS

The hyperkinetic child is overly active, restless, and fidgety. He talks excessively and loudly, laughs too long and hard, and prefers to play with younger children. At school he is often disruptive, forgets facts that he seemed to have learned, rushes headlong into his work and does it incorrectly, and skips or adds words when he reads. He is impulsive, has a short attention span, and may appear uncoordinated.

Since symptoms that characterize hyperkinesis can be found to some degree in all children, it is important that an accurate diagnosis be made. Hyperkinesis itself is rather vaguely defined and there are no physiological tests that can detect it.

One researcher has indicated that it is the "quantity, intensity and long duration of immature behavior" that set hyperactive children apart from those who may have behavior problems, who are afflicted with more serious illnesses, or who are simply bored and unchallenged by school.

TREATMENT

Doctors who adhere to the theory that hyperactivity is

caused by food additives may prescribe a special diet that attempts to eliminate these substances entirely. Many studies have been performed to examine the effectiveness of this treatment, and the results have been either contradictory or inconclusive. Still, many parents report a dramatic improvement in their children's behavior after following the diet, although this may be due in part to all the extra attention lavished on a child when his food is specially prepared.

Although parental attitudes cannot cause hyperactivity, the way the child is cared for can influence or even improve behavior. Good behavior should be praised and rewarded and bad behavior punished or ignored. When the child becomes too wild or overactive, he should be sent to a quiet room where nothing is happening until he calms down.

The most successful and most controversial treatment for hyperkinesis is drug therapy. A number of stimulant drugs seem to have a calming effect on hyperkinetic children because they work by stimulating the neurotransmitters which activate the brain's contemplative response (the response in that system of the brain that causes the person to hesitate while contemplating the outcome of proposed activity). Although the drugs may produce a significant improvement in behavior, they also may cause stomach cramps, colds, nervous mannerisms, and may stunt growth. Most doctors recommend that children taking these drugs should be given drug "holidays" during which their behavior while they are off the drug is assessed and during which they have a chance to allow their growth to catch up to normal.

MENINGITIS

Meningitis is an infection and inflammation of the meninges, the membranes that cover the brain and spinal cord.

The disease causes fever, headache, and swelling of the brain.

Although death from meningitis has become more and more unusual because of the development of so many antibiotics and other infection-fighting medications, it is always a possibility. The disease, when not properly treated, can also lead to epilepsy, blindness, amnesia (loss of memory), and deafness.

The meninges are three layers of protective membranes. The dura mater is the outermost—and toughest—membrane, and it is in contact with the inner surface of the skull. The middle membrane is called the arachnoid; the innermost layer, the pia mater, is in direct contact with the surface of the brain. These layers surround the brain and continue uninterrupted down the spinal cord. Meningitis is an inflammation of these membranes, particularly the inner two — the arachnoid and the pia mater.

There is a space called the subarachnoid space between the inner two layers. The subarachnoid space is filled with a clear fluid called cerebrospinal fluid which is produced in the brain. Meningitis results when bacteria (or sometimes viruses) invade and multiply in the cerebrospinal fluid, causing it to become filled with pus. The infection may enter the system through a severe head wound or through the bloodstream (for example, from another source of infection in the body such as the respiratory system). Occasionally, though rarely, the bacteria reach the meninges from an abscess (localized infection) of the brain itself.

Males seem more susceptible to meningitis then females. It is more common in children up to age four and in elderly persons over the age of 60. Newborns may be at higher risk for the disease if membranes surrounding the baby in the uterus have ruptured prematurely, if the mother has had certain genital infections during the last week of pregnancy, or if there has been prolonged labor. Inherited or acquired deficiencies in the body's immune (protection)

system can also increase the risk of developing meningitis.

SYMPTOMS

The symptoms of meningitis are a "bursting" headache, with pain that radiates down the neck into the back and lower limbs. This is accompanied by a high fever, rising pulse, irregular breathing, and vomiting. The patient's neck typically will become stiff and unable to be bent forward. Sometimes the patient's eyes are extremely sensitive to light. Convulsions (abnormally violent and uncontrolled muscle spasms) and coma can develop as the disease progresses.

A lumbar puncture to test for the precise infecting organism may be done if the doctor does not think there is increased pressure in the brain. A hollow needle is inserted between two of the lumbar vertebrae (bones in the lower backbone) to draw off a sample of the spinal fluid in the subarachnoid space surrounding the spinal cord. This sample is then examined to see if it is clear (normal) or cloudy (pus-filled). It is also examined under a microscope for specific bacteria that cause meningitis.

However, since prompt treatment is vital, the doctor may start the meningitis patient on some medication before definitely determining the nature of the infection. The doctor will also perform a physical examination to search for the source of the infection. Blood cultures will be taken, as well as cultures from the secretions of the respiratory tract. X rays may also be necessary to assess the effect of the infection on the brain.

Viral infections are much harder to detect and may, in fact, not show up on any standard tests even though the symptoms indicate that disease is present.

TREATMENT

The type of antibiotic drug prescribed depends on the type of microorganisms causing the in-

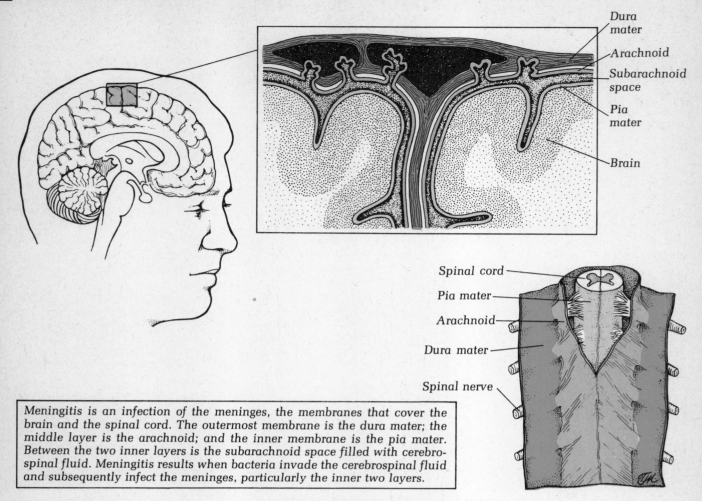

Dura mater
Arachnoid
Subarachnoid space
Pia mater
Brain

Spinal cord
Pia mater
Arachnoid
Dura mater
Spinal nerve

Meningitis is an infection of the meninges, the membranes that cover the brain and the spinal cord. The outermost membrane is the dura mater; the middle layer is the arachnoid; and the inner membrane is the pia mater. Between the two inner layers is the subarachnoid space filled with cerebrospinal fluid. Meningitis results when bacteria invade the cerebrospinal fluid and subsequently infect the meninges, particularly the inner two layers.

fection. The patient will be hospitalized and supportive measures will be taken to lower fever and control brain swelling.

Viral infections of the central nervous system are much harder to treat. There is no medication that can kill the invading virus after it has caused the infection. Treatment is limited to supportive therapy until the disease runs its course.

There are vaccines available against some of the bacteria strains that cause meningitis. In addition, researchers are working on new vaccines that will protect against additional groups of bacteria. (A vaccine is a preparation containing the microorganism that causes the disease. When the vaccine is introduced into the body, it stimulates the body to produce its own protective substances to fight and prevent the disease.)

PARKINSON'S DISEASE

Parkinson's disease is a progressive disorder affecting the nerve centers within the brain that control movement and posture. The disease causes tremors or shaking in the head and limbs as well as stiffened muscles. It occurs most frequently in persons over the age of 60.

Although the disease may be present in a mild form for 20 or even 30 years, a severe case may lead to serious disability within five or ten years. Parkinson's disease is often accompanied by depression, as the patient becomes upset over the loss of control of movements. Ironically, emotional upset can cause the symptoms to worsen, leading to further depression.

Parkinson's disease in itself is

not usually fatal, but it weakens the body generally, making the person more susceptible to other afflictions.

The causes of Parkinson's disease are unknown. Researchers believe that muscle control is governed by the balance of neurotransmitters in the brain. Neurotransmitters are chemicals whose job it is to transmit impulses across the junctions between nerves. Persons with Parkinson's disease will show a deficiency of one of these neurotransmitters called dopamine. However, there is still no indication of what causes this underlying imbalance.

Since scientists do not know exactly why Parkinson's disease occurs, they do not know why certain people develop the disease. Thus far, no one has found that any particular inherited, medical, or environmental factors predispose a person to Parkinson's disease.

SYMPTOMS

The symptoms of Parkinson's disease are tremors in the extremities and the head, muscular stiffness, drooling, a reduction in blinking and a general lack of expression in the face, a stooping posture, and a shuffling walk. Tremors often come on when the patient is resting and may lessen as the person reaches for an object. The tremors may cease during sleep.

As the disease worsens, speech may be slurred, with the ends of sentences trailing off into unintelligible muttering. Small muscle movement is affected more dramatically, reducing the ability to write, eat, chew, and swallow. All purposeful movements are slow and seem very stiff and deliberate. For example, the term "cogwheel rigidity" is often applied to typical movements in the arm of a patient. When pushed, the arm moves up and down in a jerky fashion as if controlled by a rachet like that found in a cogwheel. Excitement and tension can make the symptoms worse.

Diagnosis is made chiefly through physical examination and observation of symptoms. Tests may be performed to rule out the possibility of another source of the symptoms, especially if tremors are the only signs present. Liver disease, multiple sclerosis, chronic alcoholism, drug addition, and overfunctioning of the thyroid gland can all cause tremors.

TREATMENT

Since Parkinson's disease results from a chemical imbalance in the brain (chiefly lowered levels of the substance dopamine), the most effective treatment revolves around restoring normal dopamine levels. Dopamine itself cannot be absorbed directly from the blood into the brain, so a substance called levodopa (L-dopa) is administered. Levodopa helps the body manufacture its own dopamine.

Although levodopa relieves symptoms to a remarkable extent, it is not always the proper treatment for every case of Parkinson's disease. Because the drug has some side effects like nausea and an "on-off" effect (causing symptoms to disappear, then appear again), it is not always recommended. Furthermore, levodopa tends to lose its effectiveness over time, so it should not be administered at the first sign of mild symptoms, but should be held back for use after other treatments have ceased to be helpful.

Other milder drugs used in the treatment of Parkinson's disease are muscle relaxants and drugs that will help alleviate the drooling associated with this disease.

Certain exercises may also be recommended to help improve coordination. Physical therapy and exercise are extremely important, since lack of physical activity can lead to immobility.

REYE'S SYNDROME

Reye's syndrome is a relatively rare, noncontagious disease that strikes children under the age of 18. It is a type of encephalitis, or inflammation of the brain, but it is distinguished from other forms of encephalitis by the accompanying involvement of the liver. It usually starts after the child is recovering from a viral infection, most commonly influenza or chicken pox. Reye's syndrome affects all the organs and muscles of the body, doing the most damage to the brain and liver.

The disease causes the brain to swell and fatty deposits to collect in the liver, thus impairing the function of both organs. Early diagnosis and treatment is essential to prevent permanent brain damage, coma, or death. Approximately 25 percent of all cases of Reye's syndrome are fatal.

The precise cause of Reye's syndrome remains a mystery. Since it almost invariably follows a viral infection, it is thought to be viral in nature. It may be that the virus, in conjunction with some other unknown substance, produces a toxin (poison) that damages the body.

On the other hand, Reye's syndrome has been linked to the use of aspirin in treating the original viral infection. Although it has not been proven that aspirin causes or promotes Reye's syndrome, it is recommended that aspirin not be given to children

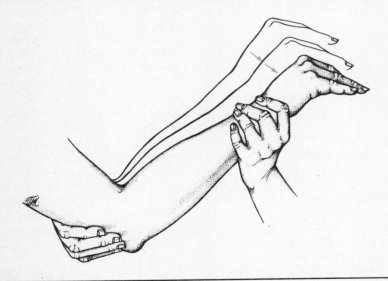

The term "cogwheel rigidity" is often used to describe the typical movements in Parkinson's disease. For example, a patient's arm, when pushed, may move up and down in a jerky fashion as if controlled by a ratchet like that found in a cogwheel.

Reye's syndrome has been linked to the use of aspirin in the treatment of viral infections. A fever can be reduced without using aspirin by sponging the patient with lukewarm — not cold — water. Between spongings, the patient should be covered with a sheet.

with viral infections. Instead, sponge baths and aspirin substitutes — which have not been linked to this disease — are advised as safer methods of managing fever and other symptoms.

Children between the ages of five and 11 who have just had a viral infection are at the highest risk for Reye's syndrome. Most of the reported cases occur in the months of December through March.

SYMPTOMS

Reye's syndrome is indicated if a child who has been recovering from a virus suddenly develops severe vomiting, abnormal drowsiness or hyperactivity, and confusion. As the disease progresses, convulsions (abnormally violent and involuntary muscle spasms) and coma may result.

If your doctor suspects Reye's syndrome after observing the symptoms, he or she may conduct several other tests to verify the diagnosis. Blood tests may reveal abnormalities that indicate liver damage. Also, in younger children, the blood sugar level will

often be very low. A sample of cerebrospinal fluid may be taken from the spinal column to rule out the possibility of other kinds of diseases, although this will be done only if the doctor does not suspect that there is increased pressure in the brain. Accurate diagnosis is crucial so that proper treatment can begin immediately.

TREATMENT

There is no cure for Reye's syndrome. Treatment consists of supportive therapy to help the patient withstand the disease until it runs its course. The patient is usually hospitalized. Usually, if a child survives for three or four days, recovery will be complete.

Children with Reye's syndrome will often develop very low blood sugar levels referred to as hypoglycemia. Treatment is therefore aimed at maintaining near normal blood sugar levels. This will be done through administration of glucose, a kind of sugar, into the vein. Doctors will also attempt to prevent increased pressure in the brain due to swelling by the use of certain medications.

STROKE

A stroke is damage to brain cells that results from an interruption of their blood supply. When the flow of oxygen-carrying blood to a given part of the brain is obstructed, neither those brain cells nor the part of the body they control can function. Because of the way the nervous system is arranged, each side of the brain controls the opposite side of the body. Thus, for example, when a stroke affects the right side of the brain, the resulting symptoms of paralysis or numbness will affect the left side of the body. In some cases of stroke, however, when the cells of the lower part of the brain are affected, symptoms may occur on the same side of the body as the stroke.

Stroke not only damages the brain, but it can also lead to temporary or permanent memory loss, difficulty in speaking or walking, and trouble controlling emotions. The individual may even lose the use of an arm or leg or even of an entire side of the body.

Stroke is caused either by a blocked artery leading to or within the brain (cerebrovascular occlusion), or by a burst artery in the brain (cerebral hemorrhage). If the arteries supplying the brain are already damaged by atherosclerosis (a narrowing of the arteries because of deposits of fatty and fibrous substances), there is an increased likelihood that a clot will form entirely blocking that artery. Furthermore, the possibility exists that a wandering clot, formed elsewhere in the body and carried through the circulatory system, will ultimately lodge in one of the cerebral arteries.

Cerebral hemorrhage, on the other hand, occurs when a diseased artery in the brain bursts, flooding the surrounding brain tissue and depriving the cells nourished by that artery of blood. Accumulation of blood from the burst artery soon forms a clot which, by displacing brain tissue, may interfere with brain function. This type of stroke is more likely to occur when the patient suffers

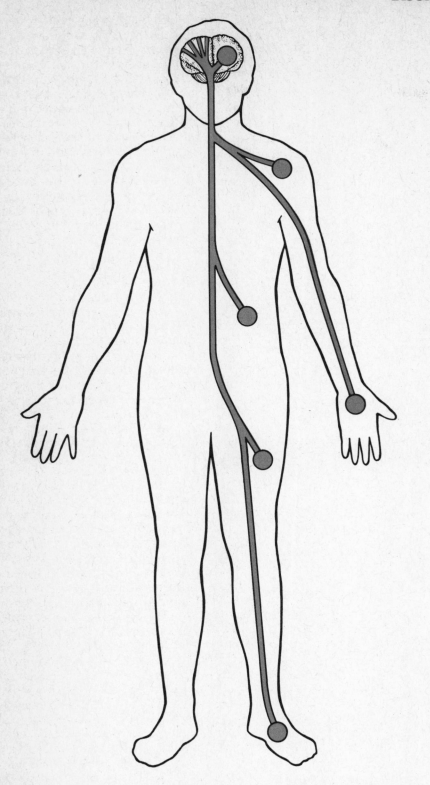

A stroke affecting one side of the brain may cause numbness or paralysis in the opposite side of the body. This is because each side of the brain controls the opposite side of the body.

pressure, are blood-filled pouches that swell out from a weak spot in the artery wall. They are not always dangerous, but if they burst, a stroke results.

Stroke is most likely to occur in persons who already have both hypertension and atherosclerosis, since both diseases weaken the arteries. Atherosclerosis promotes the formation of clots, while hypertension can encourage hemorrhaging. Since a tendency to develop atherosclerosis and hypertension seems to be inherited, heredity can also play a part in your chance of having a stroke.

Anyone who has a history of brief, intermittent stroke episodes called TIAs (transient ischemic attack) is at a greater risk for stroke. TIAs are characterized by a feeling of weakness, faintness, dizziness, ringing in the ears, and numbness in an arm or leg, all of which pass in several minutes.

Diabetes, high blood cholesterol, and smoking can also contribute to stroke. Blacks are at a greater risk for stroke because they are twice as likely to suffer from high blood pressure than the general population.

SYMPTOMS

The signs of stroke are a sudden, temporary weakness or numbness of the face, arm, or leg on one side of the body; temporary loss of speech or trouble in speaking or understanding the spoken word; temporary dimness or loss of vision; and unexplained dizziness, unsteadiness, or sudden falls. Severe headache, nausea, and emotional instability may also be present. The stroke victim may experience many of these symptoms or virtually none at all, depending on the seriousness of the attack. It is possible to have a mild stroke without knowing it.

Several diagnostic tools are used to determine the extent and nature of damage to the brain caused by stroke. The electroencephalograph (EEG) makes a visual recording of electrical impulses generated by the brain. A

from a combination of hypertension (high blood pressure) and atherosclerosis.

A burst aneurysm in the brain can also cause stroke. Aneurysms, often associated with high blood

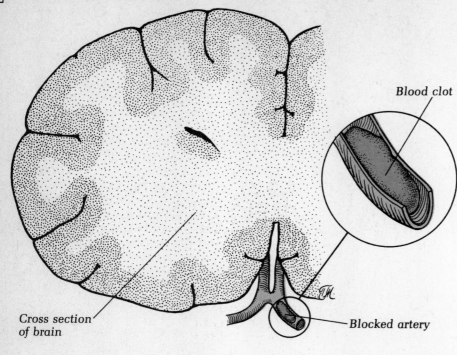

Blood clot

Cross section
of brain

Blocked artery

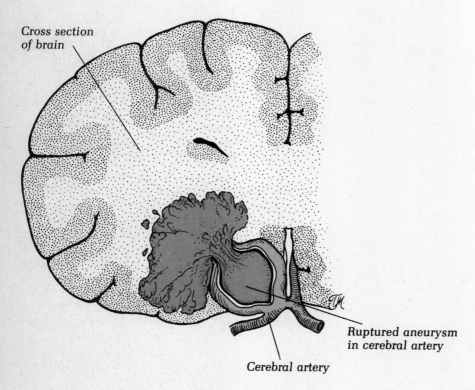

Cross section
of brain

Ruptured aneurysm
in cerebral artery

Cerebral artery

A stroke is damage to brain cells because of an interruption of their blood supply. This interruption may be caused by a blocked cerebral artery leading to the brain or by a ruptured aneurysm, a blood-filled pouch that swells out from a weak spot in the artery wall.

regular head X ray will be taken, but more sophisticated X ray techniques may also have to be employed.

If your doctor suspects a clot in an artery of the neck leading to the brain, he or she may perform arteriography, the injection of X ray opaque dye into the bloodstream to outline the artery and point out damage or clots. Or, if a problem is suspected within the brain, a CAT (computerized axial tomography) scan, which provides a three-dimensional view of the area, may be required.

TREATMENT

Stroke treatment involves a team approach to rehabilitation. Speech, physical, and occupational therapists, as well as doctors, are all involved in bringing about the recovery of a stroke patient. Although recovery is gradual, you will be encouraged to do as much as you can.

Immediate hospitalization is usually required for stroke patients. Oxygen will probably be administered after the attack to prevent further damage to the brain, and medications to prevent brain tissue swelling may be prescribed. An anticonvulsant drug may be given to prevent seizures.

If you have suffered only the warning signs of stroke, several preventive measures can be taken. The most important is to be certain that your blood pressure is normal, and, if not, to try to lower high blood pressure through improved diet and the administration of appropriate drugs. Smooth muscle relaxants and vasodilators, which improve the flow of blood to the brain, as well as anticoagulants which thin the blood and prevent clotting, may also be prescribed. Some studies have shown that taking aspirin regularly helps prevent stroke in men, but a benefit to women has not been proven. This should be discussed with a doctor, however. Finally, surgery may be recommended for persons with obstructions in the arteries leading to the brain.

CANCER

The word cancer actually refers to a class of diseases, all of which develop in a similar way, although they strike different parts of the body. Normal cells in the body reproduce only when it is necessary for them to do so. The new cell is an exact copy of the parent cell and is capable of performing the same functions. A cancer cell, however, is one that begins to reproduce wildly. The reason for this unrestrained growth is not really known, but it seems to result from a change in the basic structure of a normal cell.

As cancer cells multiply, they become less and less like the normal cell and lose any ability to function usefully. If the growth of cells is unchecked, they will form a mass known as a malignant tumor. Not all tumors are malignant. A benign tumor is one that develops from a cause other than cancer.

A tumor itself is seldom the cause of death of a cancer patient, although the presence of a tumor can sometimes interfere with bodily processes or block passages in the body. As long as cancer is confined to a single tumor, it can usually be contained or removed by surgery. A far more dangerous aspect of cancer is when the cancer cells spread from their original location. This can begin with the invasion of neighboring tissue by the cancer cells. In some cases, cancer cells may be taken up by the circulatory system and carried to distant locations in the body. This process is known as *metastasis*. Once a cancer has metastasized, chance of cure is greatly reduced. A tumor in the body can be present for quite a long time before the cancer cells begin to move to other sites in the body. This is why early detection is the single most important weapon against cancer. Early forms of the disease always respond better to treatment.

Twenty percent of the deaths in the United States result from cancer, making cancer second

Benign tumor

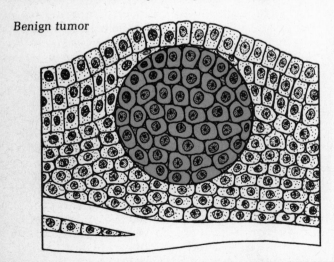

Malignant tumor

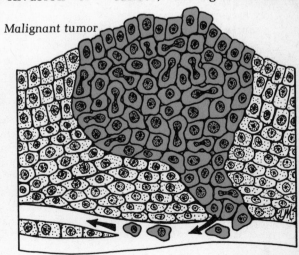

There are certain characteristics of a tumor that help in diagnosing whether it is benign (noncancerous) or malignant (cancerous). A benign tumor, shown on the left, is usually enclosed within a capsule, grows slowly, and does not invade surrounding tissue (metastasize). A malignant tumor, shown on the right, is not encapsulated, grows rapidly, and metastasizes.

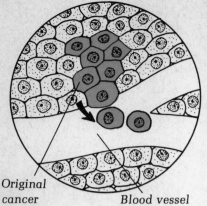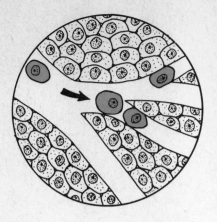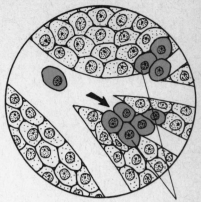

Original cancer

Blood vessel

Metastasis in new location

Metastasis is the spread of cancer from its original site to other locations in the body. In some cases, cancer cells are taken up by the circulatory system, as shown in this illustration, and carried to distant organs.

only to heart disease as a cause of death in this country. However, the outlook for the cancer patient constantly improves — if you are diagnosed with cancer today, your chance of cure is close to 50 percent. With certain kinds of cancer the percentage is much higher. In cancer a cure usually means a five-year period after treatment with no sign of the disease.

Scientists do not know why cancer cells develop, nor, once they have developed, why the body does not recognize them as foreign material and destroy them. But research comes continually closer every year to understanding cancer. Many factors that contribute to cancer have been identified. Some authorities believe that up to three quarters of all cancers result from cancer-producing substances in the environment known as carcinogens. For example, cigarette smoke is now clearly identified as a carcinogen that causes lung cancer. Yet not every heavy smoker will develop this disease. Thus it appears that cancer results not from a single source, but from a complex interaction of several factors. Certain people are more sensitive to particular environmental carcinogens than are others. In some cases this susceptibility may be inherited.

Most cancers develop in people without a family history of cancer. However, certain families do show a greater incidence of particular forms of cancer. If cancer has occurred in your family, you may have a hereditary disposition to it. Therefore, it is important to know the medical history of your family. If a particular form of cancer is present in your family, you should become aware of its symptoms and of the tests available for this disease that a doctor can perform during routine examinations.

We are surrounded by substances that are connected with cancer, such as industrial pollutants, auto emissions, insecticides, and nuclear fallout. Some scientists believe that cancer may be on the rise in industrial countries because of increasing numbers of these pollutants in the atmosphere. However, it may be that these substances are only dangerous after prolonged contact with highly concentrated forms. The most clear-cut examples of environmentally caused cancers have occurred among industrial workers. Persons who have worked with asbestos, for example, are especially vulnerable to lung cancer. Plastics workers exposed to vinyl chloride risk developing liver cancer later in life. Victims of radiation poisoning, especially Hiroshima survivors, show a high cancer rate. It is often many years

after exposure to a carcinogen that symptoms begin to develop, making it much harder to identify environmental carcinogens. Sometimes, as with the drug DES (diethylstilbestrol) taken during pregnancy to prevent miscarriage, the cancer develops in the next generation.

Recently numerous food additives, such as saccharin and cyclamates, have been identified by scientists as carcinogens. Often producers of these additives argue that the experiments that produce cancer in laboratory animals involve greater amounts and higher concentrations of the product that would ever be consumed by a human. It may be true that there is little risk from small amounts of these additives; however, since most of these additives are of little value it seems wisest to avoid them. It is not true that a large dose of *any* substance will produce cancer. A non-carcinogen will not cause cancer no matter how much is administered.

All carcinogens cannot be avoided, but it is important to cut down contact with known carcinogens. Industrial workers should be very careful about the substances they come into contact with at work. Anyone who has been exposed to concentrated forms of a known carcinogen should be on the lookout for symptoms of the form of the disease caused by this material and should also have regular examinations by a doctor.

Research also indicates that diet may be linked to certain forms of cancer. Cancer of the colon and rectum is most common in industrialized nations, and diet is probably the reason for this. In these countries great amounts of fats and very little fiber (nondigestible parts of fruits and vegetables) are consumed. Certain by-products of the digestion of fat encourage cancer formation, and in a low fiber diet these by-products are evacuated from the colon less effectively. Nitrates and nitrites, present in processed meats, can react with other substances in the stomach to form nitrosamines, known carcinogens. It is probably best to avoid foods that contain these substances. The longer the exposure to a carcinogen, the greater the risk; thus children in particular should be protected from carcinogens in the diet.

A direct relationship has been shown between smoking and lung cancer. Smokers also show a higher incidence of cancer of the mouth, throat, and bladder. If you smoke and are also exposed to other carcinogens such as asbestos and coal dust, you are more likely to develop lung cancer. Low tar and nicotine cigarettes may reduce the risk of cancer, but it is best simply to stop smoking. Some authorities believe that ten years after a person has stopped smoking, his or her chance of developing lung cancer is about the same as that of a person who has never smoked. On the other hand, once the disease develops, the chances of survival are not good.

SYMPTOMS

Because early detection is the single most important weapon against cancer, you should be aware of the seven warning signals of cancer: change in bowel or bladder habits; a sore that does not heal; unusual bleeding or discharge; thickening or lump in the breast or elsewhere; indigestion or difficulty in swallowing; obvious

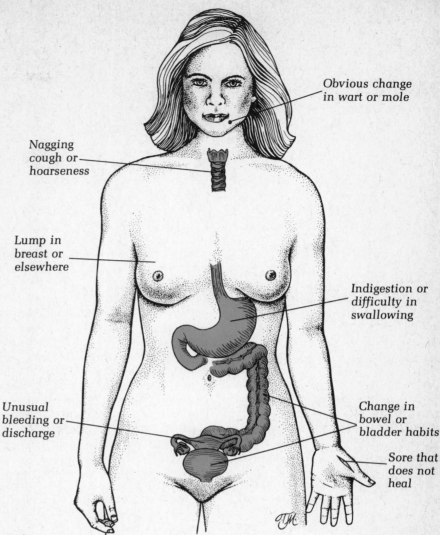

The seven warning signals of cancer.

change in a wart or a mole; and a nagging cough or hoarseness.

Regular checkups are essential for detecting cancer early enough for successful treatment. If you note any of these warning signals, consult your doctor immediately.

The specific symptoms of some of the more common types of cancers will be found within the discussions of the individual cancers. These types of cancer are discussed, in alphabetical order, at the end of this section.

TREATMENT

If cancer is suspected, the doctor will perform several tests before making a diagnosis. In many

cases, an X ray may be the first means of locating a tumor. Sometimes it is possible to introduce into the body a scope, or lighted tube, that can examine body passages from within, such as a sigmoidoscope for the colon. If a tumor is found, your doctor may want to perform a biopsy. A biopsy is the surgical removal of a piece of the tumor in order to test it for the presence of cancer. If cancer is indicated, additional tests, such as the bone scan, may be administered to see whether the disease has spread. If cancer is diagnosed, the first step is selecting the appropriate treatment. There are several types of cancer therapy.

Surgery. Surgery is the most common method of dealing with cancers that form tumors. If cancer is confined to one area, surgery can sometimes completely eliminate it. New surgical techniques are continually increasing the range of tumors that can be safely removed; and if the surgeon is able to remove only a part of the tumor, the reduced tumor can often be successfully controlled with radiation or chemotherapy.

More precise surgical techniques mean that surgery today is often less disfiguring than in the past. New developments in skin grafting make it possible to begin reconstructive work on patients—for instance, those with cancer of the head and neck — simultaneously with the cancer surgery.

Sometimes surgery is performed on a patient even though it is known that surgery will not cure the cancer. The removal of a tumor may simply make the patient more comfortable. In other cases, nerve pathways to the pain center may be cut. Certain growths that are not cancerous may be removed by a doctor because they are a kind of growth that in some patients may develop into cancers.

Chemotherapy. Chemotherapy, or the treatment of cancer with drugs, has gradually become more and more important. More than 12 kinds of cancer can now be effectively treated by chemotherapy alone. But most often cancer drugs are used as an adjuvant, that is, as a backup to primary treatment such as surgery. Once surgery has diminished a cancer, chemotherapy can often eliminate it. Chemotherapy has proved effective against some forms of cancer that used to be almost always fatal, particularly Hodgkin's disease, acute lymphocytic leukemia (a blood disease of children), and cancer of the testes (the male sex glands).

Most cancer drugs attack any fast-reproducing cells in the body whether they are cancerous or not, producing some of the well-known side effects of chemotherapy. Destruction of normal cells that reproduce frequently, such as those in the digestive tract, the hair follicles, and the bone marrow can lead to nausea, hair loss, and lowered red blood cell count.

Usually in chemotherapy several drugs are administered in combination. If the cancer does not respond, or a resistance to a drug develops, another combination may be attempted.

Radiation. Radiation destroys the ability of cells to divide. Cancer cells are far more susceptible to radiation than normal cells, although not all cancers respond to radiation. Like surgery, radiation therapy is a localized form of treatment, which means it is directed at a particular cancer site. Radiation treatment may also involve directly implanting into a tumor a radioactive pellet that destroys from within. Radiation can be used before surgery to reduce a tumor to operable size, and frequently a patient receives radiation therapy after surgery to destroy any cancer cells that might remain near the cancer site. In addition, some tumors can be treated by radiation alone.

Radiation can be especially useful in cancers where surgery will impair basic bodily functions. For example, surgery for cancer of the testes may leave the patient impotent, while radiation treatment avoids this; radiation treatment of cancer of the larynx preserves the voice box; and in the case of breast cancer, radiation can prevent the disfiguring effects of surgery. However, even in these forms of cancer, surgery may often be necessary.

Radiation therapy is being continually refined. Drugs have been discovered which make cancer cells more sensitive to radiation. Different forms of radiation are being tested on resistant cancers. In addition, radiation today can be directed more precisely, and in stronger forms, with little harm to overlying tissue. However, there are still side effects including loss of appetite, nausea, and temporary hair loss. It is not certain how dangerous it is to be treated with radiation, which is itself a carcinogen; however, it is believed that a cancer in the body is far more threatening than the future effects of radiation therapy.

Immunotherapy. The aim of immunotherapy is to help the patient's own body produce substances that resist the growth of cancer. The basis of immunotherapy is the theory that cancer develops when, for some reason, the body fails to destroy abnormal cells. So far, immunotherapy is still in the experimental stage.

Interferon is a natural substance produced by the body to resist viruses. In the laboratory interferon has been observed to prevent cancer cells from multiplying. Yet, so far, interferon has been very costly to produce artificially, and in tests it has not been as effective as standard treatments. It is likely that in the future strengthening the body's defenses will become an important tool against cancer.

Heat Therapy. Heat therapy, or hyperthermia, now being used experimentally, may soon become standard treatment for some kinds of cancer. Tumors have been shown to shrink when their temperature is raised. The circulation inside tumors is much more sluggish than in normal tissue—thus a tumor can usually endure far less heat. Temperatures tolerable to normal cells can be deadly to cancers. Heat therapy is largely painless. An instrument called a Magnetrode can deliver heat to inner portions of the body without harming overlying tissue. However, not all patients can be treated with hyperthermia — the location of the tumor or the weakened health of the patient may rule out heat therapy. At this point, heat therapy has been most effective when used in combination with radiation or chemotherapy.

Laetrile. Laetrile is an extract of apricot pits that some have proclaimed is a cure for cancer. This substance has been banned because it has been shown to be of no value against cancer in laboratory animals and has yet to be adequately tested in humans. Most patients who have shown a response to laetrile have also received conventional cancer therapy. Furthermore, laetrile has been shown to be poisonous in some patients.

Specific treatments of the more common forms of cancer will be found in the following descriptions of these cancers.

TYPES OF CANCER

Bladder Cancer. This is the most common cancer of the urinary tract. It occurs most often between the ages of 50 and 70 and is the fourth leading cause of cancer death among men. Four times as many men as women are afflicted.

Incidence of bladder cancer has been connected with exposure to a number of carcinogens. This may be because the urinary tract comes into contact with so many foreign substances because of its excretory function. For many years it has been known that those who work with aniline dyes have a high incidence of cancer of the bladder. Bladder cancer is also associated with tar from tobacco smoke and schistosomiasis infestation, a tropical parasite.

Blood in the urine is usually the first symptom of bladder cancer. In addition, urination may be difficult, painful, and frequent. The appearance of blood in the urine may be intermittent, and sometimes, if this symptom disappears, a doctor is not consulted. However, anyone with blood in the urine should consult a doctor, since in early stages this disease is highly curable, and treatment is far more difficult later on. If your doctor feels the symptoms suggest bladder cancer, he or she may order a cystoscopy. Under local anesthesia a lighted tube called a cystoscope is passed into the urinary tract through the urethra (the passageway from the bladder to the outside), through which the interior of the bladder can be examined. This instrument can even take a biopsy (removal of a small piece of tissue for analysis) of a suspicious growth.

Treatment of bladder cancer depends on how far advanced the disease is. A small tumor can sometimes be completely removed by a cystoscope. More advanced cases are treated by surgery or radiation or a combination of the two.

Bone Cancer. This is a rare form of cancer most common in children between the ages of five and 15. Predisposing factors to bone cancer are bone diseases, bone fractures, and exposure to radiation. Bone cancer begins with a sarcoma, the name for a tumor that develops in muscle, bone, or cartilage (the elastic tissue at the ends of bones).

Bone cancer usually develops first in the arms or legs. Pain, swelling, or brittleness of the bone may be its symptoms. Often it is far advanced by the time it is discovered. The first tool in diagnosis is the X ray, which can often tell whether the bone is cancerous and if the disease has spread. If cancer is indicated, an orthopedic surgeon should perform a biopsy. Bone cancer is usually treated by a combination of surgery, radiation, and chemotherapy.

Brain Cancer. Any tumor in the brain, whether cancerous or not, is very dangerous. Because the brain occupies an enclosed space within the skull, even a small tumor that weighs more than a fifth of a pound can cause crowding sufficient to bring on death. Brain cancer is most often the result of metastasis from other cancer sites, particularly the breast, lung, and skin.

Symptoms of brain cancer are of two kinds. Increased pressure in the skull can cause seizures, headaches, nausea, forgetfulness, and personality changes. However, symptoms may also arise in the part of the body controlled by the affected area in the brain. For instance, coordination, vision, or strength of limbs may be affected. In the past, brain tumors have not responded well to treatment because their presence is so difficult to detect that diagnosis occurred late in the development of the disease. Recently, however, diagnostic techniques have improved. The CAT (computerized axial tomography) scanner produces a three-dimensional image of the brain which can clearly determine the size and location of a tumor. By using a CAT scanner, doctors are also able to monitor carefully the progress of any treatment.

Surgery is the primary treatment for brain cancer when the disease has not spread throughout the body. Surgery in the brain is a delicate procedure; often a tumor deep in the brain cannot be totally removed without risking impairment of body function. However, new techniques in brain surgery —sometimes with the use of a microscope — permit treatment of tumors once considered inoperable. Radiation or chemotherapy will often follow surgery, though the sensitivity of brain tissue demands that these be administered cautiously. Steroid drugs will often be given to reduce the dangerous swelling that a tumor can produce.

Breast Cancer. About one woman in 13 will develop breast cancer at some time in her life. It is the leading cause of cancer death in women, and the leading cause of all death in women between the ages of 40 and 44. The high risk group includes women over 35, women who have never had children or who have had a child for the first time after the age of 30, and women who began menstruation early or who experienced late menopause. Breast cancer also occurs more frequently in chemical workers, women with a family history of this disease, and women who have already had breast cancer.

Self-examination of the breast can often lead to early detection. All women—particularly those in the high risk category — should perform these examinations monthly at the end of the menstrual period. Approximately 90 percent of all breast tumors are first discovered by self-examination. The recommended tech-

In the shower, keep one hand overhead and examine each breast with opposite hand. Wet, soapy skin may make it easier to feel lumps.

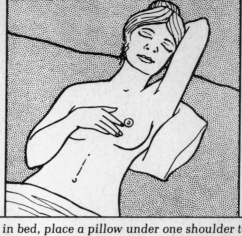

Lying in bed, place a pillow under one shoulder to elevate and flatten breast. Examine each breast, with the opposite hand, first with arm under head and again with arm at side.

In front of a mirror, stand with hands resting on hips. Examine breasts for swelling, dimpling, bulges, and changes in skin.

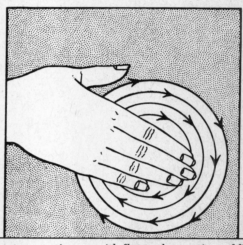

Make rotary motions—with flat pads, not tips, of finger, in concentric circles inward toward nipple. Feel for knots, lumps, or indentations. Be sure to include the armpit area.

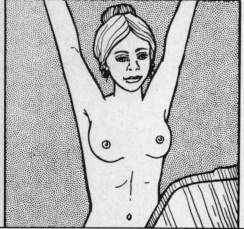

In front of mirror, examine breasts for changes with arms extended overhead. This position highlights bulges and indentations which may indicate a lump.

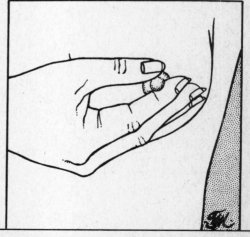

Squeeze nipples gently to inspect for any discharge. Report any suspicious findings to your doctor.

nique for breast self-examination is shown in the illustration in this section.

If a lump is discovered in the breast, your doctor will probably order an X ray of the breast, known as a mammogram. The doctor may also recommend a thermogram which can detect growths by measuring body heat. This test is based on the premise that new growths may generate more heat than the surrounding tissue. The doctor may then take a biopsy (a tissue sample) of the lump to test for the presence of cancer. If cancer is indicated, surgery will probably be performed. Women with breast cancer often dread surgery because of the disfigurement that can result; however, today surgery for a breast tumor is often less extensive than in the past. At one time all breast cancer patients received a radical mastectomy, or removal of the breast, underlying chest muscles, and lymph glands in the armpit. Now it is known that in many cases the removal of the breast, or even the tumor alone, may be equally effective. In addition, there are techniques for reconstruction of the breast after surgery and rehabilitation of muscle tone in an arm that has been weakened by surgery. In some cases radiation therapy will be used after surgery to destroy any remaining cancer cells.

Cancer of the Colon. About 40,000 Americans die every year of cancer of the colon and rectum. About half of all cases of cancer of the colon can be cured by surgery, and early detection can greatly improve this percentage. A simple test for blood in the stool can indicate whether further tests should be made for the presence of this cancer. Everyone over 40, or with chronic digestive problems, should have this test regularly. Chance of cure is twice as likely if the disease is discovered before symptoms occur.

Symptoms of cancer of the colon include a change in stools or in bowel movements, bleeding from the rectum, pencil thin stools, and abdominal discomfort not eased by bowel movement. If you have any of these symptoms your doctor will probably perform a rectal exam, inserting a finger into the rectum to search for unusual growths. If further examination is necessary, the doctor may introduce a sigmoidoscope (a lighted tube) into the colon through the anus, the opening at the end of the intestine. This instrument permits examination of the inside of the colon and can also take a biopsy of suspicious growths. Sometimes a noncancerous polyp is removed by a similar instrument, because such polyps may sometimes develop into cancer.

Surgery is the usual treatment for cancer of the colon. If the cancer is near to or in the rectum, the surgeon may remove all the rectum and create an artificial rectum, or colostomy, in the lower abdominal wall. A colostomy is usually covered with a bag to collect waste material.

Cancer of the Cervix. The cervix is the lower part of the uterus, or womb, that extends into the vagina. Cancer of the cervix is the second most common cancer among American women. The death rate from this disease has decreased 50 percent over the last 50 years, largely as a result of early diagnosis. Early cervical cancer has no symptoms but can be detected by a Pap smear. A Pap smear is performed routinely in a doctor's office by scraping the surface of the cervix. The collected material is then tested for indications of cancer. Today two out of three cases of cervical cancer are detected by a Pap smear before they display symptoms.

Cervical cancer has a higher incidence among black women and poor women. This cancer also occurs more frequently among women who were sexually active early with many partners, and among those with genital herpes.

If a Pap smear indicates the possibility of cervical cancer, a biopsy of the affected area will probably be performed. Treatment depends on how far the disease has advanced — early forms are almost always curable by surgical removal of the cervix and uterus, called a hysterectomy. If a patient still hopes to bear children, and the cancer is in an early stage, sometimes this surgery can be put off till after children have been born. However, this is possible only if the disease does not seem to be progressing, and the cancer must be monitored carefully during this phase. Eventually the uterus should be removed. More advanced forms of the disease are treated with radiation as well as surgery.

Leukemia. This is a disease of the bone marrow, the site of blood cell production. Blood cells called platelets control clotting; white blood cells fight infection; and red blood cells carry oxygen throughout the body. The symptoms of leukemia result from the impairment of these functions.

Leukemia is the most common form of cancer in children. In recent years the outlook has improved dramatically for children suffering from leukemia. Twenty years ago nearly all children diagnosed as having leukemia died. Today close to 50 percent are cured—and the lives of many more are prolonged.

More than half the people diagnosed as having leukemia first consult a doctor with complaints of being easily tired, a result of low red blood cell count. Other symptoms are easy bruising, bleeding from the gums, blood in the stool, fever, and frequent infections. The spleen and lymph glands are usually enlarged.

A diagnosis of leukemia should be made by a cancer specialist. The doctor will probably insert a needle into the hipbone to withdraw bone marrow cells that will be tested for the presence of cancer.

Leukemia is often treated first with intensive chemotherapy to kill all cancer cells in the body. The patient may become even sicker during treatment because of the large dosages of cancer-fighting drugs. After this initial treatment phase, radiation and additional drugs may be administered to be sure all of the disease has disappeared.

Liver Cancer. Liver cancer usually results from the spread of cancer cells from another site in the body. However, cancer that originates in the liver can sometimes be traced to environmental carcinogens. It is known that anyone who has worked with vinyl chloride, a chemical used in plastics manufacture, has a higher risk of this disease. It also appears that cirrhosis of the liver, a disease in which normal liver cells are replaced by fibrous tissue, may cause an individual to be more susceptible to cancer of the liver.

Symptoms of liver cancer are difficult to identify. Often they resemble the signs of a peptic ulcer — aching or burning pain in the upper abdomen, nausea, and vomiting. A swollen or hardened liver often indicates to the doctor the need for further testing.

In the rare cases in which this cancer is diagnosed early and is confined to the liver, it can be treated surgically, but most often the prognosis is not good.

Lung Cancer. Cigarette smoking is generally accepted as the major cause of lung cancer. Lung cancer is the leading cause of cancer death in men, although in recent years the incidence of lung cancer in women is growing, probably as a result of increasing numbers of women who smoke. In addition, lung cancer is also increasing among nonsmokers. This may be due to improved diagnostic techniques (many lung tumors were once diagnosed as tuberculosis), as well as to increased environmental pollution.

If you smoke, and are over 45, or have a family history of this disease, you should be on the lookout for symptoms, since the early signs can be very mild: a persistent cough or lingering respiratory discomfort. Later, coughing will increase as will chest pain and shortness of breath. The patient may also cough up blood.

A cancerous tumor in the lung is usually removed by surgery. To eliminate the entire tumor, it may be necessary to remove an entire lobe of the lung. Because lung cancers are usually not detected until they are well advanced, surgery alone may not be able to eliminate them, and radiation and chemotherapy will be used in combination with surgery.

In recent years the deadliest form of lung cancer, small-cell carcinoma, has yielded to a new drug therapy which has produced significant remission in some patients.

Lymphoma. This cancer attacks the lymphatic system, particularly the lymph nodes and the spleen. These organs manufacture lymphocytes, cells which protect the body against infection.

The first symptoms of lymphoma are usually a swollen spleen or swollen lymph glands in the neck, armpit, or groin (the juncture beween the lower abdomen and the inner thigh). Fever and sweating are later symptoms. If these symptoms persist, a doctor should be consulted. If the doctor suspects cancer, he or she will probably order a biopsy (tissue sample) of the enlarged organ.

There are two major forms of lymphoma: Hodgkin's disease and non-Hodgkin's lymphoma. In recent years there have been dramatic strides in the treatment of Hodgkin's disease. In early stages, radiation alone can be very effective. Later in the development of the disease more extensive radiation may be required, or a combination of radiation and chemotherapy. Treatment of non-Hodgkin's lymphoma is much the same as that of Hodgkin's, but far fewer patients are cured. This form of the disease is usually discovered too late for treatment.

Cancer of the Ovary. This is the most dangerous form of cancer of the female reproductive organs, because it is so difficult to diagnose in its early stages. Women over 50 have a higher incidence of the disease, as do childless women and those with a family history of ovarian cancer.

Symptoms may include pelvic discomfort, constipation, abdominal swelling, and irregular menstruation. Often a diagnosis cannot be made without an exploratory operation known as a laparotomy, during which the disease can be evaluated and, in some cases, treated. In ovarian cancer usually both ovaries and the uterus are surgically removed, although sometimes it is possible to remove only one ovary. After surgery, radiation or chemotherapy may be administered.

Prostate Cancer. After lung cancer, this is the most common cancer among men. Black Americans have a higher incidence of prostate cancer than any other group in the world. In general, it is more common in men over 55. Prostate cancer can develop very slowly and it often produces no symptoms until the disease is far advanced. Sometimes a routine examination turns up a lump in the prostate, which will prove to be cancerous in about 50 percent of the cases. Prostate examinations should be included in medical checkups of all men over 50.

When symptoms occur, they are usually the result of an enlarged prostate, the male gland that lies at the base of the bladder. The enlargement causes difficult urination or blood in the urine. Prostate cancer often spreads to the bone, and patients may complain of bone pain before they show any other symptoms.

In the small percentage of cases in which prostate cancer is discovered before it has begun to spread, the cancer can be removed by surgery or radiation. Since surgery may cause the patient to become impotent and unable to control urine flow, radiation is the preferred treatment for small tumors. When the disease has spread, usually only its symptoms are treated as they occur. Often a patient can live a long time with this form of treatment.

Skin Cancer. About 300,000 cases of skin cancer are discovered every year. Its incidence increases every year, particularly among women, perhaps because people currently are getting more exposure to sunlight. The ultraviolet rays of the sun are a major cause of skin cancer. Fair-skinned people, lacking in a protective substance in the skin called melanin, are more susceptible to the effects of these rays than are dark-skinned people. Skin cancer can also result from prolonged exposure to certain chemicals such as arsenic compounds. Burn scars and skin diseases sometimes develop into cancer.

Most skin cancers are highly treatable. Some can be removed in a doctor's office or an outpatient clinic. But since some forms of these cancers can spread throughout the body, it is important that they be treated early. The most dangerous skin cancer, the malignant melanoma, can metastasize through the lymph glands. Melanomas usually develop from moles, though only about one mole in a million ever becomes a melanoma.

Symptoms of skin cancer are a change in the surface of the skin, wounds that do not heal, and a sudden major change in a wart, mole, or birthmark. All such suspicious signs should be examined by a doctor.

Skin cancer is an unusual form of cancer in that it can be prevented easily. Fair-skinned people and anyone with a family history of skin cancer should avoid exposure to the sun. Additionally, everyone who spends time in the sun should apply a protective sunscreen to exposed portions of the body. It is important to remember that the use of certain drugs, such as barbiturates, antibiotics, and birth control pills, can increase the sensitivity of the skin. In addition, children with their more sensitive skin should be protected against the sun.

Stomach Cancer. Stomach cancer has decreased 50 percent in the last 25 years. A change in diet may account for this. Stomach cancer is more common in men than women and usually occurs between the ages of 50 and 70. The high risk group includes those with a history of pernicious anemia or alcoholism, and persons with a diet rich in smoked, pickled, or salted foods.

Symptoms of stomach cancer are similar to those of peptic ulcer (heartburn and abdominal discomfort), making diagnosis more difficult. It may not be until the disease is well advanced that identifying symptoms of a bloody stool or vomit appear. To find a tumor a doctor will take a special X ray that involves swallowing barium, a substance that coats the lining of the stomach so that it will show up on a photograph. If a tumor is indicated, a flexible tube known as an endoscope may be inserted down the throat into the stomach to examine the tumor more closely and perhaps take a biopsy of it. Surgery is the most effective treatment of this disease, but only about 10 percent of victims survive more than five years after diagnosis. Surgery is most useful when the tumor has not begun to spread. Sometimes it is necessary to remove all or part of the stomach. After such surgery a patient will have to consume a low-bulk, high-protein diet.

Cancer of the Uterus. This disease is most common in women over 50. Especially susceptible are women who have never borne children, and those who are obese, diabetic, or suffer from high blood pressure. Women who have taken the female hormone estrogen to control symptoms of menopause are also in the high risk group.

Vaginal bleeding after menopause is the most common symptom of uterine cancer. If a Pap smear shows no abnormalities, then minor surgery, known as dilation and curettage may be performed. This involves scraping the interior walls of the uterus in order to examine the tissue for the presence of cancer. If cancer is indicated, a hysterectomy (surgical removal of the uterus and the ovaries) is usually performed, although hormones may be an effective treatment against this form of cancer. Cancer of the uterus is far harder to detect than cancer of the cervix; thus it is often discovered after it is too far advanced for successful treatment.

Cancer of the Vagina. Once a disease confined to women over 50, in recent years cancer of the vagina has also begun to appear in some women between the ages of 17 and 20. The mothers of most of these young women took artificial estrogens during pregnancy, particularly the drug DES (diethylstilbestrol), in order to prevent miscarriage. Any woman whose mother took artificial estrogens during pregnancy should have a Pap smear twice a year. Symptoms of vaginal cancer include vaginal pain and bleeding. The disease is usually treated by radiation.

INDEX

Page numbers appearing in **bold type** refer to the main entry for that topic.